Africana Studies

Africana Studies

A Disciplinary Quest
for Both Theory and Method

edited by
JAMES L. CONYERS, JR.

McFarland & Company, Inc., Publishers
Jefferson, North Carolina, and London

British Library Cataloguing-in-Publication data are available

Library of Congress Cataloguing-in-Publication Data

Africana studies : a disciplinary quest for both theory and method /
    edited by James L. Conyers, Jr.
        p.   cm.
    Includes index.
    ISBN 0-7864-0278-4 (library binding : 50# alkaline paper) ∞
    1. Afro-Americans—Study and teaching (Higher)—United
States.   2. Afro-American—Historiography.   3. Blacks—
Study and teaching (Higher)—United States.   4. Blacks—
Historiography.   5. Afro-American women—Study and teaching
(Higher)—United States.   6. Afro-American women—Histori-
ography.   I. Conyers, James L.
E184.7.A315   1997
973'.0496073'0071173—dc20   96-36256
                                                             CIP

Manufactured in the United States of America

McFarland & Company, Inc., Publishers
    Box 611, Jefferson, North Carolina 28640

To the memory of Sonia D. Pierce:
Your memory and spirit live with us

Acknowledgments

I am extremely grateful to the countless numbers of scholars, students, and friends who have been of valuable assistance in organizing this study. Importantly, my family is the primary base of my intellectual, common-sense, and critical perspective on examining the African-diasporic experience. My mother, Agnes Conyers, and my wife, Jacqueline I. Conyers, are the matriarchs who provide balance and wisdom to my continued learning. Also, I would like to thank my children, Chad Anthony Hawkins, Khalfani Sekou Conyers, and Kamau Abotare Conyers, for their patience, support, and love.

I would like to especially thank: Dr. Julius E. Thompson, for providing mentorship to me for over a decade, and still continuing to do so; Dr. James B. Stewart, who as director of the NCBS Summer Institute, provided the suggestion for taking on such a project; Dr. Molefi Kete Asante, Dr. Shawn R. Donaldson, Dr. Jerry W. Ward, Jr., Dr. Delores Aldridge, Dr. Gerald L. Davis, Dr. Jacqueline Wade, and Dr. William Nelson for their continued support and encouragement. Also, I would like to thank Ms. Candi Hoffman for her typing services, in completing this manuscript.

I want to express a special debt of gratitude to my support network, whose friendship I have had the opportunity to enjoy for over twenty years: Mr. Zane Corbin, Mr. Anthony Robinson, Mr. Qawi Jamison, Mr. Henry B. Robinson, Mr. Wayne Mustafa Harper, and Mr. Joseph E. Taylor. These men have provided kinship, loyalty and absolute love for me as a brother.

Others to whom I am grateful are the following: Mwalimu Abdu Nanji, Dr. Norman Harris, Dr. Darlene Clark Hine, Dr. Kariamu Welsh-Asante, Dr. Houston Baker, Dr. Warren Swindell, Dr. Wilson J. Moses, Dr. James E. Davis, Professor Andrew Smallwood, Professor Joye Knight, Gwen Woods, Khalis Woods, Shaheed Woods, Lois Owens, Theodore Nixon, Clyde Robertson, Clifford DaVis, Jeannine Morell, Dr. Frank G. Pogue, Dr. Ida Young, Larry Hopson, Ardel Hopson, Silvia Corbin, Kim Robinson, Lizbeth Jamison, Pam Jamison, Mike Ennis-Thompson, Thomas Hughes, Guiffre Hollingsworth, Willie Davis, Robert Marion, Karen Marion, Chris Slocum, Terri Slocum, Russell Jackson, Bettye Jackson, Cassandra McKendall, Amir Aburahaman, Janet Phillips, James Phillips, Sr., Doris Clowney, Dr. Nate Norment, Dr. Maulana Karenga, Dr. James Turner, Rae Harper, Gail Fisher Scott-Bey, Leslie Carter, John Dunning, Victor Vega, Fannie Gordon, Payton

Allen, Dr. Arnold Hence, Reggie Blue, Inger Pierce, Fredrick Pierce, Shawn Pierce, James Truesdale, Mustafa Rasool, Tishona Watson, Thurman A. Baker, Dr. Leslie Wilson, Dr. David Katzman, Dr. Wendel Holbrook, Dr. Barry Truchil, Dr. Curtis Smith, Dr. Michael Murphy, Dr. Abu Abarry, Dr. Alfred Attunda, Docia Attunda, Professor Silvester James Aji, Professor Patricia Hult, Dr. Edward Andrews, Dr. John Flocker, Dr. John Wanzenreid, and my department chair colleagues in the College of Arts and Sciences at the University of Nebraska at Omaha.

Contents

A Note to the Reader

The history of changes in nomenclature in African American Studies illustrates the political and social mandates in the academic study of the African diaspora. Thus, "Africana Studies" is used as the title of this book. This term is a descriptor that identifies land, history, and culture as it relates to African-diasporic phenomena. The earlier term "African Studies" is at many universities now used to convey a focus on continental Africa.

The significance of the present study is two-fold: to examine Africana Studies from a disciplinary perspective, and to examine both the theory and the methodology of Africana scholars; the focus is not on nomenclatural ideology. Therefore, throughout this text the terms Africana Studies, African American Studies, Afro-American Studies, Black Studies, and Africology are used somewhat interchangeably as referring to the systematic and holistic examination of both African and African-diasporic phenomena.

Preface

The idea for this book came as result of my participation in the 1991 National Council of Black Studies Summer Institute, hosted at Ohio State University, and funded by the Ford Foundation. At that program ten scholars from various disciplines, and I, were in residence for three weeks, brainstorming on issues concerning contextual analysis of Africana Studies. During the institute, the director suggested that there was a critical necessity for anthologies that would explore a disciplinary matrix and the development of theory and methodology in establishing Africana Studies as a discipline. This book is reflective of those suggestions, and attempts to locate Africana Studies as a holistic discipline. Unequivocally, the scholars whose essays are in this study represent the forward leadership of this emerging field. My objective was to coordinate published and unpublished essays that discussed the ideological repertoires in Africana Studies, in a quest for both theory and method.

This work seeks to critically examine Africana Studies from a holistic or disciplinary perspective. It describes and evaluates the discipline in four cognitive parts: administration and organizational structure; a disciplinary matrix; womanism; and cultural aesthetics. Throughout, terms such as Africana Studies, African American Studies, Black Studies, and Afro-American Studies are used nearly interchangeably and refer variously to all forms of the systematic study of African phenomena.

Africana Studies could serve the scholarly world in a two-fold manner: providing theory and praxis in solving problems in the African American community, and presenting an alternative epistemology in the arts and social sciences for the examination of African phenomena.

The essays in Part One address the topic of administration and organizational structure. Of almost equal importance is the description of the pattern of adversity and struggle to provide functional Africana Studies units on both predominantly black and predominantly white college campuses. The structure of Africana Studies units dictates a number of issues such as autonomy, curricula, pedagogy, tenure, promotion, degree granting, and development of graduate programs.

Part Two, Disciplinary Matrix and Analysis, explores theory development, method, and the interpretative analysis of data from a common school of thought. It constitutes an examination of the ontology and origins of the repertoire of ideologies available in a Western academic setting for establishing a holistic discipline. In general, commonality in schools of thought among disparate fields of research and teaching leads to the development of a new academic discipline; such is the case with Africana Studies.

Africana womanism is a critical component of the new discipline. The essays in Part Three provide perspectives on gender studies and the positioning of black women on the margins of world history and social events. The goal of this part is to provide an alternative epistemology for examining women from their own racial and genderal historical perspectives. In fact, throughout societal discourse in gender studies, women of African descent have consistently transformed etymology and ideology by using prefixes that modify "Africana" or "black," to identify their particular perspectives on issues and schema of race, gender, and class.

Part Four, Cultural Aesthetics, focuses on two areas: culture, language, symbols, and motifs; and a critical examination of black poets.

The present work is unique in the sense that it focuses on ideology as well as disciplinary development. The holistic discipline of Africana Studies is in a very early stage of development. On the other hand, its development is aided by the many models available as a result of the dramatic shift towards multidisciplinary studies in recent decades. Most important, Africana Studies is multidisciplinary by its very nature; it stands in the vanguard of the transformation and transcendence of the intellectual schools of thought in the academy today.

Part One:
Administration and
Organizational Structure
in Africana Studies

1. Black Studies: An Overview

Darlene Clark Hine, Ph.D.
John Hannah Professor of History
Michigan State University

During the late 1960s and early 1970s, unique historical circumstances propelled the development of Afro-American and Africana Studies in colleges and universities. Few of these early endeavors were the result of careful and deliberate planning and analysis. Typically, they were established in response to political exigencies rather than intellectual and academic imperatives. These and other factors contributed to ongoing structural and organizational diversity. Today it seems that no two Black Studies programs are alike. Their diversity is evidenced in faculty size and composition, relations with university administrators and more traditional departments, curriculum, degrees offered, budgets, spatial resources, range of special programs, and the nature of their community outreach.

An important objective of this investigation was to examine the present status of these programs: How well have they been supported by their institutions? To what degree have they been able to secure productive faculty? Have they provided their faculties with the requisite resources and nurturing that encourage the quality teaching, research, and service required for success in the academy?

The ongoing debate over nomenclature is a graphic illustration of residual problems growing out of the turbulent times in which these programs burst upon the academic scene. The term "black studies" has become a generic designation, vociferously opposed by some who view the phrase as less than illuminating. Critics argue that this designation suggests that only black students and faculty should be interested in this area of intellectual inquiry. Most institutions appear to prefer the titles "Afro-American," "African and Afro-American," or "Africana" studies. On the one hand, those who insist on the term "Africana Studies" maintain that "Afro-American Studies" implies that the primary focus of teaching and research is the historical, cultural, and political development of Afro-Americans living within the boundaries of North America. Moreover, "African and Afro-American Studies" neglects the Caribbean and other parts of the Americas. On the other hand, "Africana Studies" encompasses a broader geographical, if not disciplinary, reach, spanning both North and South America, the Caribbean, and the African continent—in short, the African Diaspora. Of course, few of the current programs possess the requisite institutional resources, faculty positions, or budget lines to be truly "Africana." But the intent points in the right direction and therefore is certainly praiseworthy.

The attempt to identify and assess black endeavors accurately is further complicated by the differences in structure and mission between "department," "programs," "centers," and "institutes." Black Studies "departments" are best characterized as separate, autonomous units possessing an exclusive right and privilege to hire and grant tenure to their faculty, certify students, confer degrees, and administer a budget. Black students' "programs" may offer majors and minors, but rarely confer degrees. And perhaps more importantly, all faculty appointments in programs are of the "joint," "adjunct," or "associate" variety. These professors are in the unenviable position of having to please two masters to secure appointment and tenure.

"Center" and "institutes" defy easy categorization. As a rule, they tend to be administrative units more concerned with the production and dissemination of scholarship and with the professional development of teachers and scholars in the field than with undergraduate teaching. Unfortunately, considerable confusion surrounds the name "centers." Many people view centers as merely cultural or social facilities designed to ease the adjustment of black students to predominantly white campus life. Thus, centers are denigrated and dismissed as having little or no relevance to Black Studies, which is imagined to be purely an academic or intellectual endeavor, albeit with political-advocacy overtones. However, the good work being done at centers like those at the University of California at Los Angeles (UCLA) and the University of Michigan certainly should correct these misconceptions.

University Administrators

It was encouraging and refreshing to encounter so many white university administrators who sang the praises of their Black Studies department, program, centers, and institutes. In fact, there was scarcely a discordant note. From the perspectives of the more positively inclined administrators on predominantly white campuses, it appears that Black Studies not only has come of age but also has been making important contributions to the academy. Although it is heartening to witness this change in attitude, given the initial vehement objections to the creation of Black Studies units, it is nonetheless necessary to probe beyond the surface to assess fully the contemporary status of Black Studies.

Twenty years ago, when black students first demanded the establishment of Black Studies departments, programs, and centers, few of the beleaguered white administrators would have predicted a long life for these enterprises. Many undoubtedly wished that Black Studies would go away; others tried to thwart growth and development. Most of those who opposed the creation of Black Studies units claimed that these units would lower academic standards because they believed such endeavors lacked intellectual substance.

It is not surprising that at some institutions Black Studies units offered little intellectual challenge. Undertrained people were brought in to head programs hastily contrived to preserve campus peace. Unfortunately, the early development and subsequent evolution of Black Studies was further tainted by the media's sensationalized coverage of the armed black students at Cornell University and the 1969 shoot-out at UCLA, which left two students dead. In the minds of many, Black Studies would forever remain nothing more than a new kind of academic ghetto. University administrators who valued "peace" and "campus rest" had little inclination, courage, or will to insist on quality. Thus, Black Studies units seldom were held to the traditional modes of evaluation and scrutiny observed elsewhere in the academy.

By 1987, however, the tide had turned. There has been a discernible shift among college administrators from amused contempt or indifference to enthusiastic support of Black Studies. Now administrators are eager to improve the quality of their programs and departments. One potent factor has been the availability of a larger pool of productive, well-trained black scholars willing, indeed anxious, to head or work in Black Studies. No longer do administrators have to rely on the local minister or community activist to oversee and teach Black Studies. If they are willing to put up the money, administrators can recruit productive black scholars.

Another motivation fueling the change toward Black Studies is institutional expediency. Faced with the specter of declining black student enrollment, university administrators are increasingly using strong Black Studies departments, programs, centers, and institutes as recruitment devices. Moreover, as is often the case, the only critical mass of black faculty working at many of these institutions is housed in black divisions. It is sad but true that without Black Studies, Mexican American Studies, Women's Studies, or Native American Studies departments or programs, few colleges and universities could boast of having an integrated or pluralistic faculty.

Institutional expediency and a larger pool of black scholars notwithstanding, one fact deserves underscoring. Black Studies departments and their faculties have proven to be a continuing source of intellectual stimulation on many American campuses. Black Studies has opened up vast and exciting new areas of scholarship, especially in American history and literature, and has spurred intellectual inquiry into diverse social problems affecting the lives of significant portions of the total population. Lectures, seminars, and conferences sponsored by Black Studies units provide a threefold benefit: Students introduced to authorities from outside of the academy are impressed with the fact that there are many ways of expressing and knowing. Faculty members, black and white, have the opportunity to share their expertise, test assumptions, and receive immediate feedback on work in progress. Finally, black community residents are encouraged to view universities as more accessible and less foreign. As members of these communities begin to identify with universities, they develop a greater appreciation for learning, and a respect for the scholarship of black professors.

Black Studies Curriculum

Despite its contributions and successes over the past 20 years, Black Studies still has to contend with and resolve rampant confusion, conflict, and creative tensions. The issues being debated include nomenclature; curriculum; identity, mission, and structure; graduate programs; faculty recruitment, retention, and development; accreditation; and professionalization. There is an ongoing debate, with no signs of immediate resolution, over whether Black Studies is a field or a discipline. The problems surrounding curriculum are worthy of special attention. Even within the same departments, faculties often find it impossible to agree upon a standard or core for all sections of the same introductory course in Afro-American Studies. It is regrettable that there is no special summer institute or training program where Black Studies administrators and faculty could discuss and perhaps map an appropriate and effective curriculum.

The curriculum—whether it is called Black Studies, Africana Studies, or Afro-American Studies—should reflect an ordered arrangement of courses progressing from the introductory through the intermediate to advanced levels. In terms of content, a sound Black Studies curriculum must include courses in Afro-American history and in Afro-American literature and literary criticism. There should be a complement of courses in sociology, political science, psychology, and economics. A cluster of courses in art, music, and language or linguistics should also be made available to students. Finally, depending on resources and the number of faculty, a well-rounded studies effort should offer courses on other geographical areas of the Black Diaspora—the Caribbean or Africa. African and Afro-American and Africana Studies programs and departments should, as their names imply, offer a variety of courses on black societies in the New World as well as in Africa.

Although deciding what to name a unit and devolving a sound and coherent curriculum are challenging, a more daunting task is acquiring resources to recruit and retain an appropriate faculty—one that includes assistant, associate, and full professors. In the late 1960s and early 1970s, Black

Studies units simply drew into domain whoever happened to be available and willing to join them. Thus, little uniformity in curriculum could be achieved across the country. With the economic difficulties and retrenchment of the late 1970s, many Black Studies faculties declined in size, producing an even more fragmented curriculum. To ensure that existing courses were offered on a reasonable and routine basis, Black Studies administrators had to rely heavily on part-time, visiting, or temporary appointees. Most often those available to accept such positions were in the creative arts—musicians, dancers, poets, and fiction writers.

More recently, Black Studies departments have increasingly relied on crosslisting courses to augment curriculum. The crosslisting of courses is both reasonable and advantageous because it builds bridges between Black Studies and the more traditional departments within the university, thus somewhat decreasing tendencies towards isolation and marginality. To be sure, there are pitfalls, and cautious administrators must be ever vigilant. Adaptive "survival" measures may encourage some university administrators to reduce further the resources allocated to Black Studies. After all, if Black Studies is consistently able to "make do" with less, one could logically conclude that it needed fewer resources in the first place. This is a special concern for departments and programs with small numbers of majors and minors and with low course enrollment.

All of these factors—lack of a critical mass of well-trained faculty, excessive reliance on temporary hires, absence of a coherent curriculum and of content consensus for even introductory courses, and the increasing use of crosslisting of courses—bespeak the difficulties confronting and perhaps threatening the autonomy of many Black Studies departments. There are certainly concerns among the leadership of the National Council for Black Studies (NCBS). I suspect that the officers of NCBS will experience considerable frustration as the organization attempts to design a standardized curriculum. Although it is perhaps perverse to see anything positive in this disarray, the major strength of the Black Studies enterprise may well be its ever-changing and evolving nature. The rapid proliferation of knowledge in the field is a strong argument in support of institutional flexibility. Faculty in this area need to be free to develop new courses, experiment with different methodologies, and adopt nontraditional texts, just as quickly as new knowledge is produced.

Undergraduate and Graduate Degree Programs in Black Studies

One of the characteristics of a viable discipline is the authority to confer degrees and certificates to students who have mastered a particular body of knowledge. Black Studies faculty and administrators have been quite concerned with this issue. The majority of the more autonomous departments of Black Studies do, in fact, award B.A. degrees. Programs in Black Studies vary. Some offer majors while most offer at least minors to students receiving a degree from the more traditional academic disciplines. In other words, the students may receive a B.A. degree in history, sociology, political science, biology, chemistry, business administration, or education—with a concentration in Afro-American Studies.

Few Black Studies units offer master's degrees. Of the half dozen or so that do, the departments at Cornell and UCLA and the program at Yale are the most visible and are highly respected. Most of the M.A. degree students at Cornell and Yale go on to pursue Ph.D. degrees in traditional disciplines at some of the better institutions in the country. Others enter the labor force, working in social services agencies, businesses, or state and local governments. Cornell's Master of Professional Studies degree is specially designed to prepare students to work in community settings.

As with many other issues in Black Studies, there is no consensus about the wisdom of developing graduate degree programs in Afro-American Studies. Certainly, at this stage in the evolution of Black Studies, there is a need for a creditable Ph.D. degree program. As I traveled around the country, Black Studies scholars expressed enthusiasm about the prospects of making a Ph.D. degree program available to students.[1]

Black Scholars and the Modern Black Studies Movement

At present, there are a number of top-flight scholars, more than at any time in history. They are producing first-rate, indeed award-winning, books and articles in areas of Black Studies. By far the most exhilarating part of the entire project involved meeting these scholars and becoming familiar with their work. No assessment of the overall status and impact of Black Studies would be complete without noting the research activities of this latest generation of black professors and administrators. Because the absolute number of black professors is small and declining, it is easy to lose sight of the quality and breadth of their research and to minimize the impact that they have had on scholarship in all branches of knowledge.

The collective scholarship of black professors provides a sound foundation for the future development of Black Studies as a discipline. To a great extent, this scholarship will ensure the eventual institutionalization of Black Studies within the academy. As long as black scholars remain productive and competitive, and devote considerable attention to recruiting and training the next generation of scholars, Black Studies will enjoy a presence on America's campuses. It is, however, precisely the need to recruit, retain, and educate young black men and women in the humanistic and social science disciplines that casts a cloud over the joy and exuberance accompanying any serious examination of the quality of black scholarship in the last two decades. For a variety of reasons, fewer black students are entering graduate school with plans for academic careers. At every stop on a tour of Black Studies units, faculty members and administrators, black and white, broached the topic and admitted that this problem was of critical importance to the future of Black Studies.

The numerous monographs, articles, and manuscript editing projects produced by black scholars have fueled the movement to reclaim the forgotten or obscured dimensions of the black past. Their new interpretations of past and present conditions affecting all aspects of black life have wrought a veritable revolution, albeit a still largely unheralded one, in the ways in which even traditional historians, literature theorists, sociologists, anthropologists, philosophers, psychologists, and political scientists approach their work whenever it touches upon the experience of black people.

There is reason to be excited and pleased with the record of intellectual accomplishment evident in scattered institutions around the country. Regrettably, most of these black scholars have little contact with each other. Nevertheless, because there are so many recognizably productive and accomplished scholars, the future of Black Studies appears bright in spite of all the structural complexities and creative tensions. In the remainder of this paper, I will address several factors concerning black scholars: the role of philanthropic foundations in their development, the perspectives reflected in some of their work, and the relationship between their scholarship and Black Studies as an organized unit within universities and colleges.

Any perusal of the acknowledgments and prefaces of some of the refreshingly original recent works of black scholars demonstrates the critical importance of the scholarships and fellowships made available by foundations and other organizations, including those specifically set aside for minority group scholars. Without these special fellowships, I daresay the record of productivity in Black Studies would not be so impressive.

To illustrate this point, I shall discuss three recently published and widely praised (within Black Studies circles, that is) volumes authored by black women scholars, the most recent group to establish a viable presence in the academy. Gloria T. Hull, professor of English at the University of Delaware, co-editor of *All the Women Are White, All the Blacks Are Men, But Some of Us Are Brave: Black Women's Studies* (Old Westbury, N.Y.: The Feminist Press, 1982) and editor of *Give Us Each Day: The Diary of Alice Dunbar-Nelson* (New York: Norton, 1984), has recently published a provocative and icon-shattering book, *Color, Sex, and Poetry: Three Women Writers of the Harlem Renaissance* (Bloomington: Indiana University Press, 1987). No one who reads it will ever again be able to think of the Harlem Renaissance in quite the same way. Hull effectively unveils the rampant sexism and chauvinism of the black male leaders of the Renaissance. In her preface, Hull wrote that in addition to a faculty research grant from the University of Delaware and a summer stipend from the National Endowment for the Humanities, a Rockefeller Foundation Fellowship enabled her "to do the requisite, remaining travel and research."

E. Frances White, MacArthur Professor of History and Black Studies at Hampshire College in Amherst, Massachusetts, and author of *Sierra Leone's Settler Woman Traders: Women on the Afro-European Frontier* (Ann Arbor: University of Michigan Press, 1987), observed in her preface: "I received funding from the African American Scholars Council, the Danforth Foundation (Kent Fellowship) and the Roothbert Fund to aid me in my initial research. An A.W. Mellon Faculty Development Grant and a Fulbright Senior Research Scholar Fellowship helped me to return to Sierra Leone to collect further material" (p. x). White's brilliant study contributes a feminist perspective to the continuing debate over the impact of colonial rule on women in Africa.

I first learned of Sylvia Ardyn Boone's *Radiance from the Waters: Concepts of Feminine Beauty in Mende Art* (New Haven: Yale University Press, 1986) from black historian Nell Irvin Painter of the University of North Carolina. Painter commented, "It's a *wonderful* book that takes real black beauty, African beauty, seriously, in an academic, not a commercial way."[2] The volume is indeed dazzling. Boone noted in her acknowledgment, "The Foreign Area Fellowship Program of the Social Science Research Council funded the first part of my work in England and later in Sierra Leone. A Dissertation Year Fellowship from the American Association of University Women and a grant from the Ford Foundation National Fellowship Fund financed additional research and then the write-up" (p. ix). Boone is an associate professor of art history and African and Afro-American Studies at Yale University.

I have highlighted these outstanding examples of black scholarship because the study of black women is the current frontier in Black Studies. Combined with the historical studies of professor Jacqueline Jones of Wellesley College (*Song of Sorrow, Song of Love: Black Women, Work and the Family in Slavery and Freedom*, New York: Basic Books, 1985) and Deborah G. White at Rutgers University (*Ar'n't I a Woman: Female Slaves in the Plantation South*, New York: Norton, 1985), the novels of Toni Morrison, Alice Walker, and Paule Marshall, the literary criticism of Professor Barbara Christian at the University of California, Berkeley (*Black Women Novelists: The Development of a Tradition*, Westport, Conn.: Greenwood, 1980), and the black feminist theory of black scholarship mentioned above would make for a dynamic course. Because the curriculum in Black Studies is so flexible and fluid, unfettered by disciplinary constraints, such a course would be introduced and taught with *élan*. Moreover, it should be noted that quite a few of the directors and chairs of Black Studies—for example, at Cornell and at the University of Mississippi—have established working ties with Women's Studies.

In addition to fellowship support, foundations have provided major funding for a host of black editing projects. A few of the notable projects are: the Frederick Douglass Papers, John Blassingame, editor; the Booker T. Washington Papers, Louis Harlan, editor; and the Freedmen and Southern Society Project, Ira Berlin, editor. These projects have made accessible to scholars invaluable documents and primary sources. Their significance to Black Studies scholarship cannot be exaggerated.

An especially encouraging sign of the vitality of Black Studies is the rising number of black scholars who are contemplating or engaging in collaborative research projects. This progression from individual research to collaborative efforts involving many people from different disciplines is a natural one. A typical first book or major publication is usually a revised dissertation. Now that many black scholars are working on second and third books and, most importantly, have acquired tenure, they are eager to develop collaborative studies. This impulse should be encouraged, as it bodes well for the development of Black Studies as a discipline.

In the early years, Black Studies units justified their intellectual existence on the grounds that they shattered the confining and restrictive boundaries of traditional disciplines. Actually, as far as I have been able to discern, most of the individual scholars in these programs and departments have published works that are very much in keeping with the mythological canons of the disciplines in which they were formally trained. It was naive and unrealistic to expect the young historian or sociologist of the Afro-American experience to retool, master a new, still inadequately defined Afrocentric methodology, and then prepare publishable manuscripts and win tenure—all within a six-year period.

In sum, I am optimistic about the future of Black Studies because of the energy, creativity, industry, and achievements of black scholars. The dream that Black Studies can be in the forefront of interdisciplinary research and writing deserves all available nourishment. The contemporary Black Studies movement will be considerably enhanced and sustained by serious professional scholars engaged in research and writing of the black experience. The creative potential of Black Studies, however, will become a reality only to the extent that foundations and universities provide full support.

NOTES

1. In 1988 Temple University established the first Ph.D. program in African-American studies.
2. Painter to Hine, June 22, 1987.

2. Notes on Administration of Africana Studies Departments and Programs

Warren C. Swindell, Ph.D.
Professor of Afro-American Studies
Director of Afro-American Studies
Indiana State University

There is a plethora of literature available on chairing academic units and many of the pearls of wisdom which may be gleaned therein can be applied by the Africana Studies unit chair. On the other hand, the Africana Studies administrator must shoulder additional burdens above and beyond those borne by his or her colleagues who head traditional units. Some of the challenges which face the Africana Studies administrator are non-existent for others. A few of them, for example, include: (1) working in an environment where institutionalized white supremacy as a doctrine stands in diametrical opposition to the very mission the unit is charged with implementing; (2) working with insulated administrative structures, committee structures, and faculty governance structures which in many instances are designed to maintain the status quo; and (3) gaining the empowerment necessary to guarantee self-determination for the unit without interference from regressive individuals and groups—including well meaning paternalistic types. This essay is organized to explore these three topics.

White Supremacy

White supremacy is the systematic elevation of Caucasians at the expense of darkly pigmented persons. This systematic elevation is carried out by persons who are responsible for establishing, maintaining, expanding or refining human activity in areas such as economics, education, entertainment, labor, law, politics, religion, male-female relationships, and military endeavors (Fuller, p. 2).

Studies pertaining to Africana people will be flawed unless white supremacy is factored into each equation. Martin Luther King, Jr., cited white supremacy as the linchpin of our systematic oppression. Throughout his long career, W.E.B. DuBois continuously linked black status to the practice of white supremacy. More recently, Africana mental health professionals such as Carlene Young, Joseph Baldwin, Daudi Azibo, Francis Cress Welsing, Linda James Myers, and Wade Nobles have concluded that white supremacy is one of the fundamental causes of the myriad of problems that Africana people face. And yet, surveys of undergraduate students indicate that white supremacy, as a system of oppression, is rarely included in the content of major courses in the social sciences and humanities.

How does white supremacy function? In a chapter pertaining to the defeat of white power after the Civil Rights movements, Jack M. Bloom analyzes how the system works. White supremacy reaches into the African American community and attempts to shape that community by determining its goals and methods for achieving those goals. Part of that attempt involves efforts to select and validate the "right" leadership. Further, white supremacy seeks to control the way the community thinks of itself, and, to the extent that it is successful, African Americans may feel that personal options in areas of relationships and family are not available.

Historically, the system of white supremacy has operated by making the political rights of African Americans null and void. Second, a paternalistic patronage system was established where certain African Americans were given special privileges and almost absolute power over other African Americans, as long as they stayed in their place and did what they were told to do and followed the white supremacy code: "Reliance on powerful whites was not only a way of getting certain otherwise unattainable benefits, it was also an alternative to relying on other blacks. Many felt that their own people were simply not to be trusted" (Bloom, p. 125). White supremacy relies on its victims to turn inward on themselves and to devour themselves through divisiveness and cannibalism, thereby strengthening the system.

Over the years, white supremacy has been so institutionalized that many people, African American and white alike, believe that the system is supposed to function as it does. Above all, white supremacy is in a perpetual state of refinement. Sociologist J. Owens Smith, who is president of the California Black Faculty and Staff Association, recently concluded that a different form of white supremacy has emerged. The form mentioned above is paternalistic white supremacy, while the current form is competitive white supremacy. Competitive white supremacy, Smith asserts, is usually found in a large scale manufacturing economy based on capitalism. The division of labor in this system is more complex, and the gap between wages among groups is narrow and not strictly along racial lines.

Social stratification is more complex because social mobility is both vertical and horizontal. "As the lower class obtains a higher level of education, income, occupational status, standards of living and the like, the more pronounced race prejudice becomes" (Smith, p. 2). This causes conflict between the two classes centered around the distribution of resources. "Embedded in this process is not only needed resources, but also power, prestige, and social status—all of which, according to conventional wisdom, are the object of man's desire" (Smith, p. 2).

College and university professors are perceived to have power, prestige, and social status. The harder African Americans struggle to become established as professors in academia, the more resistance we will encounter. This resistance will stem from the psychological discomfort of the white middle class as it senses African American professors dipping into a well where there is an insufficient amount of the commodities to be shared.

Africana Studies administrators should be alerted to how the psychological discomfort of the white middle class will be exhibited.

> First white, and those non-black minority group persons who wish to be treated as white, will attempt to eliminate our ability to compete with them for scarce resources. This is done through the passages of laws and adopting stiff requirements which supposedly respect the primacy of merit under the disguise of raising standards—all of which are code words for institutional racism. Secondly, they will escalate the stereotypical depiction of African Americans that casts us as aggressive, uppity, insolent, oversexed, dirty, inferior, drug-crazed, and dangerous. Finally, we will become the scapegoat for all of society's problem—the purpose being to promote the idea that if society could only rid itself of this bad element, it would eliminate the problems. Such faulty reasoning too often leads to violent attacks and repressive measures against African Americans [Smith, p. 2].

Africana Studies professors must remain ever vigilant, for competitive white supremacy uses the classroom to degrade our cultural experience and to discount the significance of the historical contributions that Africana people have made to the American society and to world culture. Smith advises that the best weapon at our disposal to combat competitive white supremacy is effective organization.

T. Thomas Fortune understated the case when he predicted that it would take the brightest African Americans the better part of a century to gain the human rights justly owed to them in the United States. He observed the firmly entrenched opposition to the abolishment of slavery and knew that those who favored the subjugation of Africans would teach their children to teach their children to continue their systematic oppression of Africana people. When handed down through several generations, "Racism in the form of white supremacy is the greatest motivating force that exists among the people of the known universe" (Fuller, p. 23). It is the greatest motivating force because it teaches white people that they will be threatened with extinction unless they unite against a common enemy. When a people's basic needs and existence are threatened, they often become more vulnerable to manipulation.

One of the major tasks of the Africana Studies administrator is to develop strategies and tactics to resist institutionalized white supremacy. Resistance to white supremacy reflects an abhorrence of victimization. The expansion of white supremacy, too, must be resisted. Through collective work and responsibility, the job can be done. White supremacy has been around for centuries and the longer it is maintained, the greater the effect it has on the thinking of non-white and white people. Although many white people are not white supremacists, by virtue of definition, no white person is immune to white supremacy. Above all, white supremacy is a form of what Neely Fuller calls "closed-circle" racism and is practiced so deceptively that even its existence cannot be "proven" except by those who practice it, and by those who are its victims (Fuller, p. 25).

The Organization of Africana Studies Unites Introduction

To paraphrase a Peter Drucker truism, if Africana people are to prosper in the 1990s and 2000s, we must study organizations and how institutions are organized in the way that our forbearers tilled the soil. Organization can achieve goals that an individual could only dream about. In essence, organizations are social structures created by individuals to support the collaborative pursuit of both specified and unspecified goals. Individuals, then, create social structures or organize activities to achieve certain goals (Scott, pp. 6–9). The manner in which units are organized to a great extent determines whether or not it is even possible for the unit to accomplish its mission.

In order to determine how Africana Studies units should be organized in higher education, the purposes of the units have to be clearly articulated. Robert L. Harris, Jr., in an essay written for the Ford Foundation, asks the question: "Africana studies for what?" By what right does Africana Studies merit a place in the higher education curriculum? Answers to this question may be forthcoming after one understands the nature of a society and what goals that society sets for its members to become productive, self-actualized human beings whose material, spiritual, intellectual, and affective needs are met collectively.

There have been literally hundreds of studies pertaining to the purpose of education in the United States. As a case in point, one organization, the National Commission on Excellence in Education, in a 1983 report, articulated some of the basic purposes of education: to help all children secure gainful employment, and to manage their own lives thereby serving not only their own interests but also the progress of society itself (Gardener, p. 4).

Because many African American colleges and universities have been destabilized, and because increasingly larger numbers of African American students are attending historically white institutions of higher education, Africana Studies units and Africana Affairs units must work in tandem at these institutions to fulfill the role of the pre–Brown African American college and university. In other words, Africana Studies units and Africana Affairs units must function as colleges within historically white institutions. Research data reveal that African American students who attend historically white institutions do not graduate as often as their peers who attend African American colleges, nor have they fared as well in graduating from professional and graduate schools. This systemic failure is a natural consequence of the separate racial nations within the nation and the refusal of white Americans to integrate African Americans into their system.

Africana Studies aims to overcome the system that oppresses it. And so to Robert L. Harris' query, "Africana Studies for what?", we say Africana Studies for liberation and enlightenment. A Spanish university aims to liberate and enlighten Spanish people. It uses the Spanish language and assumes a knowledge of Spanish history. The present problems of the Spanish people are its major concerns or focus. Spanish education becomes universal only in so far as other peoples of the world comprehend and are at one with Spain in its history (DuBois, p. 93). Africana Studies on white campuses must function as colleges for African American people just as Spanish colleges function for Spanish people, for African Americans are a distinct nationality in the United States.

Because African Americans have profoundly influenced the development of the United States from its inception through the present, Africana Studies seeks to enlighten the larger society by enriching the curriculum with Afrocentric courses. Individuals and groups from other races who take Africana Studies courses often feel differently about African Americans than they did prior to their learning experiences.

What has the higher education institutional leadership done to ensure that Africana Studies units are so organized to achieve the goals articulated above? Robert L. Harris, Jr., Darlene Clark Hine, and Nellie McKay, the essayists who wrote the Ford Foundation's *Three Essays*, generally agree that there is no consistent discernible organizational structure for Africana Studies when one compares programs from institution to institution, from state to state, and region to region. Temple University's Department of African and African American Studies offers a doctorate in the discipline. A few other universities offer cognate doctorates in the discipline when courses of study are combined with traditional disciplines. Some institutions are organized into programs which are unable to confer degrees. Other units offer several degrees to majors and minors at both the undergraduate and graduate levels. Some units are designated as "centers," others as "institutes," others as "departments," and some simply as "programs." These terms are generally nondescriptive because there is so much inconsistency in nomenclature. The program at the University of Georgia, for example, is called "The Institute for African-American Studies." This administrative structure allows the conferring of degrees. However, all appointments are joint appointments.

The Africana Studies and Research Center at Cornell University is organized as a research institute and reports directly to the provost. The unit also functions as a department and offers its courses through the College of Arts and Science. Undergraduate and graduate degrees are offered by the unit, which combines African, African American, and Caribbean Studies. The unit limits joint appointments to no more than 50 percent of the core faculty. Robert L. Harris, Jr., the unit's director, stresses the importance of a departmental structure because experience has taught him that units without department status or faculty lines have encountered tremendous difficulty in attracting faculty and in providing a coherent curriculum.

Units which achieved department status during the early 1970s, such as Indiana University–Bloomington, the University of Wisconsin–Madison, and the University of Pittsburgh's department of Black Community Education Research and Development, seem to have more stability than those whose faculty lines and budgets have fluctuated. Indiana University, as a case in point, has retained most of its core African American Studies faculty since 1970. Out of 14 full-time tenure track positions, 12 have been in place several years. Everyone shares a similar philosophy, everyone respects each other and works in teams or at least couples. The unit works closely with the African American Affairs unit which is headed by a dean. The African American Cultural Center reports to the dean of African American Affairs, as does the director of the African American Arts Institute. African American vocal music, instrumental music, dance, and theater are taught through the institute, while outreach programs to students and the community and tutorial programs are administered through the Cultural Center. This program is designed to function as a college within a college. Its courses are inextricably bound to the general educational requirements of the university and to certain traditional departments which require African American Studies courses of their majors and minors. The chair of African American Studies reports to the dean of the College of Arts and Sciences, while the dean of African American Affairs reports to the vice chancellor of the University.

The Center for Afro-American Studies at UCLA also offers a degree in Afro-American Studies. Its approach is essentially an interdisciplinary one. The program affords opportunities for guest faculty members to teach courses on a regular basis and affords opportunities for the regular faculty to conduct research in the Caribbean and in South America in addition to North America.

There are as many configurations for Africana units as there are institutions which support such units. But among Africana Studies professionals and the leadership of the National Council for Black Studies, there is a broad consensus that a department which functions in a manner analogous to traditional departments (whether called a program, center, or institute) is superior to other configurations. An organizational structure, whereby the various courses in Africana Studies are connected with one another so that relationships may be discerned, is the proper course of action.

A cogent philosophy of Africana Studies provides direction for and inspires and clarifies the work of the professor. The massive struggle—both overt and covert—against the discipline places Africana Studies professors under stress. This causes difficulty and discouragement in their work. Teaching African American Studies involves very complex problems, some of which appear to be almost insoluble.

Nonetheless, Africana Studies administrators and professors must operate with the intellectual freedom to create vision for our people and the world. This is particularly essential because of what the late Bobby Wright referred to as the anti-black character of many other races. It is morally unjust to empower people who have historically oppressed Africana people to make the ultimate academic decisions affecting our ability to think for ourselves and to prepare ourselves for jobs.

Learning to think for ourselves will not occur until we assume the responsibility to control our discipline (Karenga, pp. 395–411). As Molefi Asante argues in his *Afrocentricity*, there can be no freedom until there is freedom of the mind. An ideology for liberation and enlightenment must find its existence in ourselves and not be imposed by others. Most importantly, it must be derived from the historical and cultural experiences of Africana people (Asante, p. 31).

Africana Studies and Paternalism: The Need for Self-Definition

Paternalism is a complex phenomenon. Thomas Kochman, a linguist who contributes to multicultural understanding, sheds light on an issue which will affect every African American administrator who labors in a historically white institution. An analysis of the following dialogue reveals a mixture of white supremacy and paternalism, as the two are generally inextricably bound. In chapter two of his *Black and White Styles in Conflict*, Kochman illustrates an interracial interaction between Monroe Trotter, an African American intellectual and equal rights activist, and president Woodrow Wilson. In November 1914, Trotter led an African American delegation to the White House to renew protests against the segregation of federal employees after Wilson had instituted a system of apartheid for the first time.

Demonstrating his mastery of one of white supremacy's codes, Wilson argued that the purpose of apartheid was to avoid friction between African American and white clerks. Trotter knew better and disputed Wilson, asserting that African American and white clerks had been working together for 50 years in peace, harmony, and friendship. It was only after Wilson's inauguration, he explained, that segregation was installed in the Treasury and Postal Departments. After Trotter's rebuttal, Kochman quotes the exchange as follows:

> WILSON: If this organization is ever to have another hearing before me, it must have another spokesman. Your manner offends me.
>
> TROTTER: In what way?
>
> WILSON: Your tone, with its background of passion.
>
> TROTTER: But I have no passion in me, Mr. President, you are entirely mistaken; you misinterpret my earnestness for passion [Kochman, p. 17].

White supremacy and paternalism have been so thoroughly institutionalized in American culture that African Americans who refuse to follow the code are often punished, while those who follow it become part of the system of oppression. Nellie McKay, in her essay for the Ford Foundation entitled *Black Studies in the Midwest*, links a renewed commitment among predominantly white institutions to strengthen Black Studies and to increase the number of Africana faculty on their campuses to what she identifies as "at least one group of black scholars inside of these universities—those who completed graduate work between the mid and late 1970s and who have proved themselves good citizens of the intellectual world..." (McKay, p. 26). These persons, she asserts, know how to deal with academic politics in sophisticated ways. McKay's language is very abstract and can be interpreted in many ways. However, she seems to imply that if one stays in one's place and follows the proper rules, one will be rewarded. If that is so, will the Africana community be rewarded, and how will it benefit? If the answers are positive, she has a point. On the other hand, under paternalistic white supremacy, conforming to the system means perpetuation of the system.

In her essay, McKay compares Africana Studies and Women's Studies and concludes: "Still, black studies has a long way to go to achieve full dignity and acceptance in the academic community—much further, for instance than women's studies" (McKay, p. 26). She does not explain why Women's Studies is faring better in academia than Africana Studies, particularly since historically women have not had to deal with lynch mobs, dogs, police brutality, and the long struggle in the courts.

The failure even to control the discipline of Africana Studies has led to the hiring of many persons who are alien to the Africana experience to teach Africana Studies courses. For several reasons, it is impossible for these persons to be effective teachers and sensitive researchers. Vice versa, many Africana children fail in school not because they are unintelligent, but because of the cross-cultural lack of synchronization.

Paul Gee, a linguist, discusses the teaching of reading to illustrate why various cultural groups fail to communicate. He explains that in order to read texts of type *x* in way *y*, one has to be socialized into a practice, a practice other people have mastered. Reading and writing per se, then, are not as important as the social institutions or social groups that have these practices. He then stresses that the practices of such social groups are never just literacy practices. It is unthinkable to separate ways of talking, interacting, thinking, valuing, and believing from literacy practices. "Literary practices are almost always fully integrated with, interwoven into, constitute part of the very texture of wider practices that involve talk, interaction, values, and beliefs" (Gee, p. 3).

In order to clarify and to make an essential concept less abstract, Gee coins the term "Discourses" with a capital "D" to refer to the social practices which involve an integration of ways of talking, interacting, thinking, valuing, believing, and often of reading and writing. The focus of work on literacy, he argues, ought to be on Discourses, not on writing, reading, or language.

The concept of Discourses as ways of being in the world is critical here for they are forms of life which integrate words, acts, values, beliefs, attitudes, and social identities, as well as gestures, glances, body position, and clothes. Gee writes:

> A Discourse is a sort of *identity Kit* which comes complete with the appropriate costume and instruction on how to act, talk and often write, so as to take on a particular role that others will recognize. Being trained as a linguist meant that I learned to speak, think, and act like a linguist, and to recognize others when they do so.... How does one acquire a Discourse?... Discourses are not mastered by overt instruction (even less so than languages, and hardly anyone ever fluently acquired a second language sitting in a classroom), but by inculturation ("apprenticeship") into social practices through scaffold and supported interaction with people who have already mastered the Discourse. This is how we all acquired our native language and our home-base Discourse. It is how we acquire all later, more public oriented Discourses. If you have no access to the social practice, you don't get in the Discourse, you don't have it. You cannot overtly teach anyone a Discourse in a classroom or anywhere else. Discourses are not bodies of knowledge like physics or archeology or linguistics. Therefore, ironically, while you can overtly teach someone linguistics, a body of knowledge, you can't teach them to be a linguist, that is to use a Discourse. The most you can do is to let them practice being a linguist with you [Gee, pp. 6–7].

Clearly, one cannot become competent in Africana Studies by writing a few articles or three or four books on Africana people, life, and culture. Other people have been writing about Africana people for thousands of years. But as Gee implies, one has to be socialized into Africana life and culture in order to teach Africana Studies, or to make decisions in higher education pertaining to Africana Studies. Many Africana Studies professors and administrators who make critical decisions which impact the discipline have not been socialized into Africana life and culture. And I am not implying that white people should not make decisions on Africana Studies or teach Africana Studies, for there are many white people who have been so socialized, while some African Americans have not been so socialized.

Several musicians acknowledge their socialization into the culture. Jerry Lee Lewis, a cousin of Jimmy Swaggert, is just one among millions of people who have been so socialized:

> I used to hang around Haney's Big House that was a colored establishment where they had dances and such.... We was just kids, we wasn't allowed in. So we'd slip around to the back and sneak in wherever we could. I saw lots of 'em in there, all those blues players. It was not because we were white that we were not allowed in the place, it was because we were kids. We didn't make an issue of race then... [Chapple and Garafalo, p. 245].

Rockabilly artist Carl Perkins offers a similar testimony:

> I was raised on a plantation in the flatlands of Lake County, Tennessee, and we were about the only white people on it. I played with colored kids, played football with old socks stuffed with sand. Working in the cotton fields in the sun, music was the only escape. The colored people would sing, and I'd join in, just a little kid, and that was colored rhythm and blues, got named rock 'n' roll, got named that in 1956, but the same music was there before, and it was my music [Chapple and Garafalo, p. 245].

The more accomplished and enlightened scholars and administrators of other races and cultures yield to competent Africana Studies professionals in matters pertaining to Africana students and to the discipline. Paternalistic individuals and the unenlightened, however, do not hesitate to make such decisions. Early on, Melville J. Herskovits argued that there was no such thing as African American culture. Within a short period of time, he was able to see the error of his ways. However, it is very doubtful whether or not he could have written *The Myth of the Negro Past* without access to the social practice. It was Zora Neale Hurston, his research assistant, who provided him with the necessary insight to do his study.

Gunnar Myrdal, too, admitted that he did not completely understand the African American community when he did his monumental study, *An American Dilemma*. Roger Shinn, who was author and theologian William Watley's major professor at Union Theological Seminary of New York City, demonstrates his sensitivity to, respect for, and awareness of cultural differences when he asserts that he would not dare attempt to explain Martin Luther King, Jr., nor claim to understand him. Yet, Shinn acknowledges that he saw King three times. He saw him enter into conversation, devise strategies, respond to critical questions and move people to act on their highest loyalties. He saw King on television several times and has read most of his published writings. But he yields to Watley when it comes to writing about King because Watley and King shared a common background as African American ministers and were culturally synchronized (Watley, pp. 7–8).

When people from one culture are taught by people from another culture, it is imperative that cultural synchronization take place. Africana Studies must help Africana students understand how the culture of the larger society differs from our culture so that they approach working in the culture of the larger society as would a foreigner. Jacqueline Jordan Irvine, an educational researcher at Emory University, is very clear when discussing the failure to synchronize cultures when Africana students are taught by others. "Because the culture of minority [students] is different and often misunderstood, ignored, or discounted, minority students are likely to experience cultural discontinuity in schools resulting in lack of cultural correspondence or 'sync'" (Irvine, p. 7). The same holds for college and university environments.

Irvine points out that many of the dysfunctional behaviors of Africana students such as underachievement and the lack of achievement can be attributed to the acceptance and internalization by our students of society's view that they are unlikely to succeed. As a matter of fact, it is commonly accepted by educators that self-concept influences the achievement of African American students. "Psychologists and sociologists have argued that the self is found to be in direct relation to how a person thinks others perceive him or her. Thus, a person in our society validates his or her identity through the evaluations of significant others" (White, p. 91). It stands to reason, then, that validation and approval for Africana people should be derived from the Africana community. Paradoxically, no matter what we do, or what our merits might be, as African Americans, we get poor reflections of ourselves in the behavior of whites (White, p. 93). Perhaps, then, it is as college president Stephen Joel Trachtenberg argues: "Multiculturalism can be taught only by Multicultural People" (Trachtenberg, pp. 610-611).

Conclusion

Africana Studies will face some extremely difficult days ahead because of what social science researchers call "in-group bias." In-group bias is a particularly thorny problem. It is only natural that competitive choices favoring in-group members tend to dominate all other choices available to the subjects. In fact, in-group bias in favor of members of one's own group and in disfavor of members of an out-group is one of the most conclusive findings of social science researchers. In-group members are not necessarily hostile toward out-group members, they simply favor in-group members. Therefore, as resources become scarce, faculty lines are reduced, status and prestige become more difficult to attain and line items must be reduced; social science researchers can predict where the ax will fall.

On any campus where the administration fails to protect Africana Studies from a biased majority, the discipline is in trouble, for the in-group sets the standards for differentiation. Whether the criterion is performance on a diagnostic instrument, longevity, educational credentials, or on less tangible criteria such as whether or not one has an accept, or whether or not one smiles frequently, or has a "pleasing personality," the in-group has a built-in advantage because its members develop the criteria. In other words, there is no win unless the in-group decides to allow a win. "As long as traditional standards or criteria for inclusion dominate, it is likely that the conditions for in-group bias will be perpetuated to the disadvantage of the out-group" (Jones, p. 33).

Jones concludes that institutional white supremacy is perpetuated when an institution fails to acknowledge the history of racial discrimination (Jones, p. 36). People who engage in white supremacist behavior do so because they are almost certain that there is support for it within their society generally or within their unit or institution specifically (Dennis, p. 72).

REFERENCES AND WORKS CITED

Alkalimat, Abdul and Associates. *Introduction to Afro-American Studies: A Peoples College Primer.* Chicago: Twenty-First Century Books and Publications, 1988.

Asante, Molefi Kete. "Book Review Essay: A Note on Nathan Huggins' Report to the Ford Foundation on African-American Studies." *Journal of Black Studies*, 17:2, December, 1986.

Asante, Molefi Kete. *Afrocentricity.* Trenton, N.J.: Africa World Press, Inc., 1988.

Bloom, Jack M. *Class, Race, and the Civil Rights Movements.* Bloomington: Indiana University Press, 1987.

Chapple, Steve and Reebe Garofalo. *Rock 'n' Roll Is Here to Pay.* Chicago: Nelson Hall, 1977.

Creigs, C. Beverly, and Robert E. Barns, "In the Belly of the Whale: Cultural Dimensions of African-American Incarceration and Rehabilitation." *Dialogue: A Magazine for American Baptist Chaplains and Pastoral Counselors*, 1989.

Cruse, Harold. *Plural But Equal.* New York: William Morrow, 1987.

Dennis, Ruthledge M. "Socialization and Racism: The White Experience," in Benjamin P. Bower and Raymon G. Hunt, editors, *Impact of Racism on White Americans.* Beverly Hills, Calif.: Sage Publications, 1981.

DuBois, W.E.B. *The Education of Black People.* Edited by Herbert Aptheker. Amherst: University of Massachusetts Press, 1973.

Finn, Chester E. "Why Can't Colleges Convey Our Diverse Culture's Unifying Themes," *The Chronicle of Higher Education*, June 13, 1990.

Fuller, Neely, Jr., *The United Independent Compensatory Code/System/Concept Revised Edition.* Washington, D.C.: The Author, 1984.

Gardener, David Pierpont (Chairman). National Commission on Excellence in Education. *A Nation at Risk: The Imperative for Educational Reform; A Report by the National Commission on Excellence in Education.* Washington, D.C.: Superintendent of Documents, U.S. Government Printing Office, April 26, 1983.

Gee, James Paul. "Literacies, Discourses, and Identities," a paper prepared for the Preconference Seminar on Multi-Cultural Perspectives on Literacy and Practice (Nov. 28, 1989) of the National Reading Conference.

Grassmuck, Karen. "A $50-million Gift Buoys Black Colleges for Ambitious Drive," *The Chronicle of Higher Education*, March 14, 1990, p. A38.

Harris, Robert L., Jr. "The Intellectual and Institutional Development of Africana Studies," in *Three Essays: Black Studies in the United States*. New York: Ford Foundation, 1990.

Huggins, Nathan I. *Afro-American Studies: A Report to the Ford Foundation*. New York: Ford Foundation, 1985.

Irvine, Jacqueline Jordan. "Cultural Responsiveness in Teacher Education: Strategies to Prepare Majority Teachers for Successful Instruction of Minority Students," a paper presented at the Annual Meeting of Project 30, December 1–4, 1989 in Monterey, California.

Jaynes, Gerald David, and Robin M. Williams, Jr., editors. *A Common Destiny: Blacks and American Society*. Washington, D.C.: National Academy Press, 1989.

Jones, James M. "The Concept of Racism and Its Changing Reality" in Benjamin P. Bower and Raymond G. Hunt, eds., *Impact of Racism on White Americans*. Beverly Hills, Calif.: Sage Publications, 1981.

Karenga, Maulana. *Introduction to Black Studies*. Inglewood, Calif.: Kawaida Publications, 1982.

Karenga, Maulana. "Black Studies and the Problematic of Paradigm: The Philosophical Dimension," *Journal of Black Studies* 8:4, June, 1988.

Kochman, Thomas. *Black and White Styles in Conflict*. Chicago: University of Chicago Press, 1981.

Leonhard, Charles, and Robert W. House. *Foundations and Principles of Music Education*, 2d ed. New York: McGraw-Hill, 1972.

Marynowski, Susan. "Blacks Should Not Fear Losses Through Integration, Florida Professor Says," *Black Issues in Higher Education*, July 5, 1990.

McKay, Nellie. "Black Studies in the Midwest" in *Three Essays: Black Studies in the United States*. New York: Ford Foundation, 1990.

Myrdal, Gunnar. *An American Dilemma: The Negro Problem and Modern Democracy*. New York: Harper & Row, 1944.

Scott, W. Richard. *Organizations; Rational, Natural, and Open Systems*. Englewood Cliffs, N.J.: Prentice-Hall, 1981.

Smith, J. Owens. "The New Forms of Racism," *California Black Faculty and Staff Association News*, September-November, 1989, 15:1.

Southern, Eileen. *The Music of Black Americans: A History*, 2d ed. New York: W.W. Norton, 1985.

Stafford, Walter W., and Joyce Ladner, "Comprehensive Planning and Racism," *AIP Journal*, March, 1969.

Trachtenberg, Stephen Joel. "Multiculturalism Can Be Taught Only by Multicultural People," *Phi Delta Kappan*, April 1990.

Watley, William D. *Roots of Resistance: The Nonviolent Ethic of Martin Luther King, Jr.* Valley Forge, Pa.: Judson Press, 1985.

Watson, Frederick. "Cooperative Education; Educational Goldmine for Minorities," *Black Issues in Higher Education* vol. 6, no. 8, November 23, 1989.

White, Joseph L., and Thomas A. Parham. *The Psychology of Blacks*, 2d ed. Englewood Cliffs, N.J.: Prentice-Hall, 1990.

3. Black Studies: A New Story

Houston A. Baker, Ph.D.
Albert Greenfield Professor of Human Relations
Director, Center for the Study of Black Literature and Culture
University of Pennsylvania

The single task that I set myself for the summer of 1991 was an essay on Black Studies and the institution of English. I was less certain about English in its daily, postmodern unfoldings than I was about Black Studies, for who can ever be certain what is happening at Duke? By contrast, everyone knows the familiar story of Black Studies. It is a narrative of Hagar's children redeemed from exile by the grace of affirmative action and the intentionality of black power. It is a vernacular tale, resonant with rhythm and blues. And it has been relegated in recent years to the briefest imaginable space in the encyclopedia of postmodern American academics. Thus it was that, in the summer of 1991, I wanted to construct a Black Studies account that would produce, perhaps, a conclusion rather different from "Negroes also spoke." I hoped, in short, to avoid "soul" narration.

A number of factors converged, however, to make my job more complicated than I had envisioned. First, the currents of the PC (Political Correctness) cavaliers were swirling, during the summer of 1991, with the energy of Edgar Allen Poe's maelstrom. Everywhere one turned, after the Modern Language Association opposed the nomination of Carole Iannone to the National Council on the Humanities, there were editorials and "op. ed." meditations denouncing a new "leftism" of "tenured radicals" in the American Academy. Professors who suggested that Alice Walker might conceivably form part of a course devoted to American literature were held to be equivalent—in the bizarre logic of the PC cavaliers—to Ku Klux Klanspersons. (Don't ask me to explain it.) And in the economies of the PC cavaliers, Black Studies was just one more roundheaded carryover from the chaotic 1960s, when mere anarchy was loosed in halls of ivy. Like other disciplinary area studies (e.g., Women's Studies) to which it lent force, Black Studies was suddenly being held accountable for a new "McCarthyism." (Again, don't ask me to explain it—at least not yet.)

There thus seemed to be at least two incumbencies if I was going to achieve a new and different story. I would certainly have to account for the new politics of PC by, at least, re-vocabularizing the familiar Black Studies tale to avoid its easy imbrication in a simple-minded, right-wing rhetoric of denunciation. Second, since Black Studies was founded as a social, scholarly, and pedagogical enterprise to deal with black culture, I would have to account for the relationship of such studies to black urban culture. Black urban culture, I believe, provided much of the impetus for Black Studies' founding; and surely in our own era, it is the locus of quite extraordinary transnational creative energy.

Having arrived at the contours of my narrative mission, I had absolutely no clear idea of how to fulfill it. I felt like Mr. Phelps in the original run of *Mission: Impossible.* I was out "in the cold," and the scholarly muses had disavowed knowledge of my proper person. In such instances, there is no recourse but improvisation. So, I found myself by midsummer trying to follow the unfolding PC debates, struggling to read cultural studies materials, and carving out time to catch up on the black urban expressivity of *Yo! MTV Raps.* This welter of anxiety and influences produced such hybrid moments as putting aside the *Wall Street Journal*'s latest diatribe against PC to take up the writings of Paul Gilroy while listening, with one ear, to the jamming lyrics of Ice-T's unbelievable *OG (Original Gangster)* album. Having concluded that the notion of "nation," as employed and analyzed by black British cultural studies, was indispensable to my narrative, I set out on a sunny Sunday in August to borrow a copy of Benedict Anderson's *Imagined Communities* from a friend who lives near Philadelphia's Benjamin Franklin Parkway. Instead of Anderson's book, I quite serendipitously discovered an energetically imagined community of interests in action, one that seemed rather like a Wordsworthian spot of time.

It was Unity Day on the Parkway. Thousands of people were assembled, and the scene seemed to offer—in its collaged multiplicity of sound and image—a foreshadowing of both the form and substance I hoped to capture in my new story of Black Studies. But I knew immediately that no written text could fully capture the gorgeously arrayed young black people in African-print shirts and dresses set off by roped-gold jewelry and *kofi* hats. Nor could academic writing make readers feel the heat and stillness as I approached what I shall call the "surveillance" or, alternatively, the "discipline and punish" tent set at the very head of the Benjamin Franklin Parkway. This tent (of which I shall have more to say later) was the largest of the Unity Day tents; it was the first among all competitors of the day's interiors. It was the Dante-esque first darkness, blocking the view (but not, of course, the sound) of stages from which the music flowed.

The brightness and energy, in combination with the celebratory rhythm and beat of Unity Day, proved as inspirational for me as a "filament of platinum" among alloying elements. The beauty, complexity, and expressivity of the blackness at work on the Unity Day Sunday afternoon were sufficient to convince even an overly influenced and anxious me that there was a new and important array of energies at work in the world that had to be accounted for in any story yet to be told of Black Studies. Like the innovated cultural workers whom I discovered on the parkway that August afternoon, I realized that I would have to take what I had at hand and, even under the astute surveillance and policing of the present day, convert it into a multirhythmic and different story of both academic and general social processes that have marked the past 25 years. I decided the term *moral panic,* from cultural studies, would nicely serve my ends. I gestured before and after, as it were, serving a useful analytical purpose with respect to both the first arrival of black urban migrants at the gates of the academy and to the belated current outcry against that arrival—Political Correctness. Less modishly, and drawing from the "normal practice" of academic scholarship, I realized that there was no theoretical or cultural studies escape from history. And so the story unfolds.

The new story that unfolds is a drama of shifting horizons, contested spaces, and simulacra. If one recalls the now defunct television show *College Bowl* (which was every thinking man's honorable pastime on Sundays during the early sixties), the image of the American university evoked is a pastoral landscape dotted with spacious buildings, well-dressed white youth smiling and chatting, and studious tweed-jacketed professors earnestly discoursing before rapt audiences. This image of a harmonious garden of knowledge overseen by sober white intellectuals was always shown in brief film clips at halftime for each of the competing *College Bowl* teams matched in rapid-fire responses to "common curriculum" questions of Western civilization: for example, "What eighteenth century British economist first announced the iron law of wages?" Usually the participants were young white males displaying a talent for "classical" learning that precious few Americans would ever need to know. *College Bowl's* pastoral image had become standard fare during the silent American 1950s, and it was not merely a product of smoke and mirrors. It carried, in fact, the specific weight of the American academy's founding. For even in the variousness of its founding, the American university was always conceived as a quiet, scenic space of disinterested thought—a territory functionally and strategically removed from everyday life. It is not accidental that seventeenth century Harvard was called the "seminary in the wilderness."

Without belaboring the point, it seems almost an understatement to say that the American academy is a direct, shaped product of founding ideologies. Sectarian colleges received their marching orders and general character from their respective ministerial governing boards. Private institutions marched to the beat of trustees like Ralph Ellison's Mr. Norton, a man who Clark Kerr called the "multiversity." United States campuses were relatively simple and sometimes indisputably pastoral gardens of Western knowledge indoctrination, conditioned always by strong and discernible ideologies. With the coming of the multiversity, these ideological interests increased in scale as big business and big government poured billions of research dollars into the academic garden, transforming it into a factory. What did not change, of course, were the fundamental whiteness and harmonious Westernness of higher education. Even when tweed-jacketed white men were no longer in front of rapt audiences but hermetically bent on highly financed "research," they were still white men. Likewise, the student body—even if it was no longer lolling in tree-shaded gardens—was still, almost to a young man or woman, "white, white, white," as they say repetitively for emphasis in most creoles of the world.

Of course, I am aware that there are exceptions to this characterization of Western knowledge production. American universities have always been marked by occasional sites of resistance. And on the whole one would be hard-pressed to discover the degree of expressive freedom enjoyed by the university in any other American institution. Moreover, Nathan Huggins has pointed out in *Afro-American Studies*, a report compiled for the Ford Foundation, that after World War II, American universities became more democratic as their enrollments soared, bringing non–middle class students and returning GIs to campuses. Catching a general impulse to reform, universities expanded their missions to include remedial education and the preparation of traditionally excluded citizens for upward class mobility. Even with such changes, however, the exclusivity of America's well-financed and traditionally all-white sites of higher learning remained a matter of policy and record. As the popular philosopher Pogo said in 1963, "Outside pressure (on the American academy) creates an inside pressure: academic conformity. The average (American) professor is no Socrates." Thus, in 1963 the American university was a very quiet, decorous, white project.

My own experiences certainly accord with Pogo's terse depiction of the American academy—I can almost feel, even as I write this sentence, the hushed decorum of the University of California at Los Angeles when I arrived for graduate study in 1965. Eucalyptus and palms shaded wide boulevards and intimate walkways. Quaint outdoor "Gypsy Wagons" supplied orderly dining places for a seemingly endless array of white people. I was thrown into black culture shock by Westwood Village, where even menial jobs were occupied by Mexican Americans, not bodacious brothers and sisters. And when I tried my undergraduate Howard University jive and juju on one of the very few Negro freshmen, greeting him with "What's happening, brother?" he replied, "Why…uh…good morning. How are you?" His eyes almost bugged from his head in *haute bourgeois* panic. Yes, even though UCLA was indisputably enveloped in the long shadow of the 1965 Watts summer rebellion, the campus maintained a signally quiet grace under national pressure for black liberation. But everything was soon to undergo a change that might have made even Negro freshmen blanch in 1965.

In the mid-sixties, the quiet of the American university—whether garden or factory—was shattered forever by the thundering "NO" to all prior arrangements of higher education in America issued by the Free Speech Movement (FSM). Witness those erstwhile docile (or robotic) young white men and women of *College Bowl* transformed into revolutionary cadres questioning the prerogatives of faculty and administrators. Firebrands demanding curriculum revision, deconstructing the rhetoric of American higher education *in toto*. Witness such rebellion spreading like wildfire across campuses everywhere. What an incongruous moment! Stupefied administrators, faculty, trustees, men and women of the cloth, and bewildered legislators wondered what dread "outside" demon had infected the halls of ivy. For by the mid-sixties it was obvious to everyone concerned that an outside "social" ambiance and an inside "academic" atmosphere had converged like giant weather fronts. And no one needed a meteorologist to know that a hard rain was gonna fall.

The silencing academic walls were socially breached at midcentury by codes, strategies, and cadences of the black liberation struggle in America. If W.E.B. DuBois speaks persuasively in *The Souls of Black Folk* about a coming of black folk to college that produced new and joyful songs of Talented Tenth enlightenment, surely we can speak today of the emergence on American campuses of strident white students who felt the wind-blown lyrics of a black American liberation spirit moving in their souls. Many of these students had participated in direct nonviolent protests for civil rights in their home states; others had made their way to Mississippi during the Freedom Summer of 1964. They were primed for protest, and it is fair to say that the FSM transformed the image of the American university from a *College Bowl* still life into a rollicking video of transgenerational conflict. The country witnessed and responded in deeply condemnatory tones.

The university was transformed, in fact, into a metonym for social chaos. If "mere anarchy" was loosed on America, virtually everyone agreed that the bonds of law and order had been severed by students. "Blame but the students!" became the rallying cry of agreement.

Now the social disorder of the United States was in reality a product of ill-conceived military adventurism in Southeast Asia and a monstrously excessive federal egotism on the home front. The attribution of responsibility that sought to withdraw attention from both American imperialism abroad and vicious United States reactions to black demands for civil rights at home. The voting citizenry of the United States decided that it was far more profitable and conforming to scapegoat the university than to assess the criminality of career politicians and their henchmen and constituents at home and abroad.

And it is here that Black Studies as a floating signifier becomes a powerful analytical tool. For the convergence of Civil Rights and the FSM did indeed produce incongruity. It was only the further development of this convergence, however, in the form of black students' immigration, that gave resonance to a revolutionary hybridity on American campuses. For with this immigration, "inside" and "outside" came into brilliant kaleidoscopic allegiance.

Black student recruitment, black student scholarships and fellowships, black dormitories, student leagues and unions, black faculty recruitment and curriculum revision, and preeminently Black Studies all became signs of new times and territories in the United States academy. Black Studies became a sign of conjuncture that not only foregrounded the university as a space of territorial contest, but also metaphorized the contest itself in a way that allowed the sign to serve as a simulacrum. That is to say, Black Studies as a sign became not only a real ground of contestation, but also a coded and generative space of values that encompassed both past and proximate, inside and outside, confrontations. In a word, Black Studies became a signifying amalgam of energies gesturing toward antidraft resistance, the FSM, Civil Rights, black power, and general American concerns for a redistribution of the resources of knowledge production. In the terms of Jean Baudrillard's *Simulations*, Black Studies was akin to the black box of the genetic code; it was capable of a seemingly endless proliferation of revolutionary "likenesses."

As a simulacrum, Black Studies generated a combinatory power of signification in profoundly black ways, mixing styles and producing a synthesis in which kitsch, retro, and other modes occupied spaces of value "all at the same time," to quote Baudrillard on simulacra in general. Before and after, now and future, were temporally coexistent in the Black Studies project, complicating any attempt either to recuperate or authenticate traditional notions of the *real*.

Black Studies was committed in the first instance of its determination to undoing all prevalent "authentic" notions of such disciplines as history and English. Hence, at the site of the university, Black Studies presented a hugely unsettling challenge. For even as it sought in its own voice to lay claim to disciplinary status as a normal academic subject, its very conjunctive and stylistically diverse energies eradicated the referential lines of subjectivity and disciplined academic knowledge.

How could the notion of traditional disciplines (bounded as they were by strict codes of nontransgression) remain unaffected by an avowedly interdisciplinary view of knowledge production such as Black Studies? And how—in the face of black immigration—could old notions of an exclusively white student subject-position be maintained? Black Studies as simulacrum became the foregrounded anomaly that arrested "normal" academic practice and produced both a paradigm shift and the moral panic and territorial contestation that always accompany such shifts.

Thomas Kuhn tells us in *The Structure of Scientific Revolutions* that such shifts are less the result of "discoveries" than of "anomalies" that can not be accounted for without mind-bending elaborations of old theoretical models and normal practices. And when there finally is no recourse but to move from a geocentric to a heliocentric view of the world, watch out! Missiles of panic and conflict are destined to fly.

By 1968, at UCLA, panic was no longer in the eyes of the young man whom I had greeted with Howard University argot in his freshman year. Rather, panic was in the eyes of multiversitycrats witnessing the profound sea change undergone by this young man between his freshman and junior years. And, Lord have mercy, how *rapid* that change was! By the spring of 1968, that same young Negro who had given me a cool "Hello" was radically hot. He had become a mega-coiffured, dashiki-clad student leader who audaciously saluted me one morning with "Hey, Brotherman! You gon' be at duh meet'n tonight!" Why even his idiolect had shifted! And it certainly brought panic to the hearts of the nation and produced territorial battles of immense proportions as the young man's fellow blacks migrated to shaded eucalyptus walks of an American university already besieged by the unruliness of FSM and a white countercultural left just awaiting a blackening simulacrum for its dark, revolutionary legitimacy.

In his report to the Ford Foundation, which I have already cited, Nathan Huggins wrote:

> Administrators deliberately set out to recruit poor youngsters from the inner city (so-called ghetto youth), imagining that the university might rectify failures in the secondary-school system and redeem these students so they might enter mainstream life. This policy implied a changing (or at least a rethinking) of standards of admission as they applied to these youngsters.

The recruitment and arrival of ghetto youth on university campuses nationwide was a moment that can only be understood in terms of immigration. Not only did the black arrivants bring radically different racial and class inflections to the discourse of the academy, they also brought a hybridity of style that scarcely matched the "reality" of the American academic garden. Their very presence on the university landscape challenged all existing norms and raised citizenship problems that not even the most imaginative members of the FSM could have anticipated. Far from "grateful" subjects, the black arrivants were vociferously cantankerous. Seeing no reflection of themselves at any of the traditional loci of the academy, they demanded, like Zora Neale

Hurston's Janie Starks, to know, "Where's me? I don't see me?" This challenging interrogative brought wide-eyed stares from white fellow students and from faculty and administrators alike. No one had imagined that if blacks were admitted to the university, they would be anything other than grateful for such an "opportunity." It was assumed that blacks, like compliant colonial subjects, would swear allegiance to Western civilization and quickly take up the business of assimilating white behavioral codes and intellectual fare. Not so, as Huggins records: "It was a time ... of open and symbolic displays of militancy. Hair styles, clothing, language, name changes all conspired to challenge and intimidate" (p. 18). In effect, a new, black academic immigrant culture evolved from the late sixties through the mid seventies. And this evolution was accompanied not only by a common black discourse across the nation's college and university campuses, but also by a series of reterritorializations at particular academic locales. Nationally, there were emergent publications like *The Black Collegian*. Locally, there were often territorial conflicts between traditional white inhabitants and a new immigrant population.

In his poem "Old Lem" the late Sterling Brown says: "They don't come by ones... They don't come by twos... We get the justice in the end... And they come by tens." Besieged state politicians and higher education guardians of the early 1970s must have felt that things were rushing at them not by ones or twos, but "by tens." For along with the transgressive black social initiatives that overleapt restraining academic walls in the sixties, there came new revolutionary feminist impulses. Vocal on-campus activism by the courageous Angela Davis and Charlene Hunter was matched by the actions and portraits of such black women social activists as Kathleen Cleaver and Ericka Huggins. At a quotidian level of the liberation struggle, Rosa Parks had by herself begun a fierce war of wills in 1955 when she sat down on a Montgomery, Alabama, bus and decided never to back off again. *The Feminine Mystique* was being quoted even at Howard University by 1964, and by 1969 even Yale was about to go coed. When women did come to American campuses like Yale, they arrived with the force of tens, and with Women's Liberation on their minds and Women's Studies as their goal. Having failed to listen to any reasonable advice to the contrary, male leaders at Yale decided that what they would do to welcome the coeds and make them happy was paint their rooms in pastel shades and install full-length mirrors. By the fall of 1970, I am happy to report, radical women had seized the mike at a Yale trustees meeting and demanded the name of the idiot who had prepared their "welcome." Women's Studies was alive, allied, and in effect. They came by tens, and they got the justice in the end.

By the 1970s Black Studies had become a point or space of territorial conflict and conjuncture, containing in its phrasing both the nominal academic imperative marked by *studies* and the innovative and surveilling adjectival imperative *blackness*. Rather than oxymoronic, the tensions in the phrase

Black Studies signaled an immigrant hybridity akin to a phrase like *black British* or *black American* uttered in semantic economies that had no word fields for them. What was required on American college and university campuses, therefore, was a re-vocabularization of academic discourse to reflect a genuine redistribution of space, time, and energy to meet Black Studies demands. What generally occurred, however, in response to the arrival of the new black immigrant population was moral panic as a function of territorial contestation.

In Isaac Julien's brilliant film *Territories*, the word *territory* is defined as "the holding of one's class privileges in a declining system of crisis." As a "holding," the dominant territory of Britishness in Julien's film is locked in struggle with a population that holds quite other than white British truths to be self-evident. The film, in fact, projects black British "Carnival" as a ludic space of cultural specificity that challenges all holdings of British authority. Voice-overs speak of territories of class, labor, race, and sex relations that have to be oppositionally re-vocabularized and uniquely sounded by a black British population.

Carnival and West Indian sound systems are portrayed as the ritual and music of black oppositionality and also as extensions of cultural-expressive forms originating in sacred rites of Africa and the Nile Valley. These sounds and rites of Carnival are captured in Julien's film by swaying masses of black revelers making their way through the stunned, threatening, or perplexed gaze of massed British police cordons. In one scene, a Union Jack's flaming disintegration segues into a shot of two black gay males dancing with each other. The scene surely represents a reordering of territories of patriotism, Britishness, and desire. In a later scene, a pearled and skittish older white British woman hurries along the street until she sees the Carnival revelers; her gaze registers panic. But suddenly the camera reverses, and she moves rapidly backward. The black art of the filmmaker thus challenges the woman's response and returns her to a parochial past from which she may never awaken.

Julien's wonderful mapping of the territories of immigration gives some idea of the stakes involved in Black Studies as black enrollment in American universities amounted to 10.8 percent of the total United States college enrollment in October of 1977—nearly matching the percentage of blacks in the country's 18-to-24-year-old population as a whole. At Cornell, Wesleyan, and San Francisco State, the new immigration and demands of Black Studies forced confrontations that brought not only panic, but also the police.

As Stanley Cohen defines it in his insightful *Folk Devils and Moral Panics*, a moral panic exists when "a condition, episode, person or group of persons emerges to become defined as a threat to societal values and interests" (p. 9). Characterizing the movement of blacks to the academy, the scholar Nick Aaron Ford writes:

> *Thoughtfully and honestly conceived, and effectively and wisely administered Black Studies are…a threat.* They are a threat to blatant ignorance of well-meaning people who are supposed to know the truth about the entire history and culture of their country and its people. They are a threat to prejudice and bigotry nourished by fear of the half-truths and unadulterated lies that miseducation has produced. They are a threat to false and distorted scholarship that has flourished without condemnation or shame in the most prestigious bastions of higher education in this nation [pp. 188-89].

The threat that produces moral panic results, according to Cohen, in a reactionary sequence of demonizing and surveillance followed by control activities that seek to exorcise the "threat."

Where Black Studies were concerned, the "demonizing" phase witnessed such intriguing figures as John Blassingame, Eugene Genovese, Sir Arthur Lewis, Bayard Rustin, and others delivering exorcising judgments. Blassingame offers a nearly ideal example of moral panic's attempts to "re-normalize" the anomalous:

> It is not enough to know that "whitey" has been, and is, oppressing blacks…. Instead, Negroes must study business practices, high finance, labor law and practices….the threat to black intellectuals is real. Not only do the black students demand that the teachers in black studies programs be Negroes, they also want them to have the right shade of "blackness." In essence, this means that the black scholar must have the right ideological leanings.

Blassingame's moral high dudgeon resonates in conservative harmony with the angry tones of President Richard M. Nixon, whose speech to (and I kid you not!) General Beadle State College in North Dakota in 1969 called the times "deeply troubled and profoundly unsettled."

The white historian and author of *The Political Economy of Slavery*, Eugene Genovese, weighed in during June of 1969, when he portrayed white students as seductive bogeymen leading poor black students down the road of reactionism. Genovese characterized these leftist students as "pseudo-revolutionary middle-class totalitarians" intent on coopting Black Studies demands in order to "reestablish the campus purge and thereby provide a moral and legal basis for a new wave of McCarthyism" (p. 108). This is moral panic demonizing with a vengeance!

But times of moral panic produce strange bedfellows, as Sir Arthur Lewis and Kenneth Clark's respective responses to Black Studies demonstrate. Lewis felt the entire Black Studies enterprise was but seedy emotionalism, having nothing to do with the intellectual advancement of black people. Clark, who like Lewis was an academic well-positioned to guide the new initiatives of Black Studies, adopted a posture of complete condemnation. He lambasted the separatist Black Studies program at Antioch College, lamented the failure of the college's administration to stem the tide of what he deemed dogmatism and intimidation, and resigned from the Board of Trustees.

But it would take more than verbal fiats to eradicate the contestatory energies of Black Studies. Thus, the next stage of panic management was launched: policing. At Berkeley and San Francisco State, the California Highway Patrol, the National Guard, and the San Francisco Tactical Squad were mobilized (in the case of Berkeley, under the direct control of then governor Ronald Reagan) to contain the threat. Suddenly American campuses had the appearance of riotous sites of Black British Carnival where settler opposition navigated its way and sounded its unique energies in the very face of the law. Even a police presence, however, could not effect the exorcism. Hence, juridical and all-out political intervention came to bear.

In California, political careers (e.g., that of the late S. I. Hiyakawa) were veritably assured by riding roughshod over Black Studies. New demands and tenuous realignments of academic power and privilege were adjudicated out of existence by politics and the courts at San Francisco State when the entire Black Studies faculty was ousted in 1974 by then President Hiyakawa. In other spaces, the outcome of policing was dramatically different. At Cornell, for example, black students occupied Willard Straight Hall, the student union building, and took up rifles and shotguns as, at least, symbolic resistance. Cornell's Black Studies arrivants established a program in 1969 with a $250,000 annual budget and an aggressively political and avowedly separatist orientation. In other institutions, Yale, for example, there was no call for policing because Black Studies was established by students akin to the UCLA freshman. By the time a militant cadre of inner-city arrivants entered Yale's gates, the matter had already been settled. Yale's Black Studies panic was a quiet one.

If moral panics can be read in one light as anxious moments of policing and control, they can also be read as boundary crises in which traditionally backgrounded social problems and actors move to the fore. The American Black Studies moment witnessed a migration of inner-city blacks to colleges and universities—a movement that disappeared much of the best and brightest energy of youth from black urban liberation struggles and placed it under the decorous surveillance of academic administration and policing.

At Yale and elsewhere, however—at Antioch, for instance, with its establishment (to Dr. Clark's utter dismay) of a Yellow Springs service station and a black bookstore as extensions of the Black Studies educational mission— the sign "community" was never lost. Programs usually contained provisos and funding for "community" internships and outreach. And the new black academic settler population in or near urban areas always moved between the community and campus. Hence, weekends were made for revolution. Both formally and informally, Black Studies forged a connection between everyday black urban life and traditionally disinterested academic provinces. Here was both a radical reconfiguration and a striking complication of white education in the United States. One might indeed make the stretch and say that after such direct manifestations of "cultural studies in action," how could any-one fail to forecast the birth of more academic programs of cultural studies?

The stronghold established by Black Studies in the American imagina-tion operated not only at local academic sites but nationwide, in such unan-ticipated spin-offs of the Black History Renaissance, for example, as the late Alex Haley's monumentally successful *Roots*. As the first television mini-series hugely promoted and financed, *Roots* brought Kunta Kinte into every living room and Kizzy into every kitchen for many nights in a row. An audience of millions watched enthralled as definitions of both *American* and *family* were permanently altered by Haley's *Saga of an American Family*.

Similarly, if there were rooted strongholds that gripped the nation through telecommunal transmission, there were also rock and reggae sitings of Black Diasporic studies. Horns, drums, and West Indian sound systems catapulted Bob Marley's *Natty Dread* to international prominence at approx-imately the same instant as *Roots*. If *Roots* was telepackaged for lightly ped-agogical American historical revisionism, Marley's reggae *dreadness* was pro-grammed for revolution. Marley, along with other Rasta-inspired artists, brought the Caribbean to us as what the black British scholar Paul Gilroy calls "a diasporic Aesthetics" grounded in memories of slavery.

No glitz and glitter and Hollywood high tech—none of this in reggae style. Reggae's motley was an assemblage of old hats, funky dreadlocks, makeshift shirts, uncreased trousers—an absorbing heterogeneity of appear-ance as Robert Nesta pumped a short burst of Rasta jumps, then seized his head in his left hand and shouted "We jah-ming/We jah-ming," as an I-and-I sound man. This rough motley of appearance was not a "found" moment, growing spontaneously out of want or deprivation. Rather, it was the dictated uniform of what Orlando Patterson has called "the children of sisyphus"—the followers of the Rastafarian way of anti–Babylonian everydayness. No frills, ornamentation, or material excess shall stand in the way of the coming deliv-erance from the land of oppression.

Reggae extended Black Studies via the young at already-panicked sites of knowledge production. First, style: the 'locks appeared. Then, a call for explanation and a threat of revolt: Why do I-and-I inhabit the provinces of *dread*? But not for long. For "If you are the big tree / We are the small axe / Sharpened to cut you down."

The spirituality of Rasta *dreadness* had more domesticated and Christ-ian representations among the black academic settler population in a gospel setting. The black church took up residence on campus as the Black Gospel Choir, complete with "young ministers" and entrepreneurially secured robes. As sites of resistance, these "choirs" were like liminal territories of sound—one mind tuned precisely to heaven and the other drawing inspiration from the "church home" in the local "community," which sometimes provided the pianist and even the choir director. Young black Christians were revolutionaries, proclaiming themselves "in no way tired" and offering consolation and strength with their frenzied, sanctified insistence that "God did not bring us this far to leave us."

Here, with the manifold, spatially expansive institutionalizations of Black Studies, was the production out of opposition and contest of an entirely different order of things. Black Studies scholarship grew and prospered, especially in history and literature. And new disciplinary initiatives provided dramatically reterritorialized spaces for black graduate students, faculty, and administrators who had not even dreamed of such academic entry during pre–Black Studies centuries.

If today there are demonstrably fewer programs than, say, in 1973, when 200 existed in the United States, there is still greater resilience and more abundant scholarly and personnel opportunities than ever before. If funding balances and shifts of ideological allegiances have diminished a *real* Black Studies, these factors have done little to diminish the spirited force of Black Studies as a simulacrum.

When Black Studies came to the university, its detractors immediately cried up an oppositional force of evil and insidious intent—whether this force was imagined as a black ideological contamination of scholarly discourse (*pace* Blassingame), a black diminution of standards (à la Clark), or a transgressive militancy. Moral panics consist in the invention of just such evil forces, or "folk devils." The irony of such invention, however, is that while it does not properly name the invisible adversary, it is nevertheless correct in its suspicion that a nontraditional "something not ourselves" is in progress. The academy's fear that there was more to Black Studies than met the contemptuously arresting white gaze has been borne out by the emergence of superb new scholarship, the creation of an immense academic following, and a tangible redistribution of institutional resources that could not have been foreseen by those sixties administrators who first opened the academic gates to Black Studies.

If inner-city youth first brought Black Studies under the gaze of the American academy, it was always, perhaps, the brilliant black scholar who was proleptically coded into the "black box" of the enterprise. In 1989 Henry Louis Gates, Jr., wrote: "We are seeing an increasing number of Black Studies programs becoming departments, complete with the right to award tenure. Over the past 20 years, research methods in Black Studies have become increasingly innovative and 'cross-cultural,' responding to the particular nature of the material and data under analysis by fashioning new tools." Gates himself is one of the best representations imaginable of the unanticipated emergence of excellence. He writes from the "seminary in the wilderness" as a chaired professor of literary studies and director of Black Studies at Harvard. He and countless fellow scholars such as Professors Molefi Asante of Temple University and Cornel West of Princeton are joined with innumerable undergraduate and graduate students to build the American Black Studies project securely for the twenty-first century.

This view of Black Studies provides at least some clue to the PC anxieties currently at work in the United States. The late Allan Bloom's influential *The Closing of the American Mind* commences with a sullen and dyspeptic account of the arrival of Black Studies at Cornell. This arrival is described by Bloom in darkly Miltonic terms as Paradise Lost, an expulsion from the academic garden of White Male Philosophical Privilege.

From a Black Studies perspective, the past 25 years have been a journey from bare seasons of migration to the flowering of scholarly innovation. From a conservative white male perspective, these same years must have seemed an enduring crisis, each new day and work of Black Studies bringing fresh anxieties of territorial loss.

And if one wonders why PC currents swirl so ferociously about English departments, one need only recall the date September 29, 1968. On that date, "the trustees of the California State College System voted 85 to 5 to fire one G.M. Murray from his post as an untenured lecturer at San Francisco State College. Murray, a member of the Black Panther Party had been hired as part of an attempt to increase black faculty; he had been teaching courses [as a member of the English department] that were, according to Murray, 'related to revolution'" (Huggins, *Afro-American Studies*, p. 22).

Many years ago, Matthew Arnold claimed that Western literary cultural capital—poetry in particular—might be the sole currency that human beings had left to invest in an age of mechanical reproduction and the untimely death of God. But the notion of preserving infinite historical value and unquestioned excellence in the referential files of the English department is at best a quixotic extension of Arnoldian cultural economics. For reliant as it is upon the fundamentally human power of the "word," "naming," "nommo," the site of English is always subject to unexpectedly defamiliarizing change.

Certainly, the rhythms of black urbanity brought to campus by Black Studies unsettled the quiet Western reserve of English through the revolutionary intentionalty of figures such as Murray, as well as the dazzling scholarly moves of an emergent Black Studies criticism and theory that quickly gained international prominence. The PC controversy swirls madly about English because it is the site that has been most dramatically altered—in axiology and method—by the energies of Black Studies. Hence, the heavy dramas of policing English through histrionic purges such as that of Murray, or through ludicrously hyperbolical jeremiads like those of the PC cavaliers should come as expected returns of the always repressed. So much of the present PC orchestration reduces, I think, to the latest *pas de deux* between black urbanity and English values begun during the sixties.

Finally, my own concluding return is to Philadelphia's Unity Day and the gargantuan surveillance tent at the top of the Benjamin Franklin Parkway during the summer of 1991. The tent was itself a kind of new simulacrum. In its yellow and white exterior gaiety, it seemed the perfect complement to Unity Day, a shaded place of conviviality, an updated version of the revival space that past black generations spiritually inhabited, a place of picnic rather than panic.

But once inside, what wonders did unfold. Around the tent's inner perimeter were display tables manned by uniformed men crisp in their appearance and concentrated in their attention to duty. Here were Philadelphia policemen, Pennsylvania highway patrolmen, Drug Enforcement Agency officers, United States Army counter-insurgency troopers, and United States Department of the Interior rangers—among others. The purpose of the tent—placed at the head of the Parkway—was the recruitment of young, black, urban men and women to the precincts of American "discipline and punishment." From the perspective of the tent's official personnel, it was possible to maintain surveillance over all of the assembled and predominantly black sharers of Unity Day. The complications of inside/outside were more intricate, though (as you might well imagine), than the officer's inner point of view.

Along one rim of the tent's interior, there was also a battery of card tables equipped with chess boards where pairs of black youngsters were serenely ignoring the recruiting officers and playing the Western board game of war with dread equanimity and deft, black style. As the music of "Rasta Timothy" and a variety of young, black male and female rap groups flooded the tent, the black youngsters at the chess boards moved with the rhythm, playing rapidly and slapping the timers with stunning low fives. No one, as far as I could detect, was interested in heading for the recruiters.

I think I truly startled, surprised, and then seemed a great opportunity to the United States Department of the Interior ranger to whom I said "Hello" after wandering away from the dynamic chess players. He saw me looking at the leaflets on his table and said: "Do you know Edgar Allan Poe, sir?"

Well, there it was! English reclaimed for purposes of police recruitment in the public sphere of surveillance. If even the devil can quote scripture, it would seem that even the police can find use value for English in the extraordinarily dynamic black youth sphere of a new public culture.

The idea driving the Interior Department's Poe moment (which was emblazoned by an 8×10 sheet containing a silhouette of the author) was that the nineteenth-century American writer's biographer had given a false view of Edgar Allan as a drug user. The ranger corps was convinced that Poe had, in fact, followed the example of Nancy Reagan's model citizen by just saying "No."

The policing and administering of a transgressive Poe by the official surveillance tent for purposes of recruitment, was not, I thought, very different from the discipline-and-punish frenzy of the new PC offensive. For like the Department of the Interior rangers, the PC cavaliers seek to contain the energies of all arrivants at the territories of knowledge production by recruiting them to a ludicrously "cleaned up" version of the Western past. Of course, what was so intriguing about the drama playing itself out on Philadelphia's Unity Day was the rhythmic motion of the black players who had the surveillance tent itself well under control and conditioned by a steady urban beat.

That beat has carried Black Studies from academic immigrancy to forceful, scholarly citizenship in the American university. And the new story of Black Studies is the amazing proliferation of its energies in a manner that makes avoidance or eradication impossible. This proliferation will not be contained through the massive doles of panic-stricken foundations, nor by the commencement rhetoric of American chief executives. Today, and in the future, the best that resisters and anxious crisis managers can hope for is rhythmic coexistence. This is both the immemorially old revelation—more nourishing than bread and more stimulating than new wine—and the stunningly new story of Black Studies in these United States. As Public Enemy might make the point: "It's like that y'all!"

4. Administration of African American Studies at Black Colleges

Clyde C. Robertson, A.B.D.
Director of African American Studies
New Orleans Public Schools

Introduction

In 1984, I moved to Montgomery, Alabama, in order to teach at Alabama State University. What I discovered about the students and faculty of Alabama State University, as well as the citizens of Montgomery, astonished me. I found students who didn't have self identity or esteem, and colleagues who were Eurocentric, which served to exacerbate the students' identity crises. I also found an indigenous African American population too Eurocentric to understand the vitalness of establishing a Civil Rights Museum in the city that served as the womb that gave birth to the civil rights struggle. When I arrived in that historic city, much to my chagrin, I found a cornucopia of European thought permeating a once proud and prominent African American center of struggle and strength. In an environment that has been so infiltrated, intellectually diluted, and Eurocentrically exploited, it is not surprising that there are not any viable African American Studies curricula existing.

Once, after telling an ASU administrator about aspirations of earning an advanced degree in African American Studies, I was told that I would be wasting my time because such a degree was unmarketable. The fact that this highly-educated "negro" suggested that I would be wasting my time while studying the true history of his and my ancestors is an odious example of his Eurocentric ignorance. What is frightening about this situation is that this "misguided" role model has turned his back on his culture and history. By his actions, he has the potential of influencing the students to do similarly. To

prevent the old adage, "those who forget their past are doomed by their ignorance to repeat it," from coming to fruition, we must start educating ourselves
Afrocentrically.

Pedagogical Transformation

If Alabama State University's administrators were to realize that an
Afrocentric African American Studies Department can be an essential element in the institution's curriculum, and secures this writer as a consultant,
the following texts would be recommended: *Afrocentricity; The African Origin of Civilization: Myth or Reality; From Slavery to Freedom,* and *The Next
Decade: Theoretical and Research Issues in Africana Studies.*

Theory

Afrocentricity would be the first text I would suggest to ASU's curriculum
committee. This explicit text would be a vital portion of the curriculum. I
would develop it because it explains how Afrocentric scholars and students
should formulate their lives, academic and otherwise. In the text, *Introduction
to Black Studies,* Maulana Karenga (1987; 72) says that, "African history is the
struggle and record of Africans in the process of Africanizing the world, i.e.,
shaping it in their own image and interests." *Afrocentricity* agrees with this
concept by viewing everything in relation to Africa, not Africa in mere geo-
graphic terms but Africa as vision, ideal, and promontory. These are very
important concepts to understand before students delve into an Afrocentric
African American Studies Curriculum. Throughout an African American's
academic life, he or she is Eurocentrically exposed to knowledge. Many unfor-
tunate students are never exposed to accurate accounts of history, math, geography, etc. Students, if exposed to African history, are exposed to diluted
material that de-emphasizes the role of the African in the development of the
world. These are the types of oversights that the students of ASU's African
American Studies Department would have to overcome.

In 1980, Cheikh Anta Diop emphasized the need to expand African culture, not defend it. This is what the text, *Afrocentricity,* does for its readers,
as well as preparing them for a comprehensive Afrocentric curriculum. After
the students have been indoctrinated to an Afrocentristic ideology, it would
be important to introduce them to the correct origins of civilization. Since the
beginning of the student's education process, he or she is misinformed about
the origin of civilization, as well as miseducated about Africa's contribution

to the civilizing of the world. Resultingly, it is of strategic importance to expose all students, regardless of race, to a text that reveals who introduced art, culture, politics, academics, etc., to the world, and where these people came from.

Diop's *The African Origin of Civilization: Myth or Reality* does what mainstream history texts fail to do. This significant text points to the fact that the Egyptians were the people who were the first to attempt to civilize the world. This splendid book also provides proof that the original Egyptians were brown Africans. Throughout the first two chapters of his explicit text, Diop offers examples of how European scholars such as Herodotus, Volney, and Pienzi exposed the fact that Egypt was an African civilization. On page four, Diop (1974) says that "Herodotus, after relating his eyewitness account informing us that the Egyptians were Blacks, then demonstrated, with rare honesty (for a Greek), that Greece borrowed from Egypt all the elements of her civilization, even the cult of the Gods, and that Egypt was the cradle of civilization." Diop (1974; 63) also offers a quote from Richard Lepsius, when he was describing the perfect Egyptian body as follows, "the proportions of the perfect Egyptian body has short arms and is negroid or negritian." Another compelling aspect of this text is that Diop includes pictures of artifacts that reinforce his literature which emphasizes Africa as being the origin of world civilization. These are very important realities that students of Afrocentricity should be introduced to when studying the origins of the world. Hence, *The African Origin of Civilization: Myth or Reality* is the quintessential historical work.

Praxis

After exposing students to the concepts of Afrocentricity and the origins of civilization, students then would be introduced to the history of African Americans. While studying African Americans, students would be required to read John Hope Franklin's *From Slavery to Freedom*. This text gives its readers a "bird's-eye view" of the history of African Americans. The text discusses the history of the African American's slavery experience. The text also examines the progress that African Americans have made from Reconstruction to the triumphs and tribulations of modern African Americans. By understanding African American history, all interested Americans will garner a new level of identity, purpose and direction. This is an important point because, according to Columbia University's Diane Ravitch (1987; 106), "It is important for us to study our history. People without a sense of history are ill-equipped to visualize a future because of an unclear picture of the past. A people without the knowledge of "having done" will have difficulty acknowledging the motivation of "can do." *From Slavery to Freedom* attempts to motivate its readers to challenge themselves, individually and collectively, to accept and cherish the historical truth about the African American.

Conclusion

Another important portion of the African American Studies curriculum is methodologies. Most Afrocentric scholars are social scientists or researchers. This is a very vital point. Most often Afrocentric scholars have dedicated themselves to establishing new research paradigms so that they can accurately depict trends in Africa or African America. Many times scholars attempt to inform their audiences Afrocentrically; however, they are using Eurocentric measuring tools. To avoid confusing the students, I would require that they use James Turner's *The Next Decade: Theoretical and Research Issues in Africana Studies*. This text gives its readers a view of social science problems in an Afrocentric manner. Social science research offers a way of examining and understanding the operation of human or social affairs. It provides points of view and technical procedures that uncover things that would otherwise escape our awareness.

According to Earl Babbie, (1986, xx) "things are not what they seem and social science research can make that clear." *The Next Decade: Theoretical and Research Issues in Africana Studies* makes complex issues clearer by studying social issues using an Afrocentric concept. When developing an African American Studies Department, one has to choose texts that will compliment Afrocentric ideology. The responsibility of an Afrocentric African American Studies curriculum is to approach a research question by centralizing it Afrocentrically. The four texts which I have chosen will help in alleviating my students' European world-view while helping them develop an Afrocentric world-view.

REFERENCES

Asante, Molefi Kete. *Afrocentricity*. Buffalo: Amulefi Publishing Company, 1988.
Babbie, Earl. *The Practice of Social Research*. Belmont, Calif.: Wadsworth Publishing, 1986, p. xx.
Diop, Cheikh Anta. *The African Origin of Civilization: Myth or Reality*. Westport, Conn.: Lawrence/Gill and Company, 1974, pp. 4–63.
Karenga, Maulana. *Introduction to Black Studies*. Los Angeles: Kawaida Publishing, 1987, p. 72.
Ravitch, Diane. "Forgotten Heroes: Black Contributions to American History," *The Black Collegian* 18, 3 (1988): 106.

5. "Can the Big Dog Run?"[1] Developing African American Studies at the University of Georgia

Norman Harris, Ph.D.
Professor and Head
Department of African American Studies
The University of Cincinnati

Perhaps no academic position held by an African American woman or man at a predominantly non–African American university is more representative of the challenges and opportunities that structure all African American life than is administering an African American Studies academic unit.

Two historical factors support this assertion: the inability of Caucasians to develop and enact systems of behavior which elevate ideas and spirit above materialism and pragmatism, and the consequent deformation of human personality—especially their own; and, the opportunistic participation of some African Americans in these systems of behavior to the detriment of most African Americans.

The systems of behavior are institutions—material structures or policies which have as their goal global white hegemony. This is colonialism. African American corroboration with such structures is neo-colonialism. In academia, colonialism and neo-colonialism usually play out at the level of perspective or orientation. The practical implications are seen in the content and structure of curricula. At the more sophisticated level, orientation is married to prejudice in a way to produce methodologies which have as their unspoken goal the maintenance of the status quo.

In general, any method which seeks first to segment phenomena for measurement, particularly without consideration for how the phenomena fits together, and how it may be related to all phenomenon, runs the risk of producing mere facts.[2] The production of discrete pieces of information that show little relation to each other (facts) is often labeled progress, a concept I will have more to say about a bit later. Accepted methods in academia glorify and elevate a kind of thinking that has no transcendent goal. Whereas in classical African civilizations the purpose of education was to make the human more God-like, the purpose of education in the West is to restrict human potential so that people and resources can be controlled. Thus you have the sorry and rather predictable confusion of humanity with the animal world through methodologies which seek one-to-one correlations between appearance and reality: this is a way to understand social Darwinism and its various offspring.

Behaviorism in the social sciences and post-structuralism (really a less fuel efficient model of modernism) in the humanities are the dominant methodologies in academia. The hard sciences seldom have to justify themselves, for they in this pragmatic society (of which academia is clearly a part) are the model to which the pseudosocial sciences and the humanities scholar aspire.

One might argue that the "wannabe" scientists in the social sciences and the humanities have done more to provide a "scientific" basis for racism than have the hard scientists.[3] Molefi Asante makes this point in his "The Painful Demise of Eurocentrism," which is a review of Arthur Schlesinger's *Dis-Uniting of America*. Asante writes: "Schlesinger envisions an America rooted in the past, where whites, actually Anglo-Saxon whites, defined the protocols of American society, and white culture itself represented the example to which others were forced to aspire. He loves this vision because it provides a psychological justification for the dominance of European culture in America over others" (305-306). Schlesinger the historian needs to write fiction and label it history in order to justify current events and their antecedents.

So it is into this fairly generic arena that this essay finds specific focus: my three years (1988–91) as an associate professor of English and director of the African American Studies program at the University of Georgia. My thesis is two part: (1) that the attitudes of some key white administrators and the attitudes of some of my African American colleagues can be understood in turn as colonialism and neo-colonialism; and (2) relieved of its genteel apparel, the stark issues facing me as an administrator are the same issues facing most African American attempts to institutionalize African accomplishments and possibilities. We are talking here about self-determination.

More directly, most African American attempts to establish self-determining institutions that have the same accountability and rights of similar non–African American units will more often than not be met with opposition from those committed to maintaining the existing system. Importantly, those spearheading the opposition seldom operate at a rational level.[4] At best, their operation derives from a kind of historical dyslexia wherein African and African American history are not necessarily denied, but that history gets scrambled up and ultimately subsumed under liberal largesse and confusion.

At its worst, the opposition is a pathology which blames the victim of racism for racism: "Just shut up. Go to the back of the bus and sit down." To develop the two sections of my thesis, I have divided this essay into background, development, and departure.

Background

In 1988, when I began my tenure at the University of Georgia, the African American Studies program had not had a director for several years; it had never offered a course under its own prefix; it did not have office space; and it did not have a budget. None of this was surprising or remarkable. More information was required.

Before accepting the job, I did some homework, primarily looking at the public pronouncements of the University's president. My colleague and friend Ron Bailey, who was then at the University of Mississippi, sent press clippings to me about the new president. When I combined the rhetoric of the president's comments about the kind of university he wished to create with the fact that confusion is a necessary part of what happens when key managers in any organization change, it became clear to me that these factors created some space for us to develop African American Studies.

Certainly, this was an ideal projection on my part. But, as I say, it was clear that the new president's statements and actions about increasing the number of African American faculty did confuse the old-line colonialists. They were not clear about the form the new colonialism would take. Among most African American staff and faculty, there was considerable jubilation about what these administrative changes might mean for black folk. I was among this group of expectant African Americans and welcomed the future in ways no doubt similar to the way some enslaved Africans welcomed Lincoln's Emancipation Proclamation. Again, my projections were idealistic. And that is precisely the point I wish to make: that a successful African American Studies administration must be idealistic; it must project and seek to implement the best possible world. Anything short of that is simply an underfinanced version of current events, and here I paraphrase Marx's quote of Hegel on the role of history: "History appears twice, so to speak: the first time as tragedy, the second time as farce." Thus, we were not concerned to replicate the tragic developments of western education into a farce in black face.[5]

Development

Development of African American potential derives from attempts to advance the quest for freedom and literacy.[6] I define freedom as the ability to conceptualize the world in ways continuous with one's history. I define literacy as the application of historical knowledge as the confluence between personality and situation dictates. These concepts depend on each other for realization: one cannot be truly free without being literate; one cannot be truly literate without being free. Know first that freedom is an ideal construct intended to link the individual to the best traditions in her past in order to project her future.[7]

The quest for freedom and literacy provided and continues to provide a filter for my administrative style. Through that filer I find practical administrative meaning in the fiction of Ishmael Reed in which he asserts a conspiratorial view of history wherein secret societies vie for ascendancy; the social commentary and poetry of LeRoi Jones, particularly his crystallized discussion of double consciousness in poems like *An Agony as Now*, and his subsequent conversion (albeit a temporary one) from integrationism to nationalism. An additional source is Sun Tzu's *Art of War*, particularly his discussion of the role of preparation in providing the warrior the ability to appear in whatever way consistent with achieving victory. Others important to my administrative method are Amilcar Cabral, Julius Nyerre, Maulana Karenga, Kwame Nkrumah and Oscar Mondy, my maternal grandfather.

The most audacious act of freedom during my administration at the University of Georgia was the projection of a Center for Black World Studies. This center would have combined the academic thrust of Black World Studies (African, African American, Caribbean, and South American) with the University's stated goal of creating a Black Cultural Center. I worked with a committee of African American (the Black Cultural Center Committee) students, faculty and staff in the development of this proposal, and, almost to their surprise, they liked the concept and the proposal. There was never a formal response to the proposal—at least not at the level of seriousness that went into producing the proposal. Rather, what the committee got from one of its members, a sister who was a special assistant to the President, was a letter commending the committee for its work and indicating that the Vice President for Academic Affairs wished to see cultural and academic components of the proposal separated.

This was an ideological decision; indeed, the Vice President for Academic Affairs told me on more than one occasion that he was displeased with the term "Black World." It implied, he said, a "White World." And with that I fully agreed, noting that in large part the University of Georgia functioned at the level of "White World Studies." He pointed out further that it would be better to have African American faculty integrated throughout the

University as opposed to having all of them in African American Studies. I still do not understand why he thought that a Department of African American Studies meant that no other department within the university could or should have hired African American faculty. I essentially took his position as one which reduced the academic function of African American Studies to one that was essentially missionary—we were to fan out and convert the heathens.

Much of what I just wrote is inference, and it must be so because there was no opportunity to clearly and fully discuss the issues our proposal raised. I took the Vice President for Academic Affairs' position to be one derived from an assimilationist view of America in which African Americans sought always to fit into an Anglo-Saxon version of reality, and, likewise, not in any way upset the present system. Again, the Vice President for Academic Affairs seemed to have been operating from an ideological stance, and no amount of discussion about the dynamics of black world culture and the ways that subsuming the culture center beneath the academic unit would be effective, would place the university in an advantageous posture for a variety of grants, or, indeed that what we were suggesting was simply the natural evolution of how African American Studies and African American Cultural Centers had developed—none of that was allowed on the table for discussion. Quite simply, the Vice President for Academic Affairs seemed unable to expand his thinking on this issue.

When the word came from above that the powers that be were not in favor of our proposal for a Center for Black World Studies, the bridled apprehensions of my African American colleagues burst forth. They seemed to have gone along with the proposal because they, too, did not know the form the new colonialism might take. Not wanting to be left outside whatever structures the new administration was erecting, they went along. Now that white hegemony had shown itself unadorned, brothers and sisters were hesitant to even suggest that the emperor had no clothes on.

What followed was simultaneously predictable and bizarre. Black student interest in the culture center—an exploratory initiative at least three years before I joined the faculty—was inflamed by their perception that the university was again reneging on its pledge. Meanwhile, the white students were denigrating the Black Culture Center, saying that it was separatist or that it had no real purpose. And, as it turned out, the white students were right on the second claim, but they were right for the wrong reasons. With considerable fanfare, the university announced that it had set aside $100,000 to renovate space for the Black Culture Center. The problem was that the hurriedly done two page proposal—I had resigned from the Black Culture Center Committee by this point so as not to give reality a bad name—essentially said all things would be cleared up as soon as a director for the center was found. The student newspaper enjoyed ridiculing the novel policy of spending money on structures for which no clear purpose had been assigned. They ran a series of racist cartoons. On this issue, the temperature was hot. Meanwhile, the African American Studies program was limping along in adjoining offices in the English Department, with an annual budget of $20,000.

Sun Tzu points out that only your enemy can provide you with the opportunity for victory. So, I wrote several columns in the campus newspaper to point out the incongruity of attention to the Black Culture Center at a time when the academic unit that had the study of black culture as its reason for being was being shortchanged. I then wrote a proposal to the Curriculum Committee of the Faculty Senate to have the status of the program elevated to that of an institute. According to the then state policies of the Board of Regents of the University System of Georgia, an institute could offer a major, grant tenure, organize itself as a college or as a department. In some measure, the situation that the university had created around the issue of the Black Culture Center limited their ability to say no to the proposal for an institute. We had not then reached (and returned) to the Rodney King stage wherein white people can refuse to see what they see. Reality and logic had to be acknowledged, even if grudgingly.

Cleveland Sellers and a number of others who write about their experience in SNCC (Student Non Violent Coordinating Committee), relate their surprise at how comfortable America feels in ignoring its own laws when it comes to African American rights, when it comes to African American self-determination. SNCC systematically documented the Mississippi Democratic Party's exclusion of African Americans from the electoral process, and then sought to have the illegally constituted and all-white Mississippi delegation to the 1964 Democratic party unseated. No one questioned the veracity of SNCC's documentation, rather they (both African American leaders and non–African American leaders) sought a compromise that would allow a few non-voting SNCC members into the delegation, and that would not upset the white folk.

What was stated as part of the Board of Regents' policy concerning what an institute could and could not do was ignored by the Vice President for Academic Affairs. It was pointed out to me that other institutes within the university did not function in accordance to Board of Regents policies; indeed, it was suggested that some institutes at the University of Georgia functioned much like padded cells for incorrigible but, at some level, useful faculty: "Just sit down and shut up. Go to the back of the bus." In any case, I suggested to the individual making this observation to me that he might wish to consult Hegel on the question of history (it appearing twice, so to speak: the first time as tragedy and the second time as farce), and that, in any case, the precedent of slow suicide which other academic units had established was not one African American Studies wished to follow.

Out of this came the formal approval of our Institute for African American Studies, a doubling of our budget (from $20,000 to approximately $40,000), and a one time grant of $10,000 to purchase computer equipment. I also earned a raise and had my teaching load structured so that the majority of my responsibility was to African American Studies. What a novel concept: the director of the Institute for African American Studies concentrating his teaching, research and service in African American Studies. This was progress? Leroi Jones writes:

> for me the idea of "progress" is a huge fallacy. An absurd Western egoism that has been foisted on the rest of the world as an excuse for slavery and colonialism. An excuse for making money. Because this progress the Western slave master is always talking about means simply the mass acquisition of all the dubious fruits of the industrial revolution. And the acquisition of material wealth has, in my mind, only very slightly to do with self-determination or freedom.

These advancements, particularly in the face of the fact that we would not be able to hire, tenure, promote or terminate faculty wholly within African American Studies, meant that I was being positioned to be a neo-colonial administrator. To be sure, few sets of objective circumstances always have necessary and incontrovertible ends, but we can make some reasonable deductions. As Julius Nyerre notes in *Ujamaa or Socialism*, it is not impossible to have a millionaire in a socialist society, but it is unlikely. What is important, he writes, is the attitude of the individual. Even so, it was become clear to me that something had to happen.

Our experience with a 1989-90 search for a faculty position illustrated most of the pitfalls of joint appointments; indeed, my own situation was illustrative. In the best of circumstances, faculty with joint appointments face satisfying the requirements of two academic units, neither of which fully understands or appreciates what it is that the other does. When one factors in the fact that Western civilization has historically sought to undermine and underdevelop African humanity, any faculty members with a joint appointment in African American Studies and another discipline may find Sisyphus the clearest companion and role model. Discussions about allowing the Institute to become a tenure-granting unit were usually cut off by convenient assertions, the most handy of which was how could this happen with only one person in the unit. I had of course suggested a variety of means for this to happen, including an increased reliance on external evaluators, a judicious use of faculty in other disciplines, and so forth. Because, however, the ideological position of the university was in opposition to African American Studies being self-determining, no amount of reasoned discussion was useful: "Shut up! Go to the back of the bus and sit down." I had, for some time, been violating the "Negro Code of Courteous Conduct" wherein the African man is expected to be grateful and to show that gratefulness by knowing precisely when to be satisfied. The successful neo-colonial administrator will know this, and will seek always to anticipate how long and how loud to bark. In this I have sought to be a failure.

Self-determination for African American Studies derives primarily from the ability to do what other academic disciplines do—hire faculty. The administration at the University of Georgia did not view African American Studies as a discipline, and, what is more, seemed to have some difficulty with the idea of African American faculty operating (defining research, teaching, and service) in ways consistent with the best traditions in African and African American history. Again, it is significant to note that the university had decided to commit funds to diversifying its faculty and to increasing the number of lines in African American Studies, so, in a sense our initiative was not at the expense of other departments. The point here is simply that African American Studies was denied the opportunity to contribute fully to the intellectual life of students and the university because of an administrative arrangement (joint appointments) which assured the marginalization of our discipline.

Departure

While the joint appointment issue was the major one affecting my decisions about how long to remain at the University of Georgia, the proverbial final straw was the university's decision to grant a part-time temporary employee access to the grievance procedure. Because the employee did not allege that any of his protected rights had been violated, and because the university's own personnel division saw no basis for this procedure, I reasoned that the purpose of granting the employee access to the grievance procedure was to compromise me.

Oscar Mondy, again, my maternal grandfather, the Imhotep of Duck Hill, Mississippi, taught me through the example of his life, the importance of creating or having access to diverse, and sometimes competing, resource bases. So, in addition to preaching, he was a carpenter, a veterinarian, a root doctor, a husband and father, and a farmer. The mother-wit can be simply stated: do not put all of your eggs in one basket. So, too, as I went about developing African American Studies at the University of Georgia, I made sure not to rely on any one group and certainly not on any one individual for anything—certainly not advice. In like manner, when I made the decision to leave the University of Georgia, I did not seek the advice of any one group as to how to do so. I went public. Athens has three community newspapers— two daily and the other a weekly. There are also two campus newspapers. The *Red and Black* and the *Campus Times*, the former being the older of the two and the paper which ran what many in the African American community considered as racist editorial cartoons during the debate over a Black Culture Center. Michael McLeod, a white student whose accent and style placed his origin well south of the Mason-Dixon line, did an extraordinary series of articles on the issues surrounding my resignation. As I was to discover from my wife, who was then an assistant professor in the College of Journalism, a couple of her colleagues in the College of Journalism helped McLeod with the articles.

What was most useful about his articles is that he did not limit his frame of reference to what I told him about the situation, nor did he limit it to what the administration told him about the situation. He called some of the key people in the field of African American Studies. In one article, "Hiring Is a Problem for Black Studies" (*Red and Black*, May 30, 1991, p. 5), he quoted Rhett Jones, head of the Department of African American Studies at Brown University: "Jones said Brown (University) eventually granted his program departmental status. 'If you're going to be serious about African American studies, you need to give them control over their own destiny.'" In another article in the same issue ("Harris: Georgia ideal for black studies"), McLeod writes: "Molefi Asante, chair of the African American Studies Department at Temple University ... and a native of Valdosta, Georgia, said, 'I'm always upset Georgia is not more progressive in black studies. So many impressive African American leaders came from Georgia, they ought to be a leader in the field'" (p. 6).

McLeod also wrote about the university's decision to allow a part-time temporary employee access to the grievance procedure. Here he quotes from Len Davis, the director of the university's Equal Employment Opportunity Office, who "said that in the 17 years he's worked here, he's never known a part-time temporary employee to be able to file a grievance with the University unless the employee claimed a civil rights violation." As noted earlier, no such charge was made. McLeod then notes that "In letters to Prokasy (the Vice President for Academic Affairs), Davis said Bekerie's (the gentleman filing the claim) complaints constituted a special case that should be heard by a grievance procedure." He quotes the Vice President for Academic Affairs: "The grievance procedure is very clear.... It states that a temporary doesn't have access to the process. However, I have the discretion to make a referral. Nobody objected to Harris firing Bekerie.... As a part time temporary employee, Bekerie could be fired at any time for any reason.... In this particular case there were a number of circumstances.... It seemed to me there was an issue that needed resolution.... I suspect if I were Harris, I might be upset" (p. 5). Indeed, indeed.

The two local papers were less thorough in their reporting, and were content to run headlines like "Harris Will Head Bigger Department in Cincinnati." One paragraph read "for the fiscal year, the budget for the Cincinnati

Department (of African American Studies) is $435,000 which includes all salaries. The University of Georgia Budget Office figures for the Institute for African American Studies for FY 1991 show an amended budget of $93,535. The original FY 91 budget was $51,931" (*The Athens Observer*, May 9, 1991, p. 1).

Postscript

I currently head the Department of African American Studies at the University of Cincinnati. Dr. Clarissa Myrick-Harris, my wife, is an assistant professor in the Department of English. The Department of African American Studies has five tenure track faculty and four adjunct faculty. Although the department has fewer than 30 majors, we teach over 500 students per quarter.

There are a variety of challenges at the University of Cincinnati, not the least of which is Ohio's poor economy and the subsequent reduced fundings to higher education (see "Drop in State Support Leaves Ohio Colleges Wondering How Much Farther They Can Fall," *Chronicle of Higher Education*, September 9, 1992, pp. A23-A24). However, the situation is less restrictive than the one at the University of Georgia because we have the kind of administrative arrangement that makes it unnecessary to justify our existence as frequently as we did at the University of Georgia. Quite predictably, the struggle continues.

My experience at the University of Georgia was extraordinarily enriching for what it demonstrated to me about myself. Those lessons are best stated and contextualized in the opening paragraph of an essay that Maulana Karenga did almost a decade ago, *Overturning Ourselves: From Mystification to Meaningful Struggle*. I paraphrase: Read into revolution what you will; it is essentially a question of enduring and transforming, of turning the negative into the positive. I am privileged to have had the opportunity to contribute to attempts to establish African American Studies at the University of Georgia.

NOTES

1. This is a paraphrase of a question asked about running backs on the University of Georgia Bulldogs football team. I first heard the question posed by Andrew Young during a speech he made at the University of Georgia when he was running for Governor of that state. He lost. The question suggested that merit (the ability to run) would be rewarded irrespective of race. I use the question here to suggest that academic merit does not enjoy the same kind of affirmative action as sports. This disjuncture is not unique to the University of Georgia. This essay will be reprinted in a volume edited by Dr. Lea See titled *Academic Terrorism*.

2. I am aware here that the hallmark of the scientific method is just what I here condemn.

My contention—similar to others like Wade Nobles, Asa Hilliard, Molefi Asante and Maulana Karenga, to name a few—is that science not wedded to morality or some higher good, particularly at the level of concept formation, manages only to brutalize even the possibility for beauty and the subsequent higher level of functioning for all humanity.

3. In addition to the observations made in Azibo's piece, consider also Social Darwinism, the various IZ tests and the subsequent claims thereby related, etc. All of these "objective scientific" inquiries worked only to justify racism.

4. See in this issue of *Word* Daudi Ajani ya Azibo's "Eurocentric Psychology and the Issue of Race." See also Frances Cress Welsing's *Isis Papers*.

5. The tragedy of Western education is its narrowness of content which leads to the falsification, omission, or deracination of the various cultures which compose this country.

6. I have been working with and expanding these terms since I came across them a decade ago while writing my dissertation. My acquaintance with the concepts of freedom and literacy come from my reading of Robert Stepto's *From Behind the Veil*, and from a variety of things I have read by Northrop Frye. While African American literary analysis was the specific reason for my usage of these terms, further reading indicated that their philosophical basis rested in what Carl Jung calls the collective unconsciousness. Additional reading indicated that Jung's notion of a collective unconsciousness is consistent with Richard Wright's prosaic, yet profound observation of things unseen, and the more fundamental African orientation concerning death, ancestor veneration, and the role of the past (if indeed it is that) in structuring the present. In short, the idea that African American life is structured by predispositions that cannot be fully explained by reference to empirical data is the basis for what I am doing here. In effect, the desire to achieve freedom and literacy is a supra-rational desire that is consistent with the African philosophical assumption that consciousness determines being. Please see my *Connecting Times: The Sixties in African American Fiction; African American Social Change: A Philosophical Approach*; and my forthcoming book, *Signposts: Reading African American Culture*.

7. Both in the way I phrase this assertion and in its content—both that which is literally there and that to which it alludes—I owe much to the work of Maulana Karenga, particularly his definition of Kuumba in the Nguzo Saba.

6. Africology: Building an Academic Discipline

William E. Nelson, Ph.D.
Professor of Black Studies and Political Sciences
Ohio State University

The term "Black Studies" has served a number of useful purposes for the black academic community. Adoption of this term illuminated in the 1960s the determination by blacks to become the subjects, not merely the objects, of serious intellectual endeavors. As the movement for human understanding popularly known as Black Studies proceeds toward the goal of becoming a discipline, it should be assigned a name that captures the essence of the enlarged perspective which the term "discipline" implies. One possible choice of a new term is Africology, a concept that evokes images of the rigorous, scientific pursuit of knowledge about individuals of African descent. Transition from social movement to academic discipline requires, of course, more than just the assignment of a new name. According to Professor Maulana Karenga, a discipline is by definition "a self-conscious, organized system of research and communication in a defined area of inquiry and knowledge" (Karenga, 1986, p. 5). The building of a discipline of Africology is uniquely challenging because of the absence of a widely accepted paradigm. The search for an appropriate paradigm is an essential precondition for the development of the discipline of Africology. An appropriate paradigm in Africology must be interdisciplinary in nature. That is, it must be a conceptual framework that can cut across routine disciplinary lines to produce order, coherence and understanding out of a vast array of social scientific materials.

Professor James Stewart has referred to such a paradigm as an "expansive, model of Black Studies." Stewart's expansive model transcends the ordinary boundaries of traditional disciplines and creates a new interdiscipline (Stewart, 1983, p. 1). An appropriate paradigm of Africology must also be an alternative and corrective to traditional scholarship. Such a paradigm must, of necessity, be Afrocentric in its basis orientation. This requirement entails more than just the substitution of black concepts for white concepts, it means the construction of a new epistemic based upon the unique position of African people in the world social order. In the words of Professor James Turner, the challenge for the new black intellectual is not "simply to pick or choose among the conceptual and methodological toys of traditional disciplines but to reconceptualize social action and rename the world in a way that obliterates the voids that have inevitably occurred as a result of artificial disciplinary demarcations" (Turner, 1984, pp. x-xi).

The discipline of Africology must give us a prism through which we can correctly interpret the world around us. It must give us the capacity not simply to ask different questions, but the right questions, and to test the truth of the answers we receive on the basis of realities emanating uniquely from the African experience. If Professor Russell Adams is right that epistemology is a social code for mapping a group definition of various levels of reality, an epistemology for Africology must be one that allows us to determine our reality and speak to the world about our plans for transforming the world as we know it (Adams, 1984, p. 208). An appropriate paradigm for Africology must be a liberating paradigm; that is, it must allow us to shed the straightjacket of Western culture and begin the quest for self-knowledge and self-realization called for by Professor Karenga.

An appropriate paradigm for Africology must also combine self-knowledge and self-realization with social action. In contrast to the parochial, self-limiting practices of traditional disciplines, Africology must move its boundaries beyond the borders of academia and begin to register a concerted impact on the broader community. Africology must symbolize not only the search for a new discipline but a new community of political activists. Traditional boxes and squares that have separated the research enterprise from the moral obligation to create social change contradicts the philosophical essence of Africology. As a reincarnation of the militant impulses of the 1960s revolts, Africology must not seek knowledge for knowledge's sake but vigorously pursue positive social change. From a practical standpoint, Africology must command the allegiance of Afrocentric scholars and promote effective communication within the discipline. As a discipline, Africology must also develop multiple avenues for communicating its accomplishments to the outside world. Issues centering on the imperative of standardization must be resolved in the context of the Afrocentric paradigm. Critical decisions will have to be made regarding disciplinary priorities with respect to undergraduate and graduate programming. The discipline must also establish minimum standards of professional conduct. It must insist that those who wish to wear the disciplinary name be committed unservingly to promoting the social and cultural objective of an Afrocentric community of scholars.

Finally, Africology must come to grips with the new methodologies and new technologies of the social sciences and humanities. The miracle of communications has made possible the creation of a global village of African people. Technological breakthroughs in this field have produced exciting new research possibilities; they have also given to us enormous challenges and responsibilities.

The task of building the discipline of Africology as an alternative and corrective to traditional scholarship is an extremely challenging one. In its quest for coherence and permanence, Africology faces obstacles not present during the formative years of history and political science. The distinctions that can be made here are quite marked. First, Africology does not trace its origins to forces within the academic establishment but emanates from an external grassroots movement designed to open doors for blacks in higher education that had been closed for more than a century. Professional educators with influence and power were not the key actors in the early campaign for Black Studies. Programs in Black Studies could not draw upon linkages with prestigious departments in foreign universities to undercut the cloud of suspicion surrounding their claims to academic legitimacy. In the eyes of university administrators, these programs represented political prizes to the black community; questions concerning institutionalization, substantive content, and longevity would be intimately tied to the mobilization of political support for the programs in arenas both within and external to the university.

Second, Black Studies was introduced at a time when the lines of power, authority and jurisdiction within the academic community had already been tightly drawn. Black Studies threatened to disrupt formal and informal organizational agreements that had been settled for decades. The artificial lines of demarcation that separated political science, history, sociology and economics had been crafted through protracted experimentation and negotiations. As an interdisciplinary enterprise, Black Studies not only blurred traditional distinctions, but sought to carve out for itself a separate and unique position by drawing into its purview courses and related activity impinging on the academic terrain of traditional disciplines. Established disciplines were not prepared to concede to Black Studies the right to teach black related courses that fell within their alleged jurisdiction without a fight.

Thus, when the Black Studies Department at Ohio State University introduced ten African history courses in 1972, the courses were seized by the History Department and added to History's course list. The rationale given by History for this action was that all courses with history in the title properly fell within the jurisdiction of the History Department and could only be legitimately taught by members of that department's faculty. A serious political struggle had to be waged by Black Studies for two years before its "right" to teach courses in African history was firmly established.

Third, Black Studies represented an innately radical critique of the ideology, ethos and objectives of traditional social science disciplines. It rejected the elitist assumptions of traditional social science, seeking instead to use education to promote the broadscale distribution of social, economic and cultural benefits across all sectors of the population. Black Studies questioned the validity of the Eurocentric assumption endemic to traditional social science that the whole of society could be effectively examined and explained on the basis of the values, needs, and interests of the dominant culture. It sought to transform the concomitant hostility toward African values, needs and interests, and to provide an intellectual forum where black activist-scholars could begin to examine black life from an African centered perspective.

The dual emphasis on social change through social action and academic creativity, and educational reform through a transformation of the values and practices of social science, serves as the pivotal touchstone for the construction and evolution of the discipline of Africology.

Given the present structure and ideological framework of American higher education, how can these objectives be realized? This question illuminates the most pivotal dilemma facing Black Studies today. If it remains firmly rooted within the structural nexus of American academic life, Africology will be required to assume some of the behavioral characteristics of other disciplines.

Members of the discipline will be required to teach, to research, provide guidance for student projects, read papers at conferences, answer requests for support by community constituents, and conform to the bureaucratic requirements and expectations of the universities where they work.

The discipline of Africology must support the work of its members and forge the kind of broad linkages throughout the academic community required to achieve respectability and influence. Can Africology achieve the practical objectives outlined above while fulfilling its challenge to radically transform traditional approaches to education? There is a great danger that as Africology seeks to become institutionalized, it will abandon its commitment to radical social change and community uplift. This danger is reflected in the tendency of second generation Black Studies scholars to change the focus of the discipline by acceding to university demands for joint appointments, and cutting their ties to student groups and community organizations. The new orthodoxy is that Black Studies can best do its work by cementing formal relations with parallel academic units across the university campus, while simultaneously relinquishing its claims to institutional autonomy and academic independence. Structural decentralization, under this formulation, becomes the functional twin of ideological disintegration. The emphasis on Afrocentric analysis is muted by a concern of "objective" scholarship which places issues germane to the black experience within the broader context of Western developments and the contributions of dominant white interests.

Clearly, the task of building the discipline of Africology is fraught with pressure, complexity, and contradictions. The American academy has not been a receptive host to those who have attempted to adhere religiously to the original goals of the Black Studies movement. Still, the challenges faced by the advocates of Africology are not insuperable. A strong, dynamic, functional discipline of Africology can be built without unduly sacrificing its commitment to educational reform and social change. In contrast to history and political science, Africology must be built from the bottom up, not the top down. The building process must begin in the broader black community with the establishment of a firm political network dedicated to quality, radical academic programming. American universities are deeply immersed in the political process. Pressure by organized interests both within and outside the university can have an appreciable affect on the ability of Africology programs to achieve their objectives without making major concessions. The community base of the Africology building process cannot be emphasized enough. The quest for Africology must be viewed as an extension of the Civil Rights campaign that first brought Black Studies into existence. Africology represents a continuing phase in the struggle for black liberation through education. Its substantive interests are coterminous with those of the community and exist in symbiotic relationship with a range of other objectives propelled by the immense power, and potential power, of community mobilization.

Africology must also establish a base of strong political support on the campus. The central target here must be undergraduate students who will be motivated not only to take courses in the program, but rally to its support on a continuous basis. Because of its history as an overtly political movement, Africology cannot afford to follow in the footsteps of history and political science by concentrating its initial efforts on graduate education. While graduate education is a critical component of the overall developmental process, a heavy concentration in this area must await the construction of a solid academic and political base at the undergraduate level.

Africology must seek to cultivate an image of disciplinary integrity through the creation of standardized curricula and the establishment of procedures and criteria for evaluation and accreditation. The clear sign that the field has begun to move toward disciplinary consolidation will be the disappearance of a multitude of approaches to Black Studies courses and the institutionalization of a uniform curriculum across the country. Such a curriculum will be important not only in clearly defining the central ideology and core subject matter of the discipline, but in erecting disciplinary boundaries so that the essence of its contributions will not be diluted through external penetration from rival disciplines.

Africology must create a nationwide institutional network to support the fundamental objectives of the discipline. Efforts should be made to establish autonomous departments of Africology. Academic departments are the lifeblood of successful disciplinary movements. They serve as important recruitment vehicles for students into the field. They are also the key instruments of power in the effort to promote the creative institutionalization of disciplines within the central structure of the university. An accent on professional growth must be a key component of plans for the long-term evolution and development of the discipline of Africology. The professionalization process begins with the initiation of sound graduate programs. It continues with the creation of a national organization, the holding of annual conferences and the publication of a national journal.

The national organization must be both a political instrument and a service organization. As a political instrument, it must coordinate the establishment of functional networks to mobilize organization support behind the discipline's premier objectives. In its service capacity, it must keep members of the discipline informed of important developments, promote their career interests and coordinate the raising of support funds from public and private sources. The unorthodox ideological perspective of the discipline may render the obtaining of government grants and major corporate support impossible. This fact may place additional weight on the capacity of disciplinary leaders to find ways to make the contributions of the discipline visible and uniquely relevant to grassroots citizens. At this moment in human history, we have reached the magical cross-section in time where human aspirations can be transformed into academic programs that can liberate the world from hundreds of years of human sufferings. African people bring to the human condition special insight and a unique gift for progressive social development. If carefully constructed, Africology can be the instrument of enlightenment and political triumph that will transform the human condition around the world into a model of social responsibility and magnificent achievement.

REFERENCES

Adams, Russell L. "Intellectual Questions and Imperatives in the Development of Afro-American Studies," in Carlene Young (ed.), *An Assessment of Black Studies Programs in American Higher Education, the Journal of Negro Education* vol. 53, no. 3 (Summer, 1984).

Ash, Roberta. *Social Movements in America*. Chicago: Markham Publishing Company, 1972.

Brisbane, Robert H. *Black Activism: Racial Revolution in the United States, 1954–1970*. Valley Forge, Pa.: Judson Press, 1974.

Chrisman, Robert. "Observations on Race and Class at San Francisco State," in James McEvoy and Abraham Miller, *Black Power and Student Rebellion*. Belmont, Calif.: Wadsworth, 1969.

Dye, Thomas R. *Who's Running America: The Reagan Years*. Englewood Cliffs, N.J.: Prentice-Hall, 1983.

Edwards, Harry. *Black Students*. New York: The Free Press, 1970.

Higham, John. *History: The Development of Historical Studies in the United States*. Englewood Cliffs, N.J.: Prentice-Hall, 1965.

Karenga, Maulana. "Black Studies and the Problematic of Paradigm: The Philosophical Dimension," unpublished paper prepared for publication in *Phylon: The Atlanta University Review of Race and Culture*. June, 1986.

Meranto, Philip J., Neida J. Meranto, Matthew R. Lippman. *Guarding the Ivory Tower: Repression and Rebellion in Higher Education*. Denver: Lucha Publications, 1985.

Parenti, Michael. *Power and the Powerless*. New York: St. Martin's Press, 1978.

Somit, Albert, and Joseph Tanenhaus. *American Political Science: A Profile of a Discipline*. New York: Atherton Press, 1964.

Somit, Albert, and Joseph Tanenhaus. *The Development of Political Science: From Burgess to Behavioralism*. Boston: Allyn and Bacon, 1967.

Skolnick, Jerome H., and Elliott Currie. *Crisis in American Institutions*, 4th ed. Boston: Little, Brown, 1982.

Staples, Robert. "What Is Black Sociology? Toward a Sociology of Black Liberation," in Joyce A. Ladner (ed.), *The Death of White Sociology*. New York: Vintage Books, 1973.

Stewart, James B. "Toward Operationalization of an 'Expansive' Model of Black Studies." Atlanta: Institute of the Black World, 1983.

Turner, James E. *The Next Decade: Theoretical and Research Issues in Africana Studies*. Ithaca, N.Y.: Africana Studies and Research Center, Cornell University, New York, 1984.

Walton, Hanes Jr. *Invisible Politics: Black Political Behavior*. Albany: State University of New York Press, 1985.

NOTES

1. For a cogent examination of the limitations of white scholarship in the analysis of the Black Experience in politics see Hanes Walton, Jr., *Invisible Politics: Black Political Behavior* (Albany, New York: State University of New York Press, 1985).

2. Interview with faculty member at South Carolina State College, Winter, 1988.

3. Interview with faculty member at Tennessee State University, Winter, 1988.

4. Interview with faculty member at Jackson State University, Winter, 1988.

Part Two:
Disciplinary Matrix
and Analysis

7. Afrocentricity and the Quest for Method

Molefi K. Asante, Ph.D.
Chair, Professor of African American Studies
Temple University

Cornel West has written in *Prophetic Fragments* that "we live in a time of cultural disarray and social decay, an age filled with ruins and fragments. Hence, our intellectual landscapes are littered with allegorical tales of deterioration rather than dramative narratives of reconciliation."[1] While I would not go quite so far as West to bemoan the contemporary intellectual landscape, there is no escaping the fact that few offers of illuminating dramas are presented for review. But circumstances such as described by West alone present fruitful times and like the ancient Africans who lived along the banks of the Nile who took advantage of whatever situation was presented to them by the river's flow, we must take full advantage of the allegorical conditions found in our societies. If the river was full of water, the Egyptians used large barges to float stones to various sites. If the river had little water, they used heavy sledges pulled by hundreds of people over constantly replaced wooden rollers.

The terrible intellectual plight of the Western world is often laid at the feet of the positivists. Surely the charge, while probably having some truth, is overrated. As a philosophical position, worked out by Saint-Simon and August Comte in the nineteenth century and carried out in the projects of the empiricists and logical positivists in the twentieth century, positivism meant simply that which is given and has to be accepted as it is found rather than going beyond to something unknown such as had been the case in some theological and metaphysical circles. The appeal of the positivist program is its commitment to a hard-headed, no-nonsense interpretation of reality. By setting up the basis for logical positivism with its verifiability tests and by extending the empiricist vision, positivism has insinuated itself into every form of modern Western thought. The logical positivists, particularly of the Vienna Circle in the 1920s and 1930s, tried to systematize empiricism's search for

69

experience by suggesting that propositions might not be false or true but meaningful or meaningless depending upon whether or not they could be verified by observation. The West, as the principal source and receiver of this philosophical view, has succumbed in many of its institutions to a rather materialist conception of reality.

Positivism has brought us to a highly technically managed and structured society where all knowledge flows upward to more efficiently control and dominate society. We are either locked in or shut out; the only action expected of us is to adapt to the situation in the name of structural necessity, rational efficiency, and technical progress. The ruling ideologies continue to abuse positions of power on questions of knowledge. That is why I have maintained that the Eurocentric West is trapped, even in its best intentions, by its concentration on itself, its selfishness, its inability to draw a wider picture. Specifically, I wrote in *The Afrocentric Idea*:

> Even in its reach for diversity, a western philosophy or science creates, *inter alia*, limitations.... The problem is not in the expounding of western categories but in the absolute manner in which they are assumed to constitute the whole of human thought.[2]

Thus it becomes possible for Trent Schroyer, writing in *The Critique of Domination*, to begin his attack on a scientized Western civilization with the following passage:

> The critique of domination, or the reflective critique of socially unnecessary constraints of human freedom, is as old as the Western concept of reason. In classical Greek philosophy the notion of reason (*nous*) was developed in relation to the "seeing" of the invisible in the visible, or of the essential in the appearing. For example, in Plato's famous cave allegory the painful re-turning to the sun (i.e., beauty, truth) involved a recognition of the mystifications and domination of conventions (*nomos*) over man's potentialities. Only a turning around of the soul could restore the knowledge of the difference between the appearances created by the false light of the fire (maintained by the guardians of convention and the true source of essential reality). In Plato's myth the unconcealment of truth, of actuality, required a reflective negation of the appearances of conventional life. Plato's concept of negative reason is best illustrated in his presentation of the person and the dialogic method of Socrates. Plato mythically depicts Socrates' "inner voice" (the symbol for reason) as always saying no, and while this does not exhaust the concept of reason it is clearly its major function. Or, the Socratic method of dialogue is presented as discovering the essential by ruling out what it is not (e.g., justice, love, etc.). With the Socratic method Plato shows the basic concept of reason as a critique of conventional mystification which releases a change praxis (action) in the individual's life.[3]

Schroyer's emphasis on the Greeks suggests why the Afrocentric method has another advantage over the critical theorists. Wilden, Habermas, Sartre,

Marcuse, and other Eurocentricists have tried to work out a critical theory with its ties firmly rooted in the Greek tradition. But I am loosed from that tradition. I claim it as a part of my intellectual heritage; but since I share other classical traditions as well, I have no reason to be trapped in the European past. Essentially, Sartre and Marcuse found that the foundations of a critical theory associated with the concept of negative reason (i.e. the knowledge of something because you know what it is not) were elusive. My claim is one of freedom from the constraints of Eurocentricists in connection with critical theory; yet I do not claim that the final emancipatory moment will have come when I am finished. For the time being, I think that we are on a different road. Stepping outside of the historical moment might permit new interpretations, new criticisms, ultimately the acquisition of new knowledge.

However, one steps outside one's history with great difficulty. In fact, the act itself is highly improbable from true historical consciousness. There is no anti-place, since we are all consumers of space and time. There is, of course, the unknown that we presume is "out there" until we know it by "being there." Our place is the constantly presenting and re-presenting context, the evolving presentation context, the perspective—that is, history to us.

The Afrocentrist sees knowledge of this "place" perspective as a fundamental rule of intellectual inquiry because its content is a self-conscious obliteration of the subject/object duality and the enthronement of an African wholism. A rigorous discipline is necessary to advance the intellectual movement toward a meaningful concept of place. In saying this I am challenging the Afrocentrist to maintain inquiry rooted in a strict interpretation of place in order to betray all naive racial theories and establish Afrocentricity as a legitimate response to the human conditions. All knowledge results from an occasion of encounter in place. But the place remains a rightly shaped perspective that allows the Afrocentrist to put African ideals and values at the center of inquiry. If this does not happen then Afrocentricity does not exist. Now what are African ideals and values? The answers to this question provide the arena for Afrocentric debate, discussion, and endarkening. The Afrocentrist will not question the idea of the centrality of African ideals and values but will argue over what constitutes those ideals and values. The Afrocentrist seeks to uncover and use codes, paradigms, symbols, motifs, myths, and circles of discussion that reinforce the centrality of African ideals and values as a valid frame of reference for acquiring and examining data. Such a method appears to go beyond Western history in order to re-valorize the African place in the interpretation of Africans, continental and diasporan.

A collection of data, for example, for an Afrocentric project will consider cognitive and material systems, direct and indirect data-gathering measures, myths, tape or video-recorded conversations, and unobtrusive acquisition processes based on the African culture, e.g., the style of male address used in long-time-no-see greetings. Knowledge relates ultimately to some human interest even if it is only to "see" the person who conceives of a problem.

Africanists, much like Egyptologists who deal with ancient Egypt, tend to be Europeans whose interest in Africa serves European Studies. Where Africans participate in such enterprises, for example, under the aegis of the African Studies Association, they are bound by the same protocols as the European scholars. At the 1988 African Studies Association conference held in Chicago, Illinois, not one panel dealt with (Egyptian) Kemetic traditions or the relationship of the Kemetic culture to the rest of Africa. One asks, how can you have hundreds of scholars participating in an intellectual conference on Africa and no one discusses ancient Egypt or Nubia? During the same week that the African Studies Association was meeting, the American Studies Association met in Miami. The latter conference has numerous panels and papers that referred to the Greeks and Romans.

What many scholars who participate in African Studies do is not properly African Studies but European Studies of Africa. This has little to do with the racial background of the scholar but rather with the perspective from which the person examines data. On many local trains in the northeast of the United States, half of the seats face the direction of travel and half face the opposite direction. You may ride with your back to the direction of travel or in the normal direction facing forward. Although you are moving in one direction, depending upon which way you are faced you get a different view of reality. In the face forward position, you see things going. On some trains they have seats against the sides of the wall—in those cases you see things coming and going. Well, we are like that at this moment in history: we see things from both vantage points—coming and going—and what we see going are the vestiges of a system of racial domination—it was a wrong headed system in the first place; what we see coming is a post-modern society that is sympathetic to diversity and committed to pluralistic views. Thus, no longer can European Studies of Africa parade as African Studies; the overthrow of the dominating canon has already begun.

A person who studies the economics of Tanzania in an economic department and then completes a dissertation on some aspect of the Tanzanian economy cannot automatically be considered an Africanist. In fact, such a person is essentially an economist, albeit one who employs the assumptions, predispositions and methods of economics to the Tanzanian economic sector. Application of the protocols of the economic discipline to an African nation is a matter of selection, not of philosophical outlook; it is a matter of temperament, not of methodological discipline; a matter of fancy, not of perspective.

What is difficult for some people in the field to understand is that African American Studies is not merely a collection of courses on a particular subject matter differentiated from other courses because of its emphasis on

African phenomena.[4] By virtue of the work in the field, it has become a method of human studies, equal to any other method of human studies in the prosecution of its work. African American Studies is a *human science*, that is, it is committed to discovering in human experience, historical and contemporary, all the ways African people have tried to make their physical, social, and cultural environments serve the end of harmony. Unlike most social sciences, it does not examine from a distance in order to predict behavior. Unlike some other disciplines, it is neither purely social science nor humanities but a merging of the two fields as well as the use of several approaches to phenomena stemming from the Afrocentric perspective. While it is possible for the sociologist and the anthropologist to say that their fields contain nothing new, that is, nothing that is not treated in other extant sciences, the African American Studies scholar knows that the result of the Afrocentric perspective is so profoundly revolutionary in the field of knowledge that it virtually constitutes new knowledge.

The Principal Issues

The Afrocentric enterprise is framed by cosmological, epistemological, axiological, and aesthetic issues. In this regard the Afrocentric method pursues a world voice distinctly African-centered in relationship to external phenomena.

Although I recognize the transitional nature of all cultural manifestations of a social, economic or political dimension, I also know that in the United States and other parts of the African world, culturally speaking, there is movement toward new, more cosmocultural forms of understanding. Nevertheless, meaning in the contemporary context must be derived from the most centered aspects of the African's being. When this is not the case, psychological dislocation creates automatons who are unable to fully capture the historical moment because they are living on someone else's terms. We are either existing on our own terms or the terms of others.

Cosmological Issue

The place of African culture in the myths, legends, literatures and oratures of African people constitutes, at the mythological level, the cosmological issue within the Afrocentric enterprise. What role does the African culture play in the African's interface with the cosmos? Are dramas of life and death in this tradition reflected in metaphysical terms? How are those terms translated by lunar, solar, or stellar metaphors? The fundamental assumptions of Africalogical inquiry are based on the African orientation to the cosmos. By "African" I mean clearly a "composite African," not a specific, discrete African orientation which would rather mean ethnic identification, i.e., Yoruba, Zulu, Nuba, etc.

There are several terms which might be considered cosmological in the sense that they are fundamental to any research initiative in this field.

Racial Formation. Race as a social factor remains prevalent in heterogeneous but hegemonically Eurocentric societies. In the United States, the most developed example of such a society, the question of race is the most dominant aspect of intersocial relations.

Culture. A useful way to view the cultural question Afrocentrically lies in the understanding of culture as shared perceptions, attitudes, and predisposition that allow people to organize experiences in certain ways. A student of African American culture, for example, must be prepared to deal with the complex issue of "bleeding cultures," that is, the fact that African Americans constitute the most heterogeneous group in the United States biologically but perhaps one of the most homogeneous socially. Overlaps in social and cultural definitions, explanations, and solutions have to be carefully sorted out for the Africologist to be able to determine how issues, areas, and people are joined, or differentiated in given settings. For example, something might be the result of social behaviors rather than cultural behaviors. Furthermore, the cultural behaviors may result from African American patterns from the South or from Jamaica.

Gender. Africalogy recognizes gender as a substantial research issue in questions dealing with social, political, economic, cultural, or aesthetic problems. Since the liberation of women is not an act of charity but a fundamental part of the Afrocentric project, the researcher must be cognizant of sexist language, terminology, and perspectives. It is impossible for a scholar to deal effectively with either the cultural/aesthetic or the social/behavioral concentrations without attention to the historic impact and achievement of women within the African community. Both female and male scholars must properly examine the roles women have played in liberating Africans and others from oppression, resisting the imposition of sexist repression and subjugation, and exercising economic and political authority.

Class. Class distinctions for the Afrocentrist consist in four aspects of property relations: (1) those who possess income-producing properties; (2) those who possess some property that produces income and a job that supplements income; (3) those who maintain professions or positions because of skills; and (4) those who do not have skills and whose services may or may not be employed.[5]

Epistemological Issue

What constitutes the quest for truth in the Afrocentric enterprise? In Africalogy, language, myth, ancestral memory, dance-music-art, and science provide the sources of knowledge, the canons of proof and the structures of truth.

Language. Language exists when a community of people use a set of agreed-upon symbols to express concepts, ideas, and psychological needs. The Afrocentric scholar finds the source of a people's truth close to the language. In the United States, Ebonics serves as the archetype of African-American language.

Myth. There is an idea of preconcept, pre-belief based upon the particularity of the African experience in the world. I postulate that myth, especially the central myth of the next millennia in heterogeneous but hegemonically Eurocentric societies, will be the resolution of ethnic conflict. All behavior will be rooted in experiential patterns played out in the intervention of ideas and feelings in the imposing movement of the European worldview. As Armstrong has said of the mythoform, it "is strong, viable, subtle, inescapable, pervasive—operating behind each possibility of man's relationship with the world, refracting through each sense and each faculty into terms appropriate to them."[6]

Dance-Music-Art. Performing and representational art forms are central to any Afrocentric interpretation of cultural or social reality. Indeed, the fact that dance is a way of life in traditional African life and not a leisure activity to be done when one is finished with "real work" as in the West informs any Afrocentric analysis. In the diaspora, the ubiquity of the dance finds its expression in the Africanization of the Walkman and radio. Dance and music must be interwoven with life.

Axiological Issue

The question of value is at the core of the Afrocentric quest for truth because the ethical issues have always been connected to the advancement of African knowledge, which is essentially function.

Good. What constitutes good is a matter of the historical conditions and cultural developments of a particular society. Two common expressions among African Americans relate the good to the beautiful: "Beauty is as beauty does" or "She's beautiful because she's good." The first statement places the emphasis on what a person does, that is, how a person "walks" among others in the society. The second statement identifies the beauty by action. If a person's actions are not good, it does not matter how the person looks physically. Doing good is equivalent to being beautiful.

Right Conduct. Therefore, right conduct represents a category of the axiological issue in Afrocentric analysis. The Afrocentric method isolates conduct rather than physical attributes of a person in literary or social analysis.

Aesthetic Issue

According to Welsh-Asante (1985), the African aesthetic is comprised of seven aspects which she calls "senses." These senses are polyrhythm, polycentrism, dimensional, repetition, curvilinear, epic memory, and wholism.[7]

These aesthetic "senses" are said to exist as the leading elements of the African's response to art—plastic or performing. Polyrhythm refers to the simultaneous occurrence of several major rhythms. Polycentrism suggests the presence of several colors in a painting or several movements on a dancer's body occurring in the context of a presentation of art. Dimensional is spatial relationships and shows depth and energy, the awareness of vital force. Repetition is the recurring theme in a presentation of art. The recurrence is not necessarily an exact one but the theme or concept is presented as central to the work of art. Curvilinear means that the lines are curved in the art, dance, music or poetry—this is normally called indirection in the spoken or written art forms. Epic memory carries with it the idea that the art contains the historic memory that allows the artist and audience to participate in the same celebration or pathos. Wholism is the unity of the collective parts of the artwork despite the various unique aspects of the art.

Structure of the Field

Centrism, the groundedness of observation and behavior in one's own historical experiences, structures the concepts, paradigms, theories, and methods of Africalogy. In this way, Africalogy secures its place alongside other centric pluralisms without hierarchy and without seeking hegemony. As a discipline, Africalogy is sustained by a commitment to centering the study of African phenomena and events in the particular cultural voice of the composite African people. Furthermore, it opens the door for interpretations of reality based in evidence and data secured by reference to the African world voice.

The anteriority of the classical African civilizations must be entertained in any Africalogical inquiry. Classical references are necessary as baseline frames for discussing the development of African cultural phenomena. Without such referent points, most research would appear disconnected, without historical continuity, discrete and isolated, incidental and non-organic.

Subject Fields

There are six general subject fields in Africalogy: social, historical, cultural, political, economic, and psychological.

A student of Africalogy chooses a research issue which falls within one or more of these subject fields. In any endeavor to uncover, analyze, criticize, or anticipate an issue, the Africaologist works to utilize appropriate methods for the subject. To examine cultural nationalism, for example, within the historical or political subject field would require a consonant method for research.

There are three paradigmatic approaches to research in Africalogy: functional, categorical, and etymological. The functional paradigm represents needs, policy, and action. In the categorical paradigm are issues of schemes, gender, class, themes, and files. The etymological paradigm deals with language, particularly in terms of word and concept origin. Studies of either sort might be conducted in the social context of African people, libraries and archives, or laboratories. The aim is to provide research that is ultimately verifiable in human experience, the final empirical authority.

A student of Africalogy might choose to perform a study in the general field of history but utilizing the functional paradigm. Or one might choose the general field of psychology and the etymological paradigm. Or one might study a topic in the general field of culture and use the categorical paradigm. Of course, other combinations are possible and the student is limited only by her or his ability to properly conceptualize the topic for study in an Afrocentric manner. Since Africalogy is not history, political science or sociology, the student must be well-grounded in the assumptions of the Afrocentric approach to human knowledge.

Scholars in our field have often been handicapped in their quest for clear and authoritative statements by a lack of methodological direction for collecting and analyzing data, choosing and interpreting research themes, approaching and appreciating cultural artifacts, and isolating and evaluating facts. As an increasingly self-conscious field, African American Studies has begun to produce a variety of philosophical approaches to the Afrocentric inquiry. These studies have served to underscore the need for solid methodological studies at the level of basic premises of the field and have become, in effect, pioneer works in a new perspective on phenomena.[8]

The Afrocentric psychologists have led in the reconceptualization of the field of African personality theories. Among the leaders of this field have been Wade Nobles, Joseph Baldwin, Na'im Akbar, Daudi Azibo, Linda James Myers, and others. Initially calling themselves "Africentric" scholars, these intellectuals trained in psychology have explored every area of human psychology which impinges on the African experience.

Political scientists qua political scientists such as James Turner, Ronald Walters and Leonard Jeffries have argued positions that may be called Afrocentric. Only Karenga and Carruthers, however, have transformed political science and themselves and now see themselves as Afrocentrists.

The field of sociology has remained mired in a "social problem" paradigm that does not permit a fair interpretation of African data. From the days of E. Franklin Frazier, the greatest of the sociologists, the field has exhibited a double consciousness. What does a sociologist do when there are no deviant classes or societies? In the case of most African scholars in these fields, little knowledge of African Americans or Africans is available. They neither appreciate nor understand the significance of the Nile Valley.

I have consistently argued that the African American Studies or African Studies scholar whom I shall call "Africalogist" must begin analysis from the primacy of the classical African civilizations, namely Kemet (Egypt), Nubia, Axum, and Meroe. This simply means that adequate understanding of African phenomena cannot occur without a reference point in the classic and most documented African culture. This is not to say that everything one writes must be shown to be tied to Egypt but it means that one cannot write fully without a self-conscious attempt to place the historical enterprise in an organic relationship to African history.

"Africalogy" is defined, therefore, as the Afrocentric study of phenomena, events, ideas, and personalities related to Africa.[9] The mere study of phenomena of Africa is not Africalogy but some other intellectual enterprise. The scholar who generates research questions based on the centrality of Africa is engaged in a very different research inquiry than the one who imposes Western criteria on the phenomena.

The use of African origins of civilization and the Kemetic high culture as a classical starting point are the practical manifestations of the ways the scholar secures centrism when studying Africa. Africalogy always uses the classical starting place as the beginning of knowledge. This is why Afrocentric is perhaps the most important word in the above definition of Africalogy. Otherwise one could easily think that any study of African phenomena or people constitutes Africalogy.

The geographical scope of the African world, and hence, the Africalogical enterprise, includes Africa, the Americas, the Caribbean, various regions of Asia and the Pacific. Wherever people declare themselves as African, despite the distance from the continent or the recency of their out-migration, they are accepted as part of the African world. Thus, the indigenous people of Australia and New Guinea are considered African and in a larger context subjects for Africalogists who maintain a full analytical and theoretical discussion of African phenomena.

Although the major regions of the African culture are Africa, the Caribbean and the Americas, even within those regions there are varying degrees of cultural and technological affinity to an African world voice. Africalogy is concerned with Africans in any particular region as well as all regions. Thus,

Nascimento can remind us that Brazil specifically, and South America generally, have provided an enormous amount of cultural, historical, and social data about Africans[10] (Nascimento, "Pan Africanism, Negritude and the Afro Brazilian Experience," FESPAC symposium, Dakar, December 15, 1987). In Brazil, Zumbi, the last of the kings of the Republic of Palmares, Luisa Mahin and Luiz Gama are principal figures in the making of African American history; in Dominican Republic, Diego de Camp and Lemba provide cause for celebration; in Venezuela, Oyocta, King Miguel, and King Bayano stand astride the political and social history of the region; in Colombia, there is Benkos Bioho; and in Mexico, no fighter for freedom was ever any more courageous than Yanga.

Africalogy rejects the Africanist idea of the separation of African people as being short-sighted, analytically vapid, and philosophically unsound. One cannot study Africans in the United States or Brazil or Jamaica without some appreciation for the historical and cultural significance of Africa as source and origin. A reactionary posture which claims African American Studies as "African Slave Studies" is rejected outright because it disconnects the African in America from thousands of years of history and tradition. Thus, if one concentrates on studying Africans in the inner cities of the Northeast United States, which is reasonable, it must be done with the idea in the back of the mind that one is studying African people, not "made-in-America Negroes" without historical depth.

In addition to the problem of geographical scope is the problem of gathering data about African people from oral, written and artifactal records. The work of scholars will be greatly enhanced by oral and video records that have become essential tools of analysis for contemporary African American Studies. On the other hand, studies of ancient Africa present different challenges.

Much of the data used in a reconstructive Egyptian primacy must be artifactal since written records are barely 6,000 years old. Although humans seemed to have appeared more than two million years ago, the fact that permanent records are fairly new is a limiting factor in assessing with complete certainty what their existence was like during the early period.

However, the records are abundant enough in certain concrete areas for the scholar to examine the origins of African civilizations as never before. Of course, Afrocentric approaches to these records, written or material, must be advanced. For example, because written documents are not found in a certain area does not mean that written documents did not exist. In fact, the materials upon which writing was done may not have survived. Neither can we say that in societies of priestly writing, where a limited number of scribes had the knowledge of text, that writing was unknown. It may have been generally not practiced while remaining specifically the function of a small cadre of scribes. Nor is it possible to make any assessment of the origin of writing with any certainty. Speculative answers are heuristic but not definitive. Thus in any discussion of the nature of records in Africa or among African people we must redefine the approach, perhaps to see writing as a stage in human history much like the introduction of radio or television.

Authors tend to write about what is accessible whether they are novelists or scholars. Therefore Christian Thomsen's 1836 interpretation of societies moving from Stone to Bronze to Iron Age was applicable to Denmark, the model for its development, and not to Japan. Definitions become contextual and experiential in terms of what the scholar knows; the more appreciation one has of other societies the less provincial the definitions should be. Of course, this does not always hold true, as it should.

We now know, of course, that these contextualized definitions are the results of ignorance. At one time the Europeans held that the Earth evolved through a series of catastrophes and that human beings emerged after the last general catastrophe. Without an appreciation for depth in time of the human race, all material remains were generally looked upon as the results of people the Europeans knew, like Vikings and Phoenicians. Scholars are still trying to sort out the contributions of these seafaring people. Since the seafaring Europeans of the eighteenth and nineteenth centuries spent considerable time writing about the Vikings and Phoenicians, they attributed to these people a wider array of material culture than was justified. However, since we now know of material artifacts that extend far beyond the 6,000-year history of the Earth the European biblicalists accepted as fact, we are in a better position to assess the antiquity of African civilizations.

Tournal is credited with using the term "prehistorique" in 1833 as an adjective, but it was not until 1851 when Daniel Wilson wrote *The Archaeology and Prehistoric Annals of Scotland* that the idea of a discipline emerged.[11] In fact, the idea behind prehistory seems to be when written records cease to be available as you go back in time, you have prehistory. Because Eurocentric writers often used race as a primary concept in discussing civilizations and cultures, we are frequently called upon to "make sense" out of statements of value identified with race theory.

Any Afrocentric methodology must explain racial characteristics in a realistic manner. To begin with, we must admit the strategic ambiguity of this term as it is often used. For us, race refers to the progeny of a fairy stable common gene pool which produces people with similar physical characteristics. Of course, by this definition we can quickly see that the defined gene pool may be large or small, thus giving the possibility of many races. For our purposes, however, we speak of the African race meaning the gene pool defined by the whole of the African continent, including people in every geographical area of the land from Egypt to South Africa, from Senegal to Kenya. The oceans constitute the biggest barriers to gene pool overflow, with the Mediterranean and Red Seas being relatively minor barriers. Although it is possible to have gene pool overflow in any direction, it is most likely that the major oceans serve as fairly tight boundaries.

The Sahara is not and has never been the barrier to commerce, trade, or interaction among African people as it has appeared to be to some writers. In fact, it is a culturally interactive arena itself and has been a greater context for such interaction in the past. Herodotus spoke of the Garamantes, whose capital now appears to have been Garama in the Libyan Desert as being a people who controlled areas of the vast desert.[12] But long before the Garamantes, indeed at least 10,000 years earlier, Africans whose physical features were like those of the Hausa and Yoruba built canals and villages in the desert. Thus, we cannot speak correctly of Africa north of the Sahara or south of the Sahara; the Sahara is Africa and numerous people inhabit the Sahara.

The African race stems from a continental African gene pool and includes all of those whose ancestors originated there and who possess linguistic or cultural qualities and traits associated with the gene pool. Like other definitions of gene pools, this one is imprecise. We know, for example, that in one biological sense all humans are Africans since we all possess the mitochondrial DNA of an African woman who lived about 200,000 years ago.[13] However, in the present historical epoch, African has come to mean one who has physical and cultural characteristics similar to those presently found in some region of the continent.

The definition of society useful to our discussion is an interrelated set of habits created and maintained by humans interacting. As a point of reference, culture is a cognitive concept about how humans interact, create, maintain, and develop institutions inasmuch as culture exists in the brain as well as in the execution.

Although Christian Thomsen had divided prehistory into Stone, Bronze, and Iron Ages, we now know that this division was too arbitrary. Societies did not all go through the same stages, and if they did, they went through them differentially. Furthermore, the great variety of human societies require more flexible conceptual approaches for analysis. The imposition of concepts derived from European analysis alone tends to obscure the fact that all societies have been more or less successful.

Classificatory Aspects of Africalogy

Among Africalogists the study of African phenomena is primarily an examination of cultural/aesthetic, social/behavioral, and policy issues. It is generally accepted that these three knowledge areas, judiciously studied, can be used to examine all phenomena. A growing literature in the field suggests that serious scholarship in economics or drama, history or politics, can be classified in one of the knowledge areas. Literatures are emerging around each of these cluster areas with direct interest to Africalogical issues.

Cultural/Aesthetic. By the cluster term cultural/aesthetic is meant the creative, artistic, and inventive aspect of human phenomena which demonstrates the expression of values, arts, and the good. The beautiful is a subcategory of the good and is therefore not included in the definition. To be good is to be beautiful, according to an Afrocentric perspective.

We reserve the term cultural/aesthetic for most of what is usually called in the West the arts and humanities: music, dance, literature, history, philosophy, painting, and theater. What we study in this area are the significant elements in African phenomena, whether continental or diasporan, that give meaning to cultural character. Cultural character means the essence of a people's history and icons in harmonious tension. Karenga has suggested four principal constituents: history, religion, motif, and ethos.[14] History is the coherent record of the achievements of a people. Religion or mythology is the ritualized manner in which a people present themselves to humanity. Motif represents the icons and symbols through which a people announce themselves. Ethos is how you are projected to the world. Karenga found these concepts to be central to any discussion of culture.

On the other hand, Diop has advanced a conception of culture which includes three factors: psychic, historic, and linguistic. In his view, as seen in the *Culture Unity of Black Africa*, the psychic factor is a mental factor; the historic deals with phenomena; and the linguistic is concerned with languages.[15] Diop's intention is to demonstrate the unity of African culture by examining these factors.

In order to capture Karenga's constituents while not losing sight of Diop's traditional factors, I have integrated these most prominent conceptualizations into a cultural framework with three key elements:

Epistemic: ethics, politics, psychology, modes of behavior
Scientific: history, linguistics, economics, methods of investigation
Artistic: icons, art, motifs, symbols, methods of presentation

Although I recognize the overlapping potential of certain areas, I am convinced that such a classification as has been made here is valuable for understanding areas of inquiry on the cultural question.

Many important ideas and innovations, particularly in the artistic sphere, have gone either unrecognized or been badly misunderstood because of a lack of Afrocentric methodology. There is no way to properly appreciate rap, or break dancing, for example, without a cultural/aesthetic perspective in African and African American cultural history. A child does not give birth to itself.

Some Afrocentrists like Rosalind Jeffries tie most cultural and artistic expressions of the African world to the Nile Valley civilization or show the possibility of the diffusion of the ideas over a great period of time through transformation into the present era. Niangoran-Bouah has done similar work with the gold-weights of Ghana; Diop showed the interconnectedness of the graphic systems of West African nations with ancient Kemet, Welsh-Asante has developed the *umfundalai* technique of dance essentially around the primacy of the Nile Valley civilizations, and Meyerwitz has shown the continuation of the Egyptian kingship system in the Ghanaian kingship system.[16] This field of cultural science is relatively new in the way it is being articulated and will make a major contribution to reinterpretation of African cultural/aesthetic phenomena.

Social/Behavioral. The social/behavioral cluster refers to the area of knowledge that deals with human behavior in relationship to other humans, living or dead, relationship to the cosmos, and relationship to self. It is the area normally covered in the American system by fields such as sociology, psychology, economics, political science, urban studies, religion, and anthropology, among others. As it is expressed in our discussion of phenomena, the social/behavioral cluster includes the critique of Eurocentric interpretations of African phenomena as well. Therefore, it is both an *analysis* and a *criticism* of the manner African social or behavioral data have been interpreted.

The criticism derives from the need to set the record straight. Indeed the idea found embedded in European thought, particularly in the seventeenth, eighteenth, nineteenth, and twentieth centuries, that Africans were inferior socially and behaviorally, has tainted most of what passes for social science in the West, definitionally and conceptually. Few have been able to escape Alexander Pope's dictum in the *Essay on Man* (1733), "some are, and must be, greater than the rest" and its implication for European contact and interpretation of that contact with the rest of the world.[17]

Stephen Jay Gould argues in *The Mismeasure of Man* that biological determinism, the idea that those perceived to be on the bottom are made of poor brains or bad genes, was a shared context of European and American thinking about racial ranking.[18] In fact, Gould contends that while racial prejudice may be as old as recorded history, "its biological justification imposed the additional burden of intrinsic inferiority upon despised groups, and precluded redemption by conversion or assimilation."[19]

The publication of Charles Darwin's *The Origin of the Species* in 1859 and his subsequent 13 years of publications devoted to expanding and applying his notion of natural selection (which James Chesebro has shown persuasively is an oxymoron—the combining of two contradictory terms without reducing the tension between them to form a new concept) created an intellectual climate for all kinds of racist and sexist notions about human achievement, reproduction, and worth.[20] Indeed, Darwin worked within the general anti–African canon while at the same time attempting to state a theory of evolution which was against the intellectual wisdom of the day. Thus, social and racial motivations operated in Darwin's work as a function of the European male's presentation of self as the highest human form. Of course this is a self-serving formulation for the definer. The argument is generally stated in this fashion: When individuals compete for scarce resources to survive and reproduce, those who are more successful at securing a greater proportion of the resources generate more offspring and consequently their kind is reproduced at a greater rate of increase because the fittest has survived. All of this is based upon the idea that the ratio of reproductive increase is so great that it leads to struggle. However, population may recommend some other, more humane, view of the evolutionary process.

From such damaged intellectual ideas as biological determinism came Social Darwinism, Kindly Paternalism, and a myriad of white justifications for the imposition of Eurocentrism as universal. As Michael Bradley says in *Iceman Inheritance*, the European was more aggressive than others due to, he believed, the nature of the historical evolution in Europe itself.[21] Nevertheless, the ideas of these writers have colored the minds of some of the most influential social scientists in Europe and America. A strong list could be made of the early progenitors of racial thinking: H.J. Eysenck, Louis Bolk, Cesare Lombroso, Paul Broca, Robert M. Yerkes, C.C. Brigham, Robert Bean, G. Stanley Hall, and Charles Spearman. One can find individuals such as these for any field of endeavor who contributed to the racist social/behavioral context, making it necessary for re-evaluative analysis and critique.

Policy Issues. Africalogy is necessarily an area which encompasses all political, social, and economic issues confronting the African world. The policy issue cluster includes discussion and debate around what should or ought to be political, social, cultural, or economic actions in response to critical conditions affecting African communities. Some of the policy issues involved in this field of study are health, education, welfare, and employment. Each of these issues may be researched, discussed, and resolved within the framework of an Afrocentric analysis. For example, an inquiry into health problems within the African American community must begin with an understanding of the role played by communal beliefs in various ways, e.g., how to eradicate disease, how to mask and minimize pain, how to secure the most effective health delivery to an African American community bent on having a hoodoo priest present whenever a medical doctor enters a case.

All methods of doing research have philosophical roots with specific assumptions about phenomena, human inquiry, and knowledge. The Africanist's frame of reference has too often been Eurocentric, that is, flowing from a conceptualization of African people developed to support the Western version of Africa. The problem exists because so much of the Western tradition is firmly grounded in Hegel's conception of history. Hegel elaborated three histories or three ways of writing history: original, reflective, and philosophical.[22] Original history, such as that of Herodotus and Thucydides, describes actions, events, and conditions which the historian saw with his own eyes or received reports of from others.

These primary historians are concerned with "what is actual and living in their environment."[23] Such a history is a contemporary report of events and conditions. In Hegel's sense of original history, certain sociologists or anthropologists might be said to be historians.

Reflective history may be universal, pragmatic, critical, or fragmentary. In its so-called "universal" form it seeks to survey an entire people, country, or the world. Hegel sees problems with this method of history, chief of which is the remarkable ability of some historians to not transfer their contemporary frame of mind to the period they are writing about at the moment. Thus, he describes a Livian history that makes Roman kings and generals speak in the manner of lawyers of the Livian era and not in the traditions of Roman antiquity.

The pragmatic form allows the historian to write about past events at a present time; the confluence of events and conditions assist in nullifying the past, and therefore all periods of history, in spite of themselves, must decide within and in accordance to its own age. Fascinated by the idea of spirit, Hegel does not count reflective history valuable unless it is history committed to exploring the deep patterns of a people. Hegel's condemnation of German reflective histories is not that they did not follow the French example of creating a present for themselves and referring the past to the present condition.

Critical history is the "evaluation of historical narratives and examination of their truth and trustworthiness."[24] The key contribution of this method is in the ability of the author to extract results from narration rather than events. Although Hegel is content to isolate this form as a part of the reflective method of history, he is critical of it as history. Historiography, for example, could not rightly be called history, and higher criticism was itself suspect because of what Hegel sees as its "subjective fancies" replacing definite facts.

The fourth form of reflective history is fragmentary. Hegel writes that it is "abstractive but, in adopting universal points of view for example the history of art, of law, of religion—it forms a transition to philosophical world history."[25] The aim of this kind of conceptual history is always to find the guide to the inner soul of a people. Hegel's metaphysics, the principal introduction of metaphysics for the Western world, comes out in his notions of guides of the soul; the idea is in truth, the spirit, rational and necessary will. It is impossible to understand Hegel's concept of reflective history without knowing that for him history is really spirit performing in time as nature is idea in space.[26]

The third Hegelian method of history is philosophical. He finds the need to justify this type of historical method because, unlike the cases of the original and reflective histories, the concept is not self-explanatory. The Hegelian concept of philosophical history is the thoughtful contemplation of history on the basis of data of reality. This he contrasts to philosophy which allegedly produces its own ideas out of speculation, without regard to given data.

Critics may assume that "objectivity" is compromised when the investigator uses the descriptive mode for Afrocentric research. The Afrocentricist does not accept the European concept of objectivity because it is invalid operationally. Dona Richards is correct to evaluate the concept of "objectivity" negatively in her brilliant essay.[27] I have argued that what often passes for objectivity is a sort of collective European subjectivity. Therefore, it may not serve any useful purpose to speak of objectivity and subjectivity as this division is artificial in and of itself. The Afrocentricist speaks of research that is ultimately verifiable in the experiences of human beings, the final empirical authority. Of course, the methods of proof are founded upon the principles of fairness and openness. Both concepts are based in the idea of doing something that can be shown to be fair in its procedure and open in its application. What is unconscionable is the idea that when a person makes any decision, it is "objective;" every decision, even my choice of software for my word processor, is human and consequently "subjective."

One cannot conduct an authentic debate on the political philosophies of Jefferson, Hume, or Locke without a discussion of their doctrines of racial supremacy, sexism, exploitation of other nationalities, colonialism and slavery. The true scholar must seek to assess the views of the political theorists in light of the cultural, racial class, and gender context. The point is: no field of human knowledge can be divorced from its author's involvement as a human being in a given context.

Some critics assume that the investigator may rely too much on his or her own opinions in collecting data from a social context with which the investigator is familiar. The Afrocentric method proposes the dual-collection paradigm to deal with the problem, particularly as it relates to what may be cross-cultural or cross-national research projects. This is important because in too many cases the Eurocentric method allows an individual researcher to conduct research on his or her own. In many cases in Africa, graduate students from American and European universities conduct research in communities that they have little in common with and expect to be able to make sense out of without assistance. This is probably one of the biggest sins of the Eurocentric methods. They assume they can insure "objectivity" and make some sense out of what they discover in African communities. If accurate results are obtained, it is often by default and luck, not because of some "objective" method.

The Dual-Collection Model

Two directives are invoked whenever the Africalogical researcher seeks to make a cross-cultural or trans-racial study: (1) The use of two researchers to collect similar data, at least one of whom must be from the social or cultural context; and (2) The assessment of the data by two evaluators, at least one of whom must be from the social or cultural context. In addition to the use of the dual-collection model, researchers using the descriptive approach will also employ triangulation of information and in-depth interviews.

The nomothetic model of experimental laboratory research, which insists that variable control and manipulation are able to assist in universal laws, is highly questionable. "Universal" is again one of those Eurocentric terms that has little meaning in the real world. People live in societies and operate within cultures. The aim of the descriptive researcher has to be the in-depth knowledge of a social/human context in order to be able to make some sense out of it, to appreciate it, to live in peace with it. In some senses this is counter to the experimental framework that is based on the logic of war and the market; it is essentially an imperialistic model. What is the need for the universal idea, the control and manipulation of variables, the predictive ability of the researchers? Based on the war games model, the Eurocentric social scientists went to the boards to be able to predict human behavior under adverse circumstances. This model has now been used in market research, particularly by advertising interests, in order to sell more products. The Afrocentric method must have a different goal; it must find its reason to be in the humanizing mission. This is an interactive model rather than a distant, sterile, abstract, isolated, and non-contact model. Rather, this method finds its strength in the cooperative and integrative function of human experiences.

Edmund Husserl's *Ideas: General Introduction to Phenomenology* provoked discussion around the issue of methodology in European social sciences.[28] Husserl's introduction of phenomenology was a major advance for the social sciences. In fact, taking many of his ideas from continental African philosophy, Husserl posited a wholistic view rather than a detached, isolated, disparate reality. The phenomenologist's search for essence by questioning all assumptions about reality is similar to the Afrocentricist's search for essence by questioning all assumptions about reality that are rooted in a particularistic view of the universe.

The distortion of social reality by traditional Eurocentric scientific methods occurs because of allegiance to a set of false propositions. One such proposition appears in the formulation where the researcher is separate from the object of study and in fact seeks to gain as much distance as possible from the object. Both the phenomenologists and the Afrocentricists reject the separation of the investigator/subject relationship, though for different reasons. The Afrocentricist finds the wholistic impulse naturally from the cultural environment. Whether one talks of reality in the African American church or in African dance, one sees that separation of subject/object, speaker/audience, dancer/spectators or investigator/subject is artificial. The social context of African people encourages a collective as opposed to an individual separation.

The Afrocentric method insists that the researcher examines herself or himself in the process of examining any subject. Thus, the process of examination involves introspection and retrospection. Introspection means that the researcher questions herself or himself in regards to the topic under discussion. One might write down all one believes and thinks about a topic prior to beginning the research project. The reason for this is to ascertain what obstacles exist to an Afrocentric method in the researcher's own mind. Retrospection is the process of questioning one's self after the project has been completed to ascertain if any personal obstacles exist to a fair interpretation.

The hypothetical-statistical model found in modern Eurocentric methods is interventionist in the research project because it focuses the researcher's biases on both inquiry and analysis. Afrocentric method suggests cultural and social immersion as opposed to "scientific distance" as the best approach to understand African phenomena. This process in itself is extremely difficult because it means that the researcher must have some familiarity with the history, language, philosophy, and myths of the people under study. It goes without saying that other methods often assume that the researcher need not know anything about the culture in order to undertake a project. Furthermore, without cultural immersion the researcher loses all sense of ethical value and becomes a researcher "for the sake of research," the worse kind of value in the Afrocentric approach which sees research as assisting in the humanizing of the world. In a European world, you can have intercultural communications doing intercultural research and yet do not believe in intercultural communication, except as a way to sell market products, attitudes, or beliefs.

The Afrocentric method shares some of the perceptions of the so-called "ethnomethodology" but differs in both its philosophical base and its conceptualization. What it shares with ethnomethodology is the idea that reality is a process and that the discussion of normative patterns cannot be made intelligently unless the researcher understands the social context. What I have difficulty with is the Eurocentric foundation of Harold Garfinkel's view.[29] Although Garfinkel argued correctly that researchers should not assume common meaning is shared, he incorrectly assumed that the structure that accounted for subjects' perceptions was above and beyond the contextual meaning of their particular culture.

But the principal problem with ethnomethodology is its Eurocentric bias. What is ethnomethodology conceptually but the white Western Eurocentric researcher saying to other white Western Eurocentric researchers that "we ought to study these other people from their own contexts"? "Ethno" is derived from "ethnic," which is derived from the Medieval English "ethnik" and the Late Latin "ethica," which means "heathen." Since the Eurocentric writers did not initially include white people in their conceptualization, one can only speculate that ethnomethodology, like ethnomusicology, was meant to study those who were not Europeans.

Our methodology must be wholistic and integrative; our epistemology, participatory and committed. The Africalogist is a working scholar committed to the advancement of knowledge about the African world. In pursuing a vision in Afrocentric scholarship, the Africalogist gathers facts about African phenomena, verifies them and subjects the interpretations to the strictest measures. The aim of the Africalogist is to make the world more meaningful to those who live in it and to create spaces for human understanding. Our task is not like that of the Western social scientist who seeks to predict human behavior in order to advance more direct control over nature, but rather to explain human nature as it is manifest in the African arena. All statements about objects, phenomena, and events are subjects for discussion, analysis, and action. To be a good Africalogist, the scholar must be able to distinguish between Afrocentric statements and less precise non–Afrocentric statements.

NOTES

1. Cornel West, *Prophetic Fragments*, Trenton: Africa World Press, 1988, p. 270.

2. Molefi Kete Asante, *The Afrocentric Idea*, Philadelphia: Temple University Press, 1987, p. 181.

3. Trent Schroyer, *The Critique of Domination*, p. 15.

4. See Nathan Huggins, *Report to the Ford Foundation on Afro-American Studies*, New York: Ford Foundation, 1986. I argued in a review of this monograph that Huggins confused programs and departments in his assessment of African American Studies.

5. Eric King, "The Employment of Black Males," 2nd Annual Black Family Conference, Center for the Study of Stabilization of the Black Family, Niagara Falls, New York, October 16, 1988.

6. Robert Plant Armstrong, *Wellspring: On the Myth and Source of Culture*, Berkeley: University of California Press, 1975.

7. Kariamu Welsh-Asante, "Commonalities in African Dance: An Aesthetic Foundation for African Dance," in *African Culture: The Rhythms of Unity*, edited by M.K. Asante and K.W. Asante, Westport: Greenwood Press, 1985.

8. See Linda James Myers, *Understanding Afrocentricity*.

9. Although I coined the term "Afrology" and used it in *The Afrocentric Idea* to refer to the Afrocentric study of African phenomena, after considerable discussion with my colleagues and students, I am now ready to abandon that term for the more accessible term Africalogy. It is more explicit, does not repeat the "Afro" prefix which has generated quite a lot of discussion itself, and is readily understandable by most literate Americans and Africans.

10. Abdios do Nascimento, "Pan Africanism and the South American Connection," DuBois Lecture, Accra, 1988.

11. Robert F. Heizer (ed.), *Man's Discovery of His Past: Literary Landmarks in Archaeology*, Englewood Cliffs, N.J.: Prentice-Hall, 1962.

12. Herodotus, *Histories*.

13. Rebecca Cann, *et al.*

14. Maulana Karenga, *Kawaida Theory*, Los Angeles: Kawaida Press, 1980.

15. Cheikh Anta Diop, *Cultural Unity of Black Africa*, Chicago: Third World Press.

16. Rosalind Jeffries, "African Art and Its Continuities," Colgate University, October 18, 1988.

17. See K. Welsh Asante, and Meyerwitz.

18. Alexander Pope, *Essay on Man*.

19. Stephen Jay Gould, *The Mismeasure of Man*, New York: Norton, 1981, p. 31.

20. James Chesbro, "Deconstructing Darwin's *Origin of the Species*," Speech Communication Association Conference, New Orleans, November 6, 1988.

21. Micheal Bradley, *The Iceman Inheritance*, Toronto: Dorset, 1981.

22. George Hegel, *Reason in History*, trans. R. Hortman. Indianapolis: Bobbs-Merrill, 1982, p. 3.

23. Hegel, p. 4.

24. Hegel, p. 9.

25. Hegel, p. 9.

26. Hegel, p. xxi.

27. Dona Richards, (aka Marimba Ani).

28. Edmund Husserl, *Ideas: General Introduction to Phenomonology*.

29. Harold Garfinkel, *Studies in Ethnomethodology*, Englewood Cliffs, N.J.: Prentice-Hall, 1967.

8. Africana Studies and Epistemology: A Discourse in the Sociology of Knowledge

James E. Turner, Ph.D.
Associate Professor of Africana Studies
Cornell University

Black Studies begins with the study of Black History ... because it is relevant; even indispensable to the introduction and development of all the other subject areas. Black history places them in perspective, establishes their origins and development, and thus aids in critical discussion and understanding of them.—Dr. Maulana Karenga

We can only understand the present by continually referring to and studying the past; when any one of the intricate phenomena of our daily life puzzles us; when there arise religious problems, political problems, race problems, we must always remember that while their solution lies in the present, their cause and their explanation lie in the past.—Dr. W.E.B. DuBois

A decade is actually not much time in the span of history; it is only a short period in the life of a new field of study; and it is inadequate for the full development of a discipline and its complements. But, in another sense, it has been a long ten years, and as might have been expected, along the way there have been many obstacles, serious challenges, and great demands and expectations. However, the achievements during this time have been nothing short of extraordinary.

It was during the summer of 1969 that the Institute of the Black World organized a two-month project for faculty and students to organize a curriculum prototype that would define the conceptual parameters and explain the scholarly method and purpose for what was generally being referred to as *Black Studies.*

The summer workshop was followed by a Black Studies Directors' Seminar on November 7–9 of that same year. The approximately 30 participants came from a cross section of private and public institutions of higher education, and all were involved (under different institutional circumstances) with developing program designs and instructional formats as directors for Black Studies. The significance of this meeting lies in the fact that it was, in a manner of speaking, the founding convention for the field. It was the base for professional association between initial Black Studies educators, a clearinghouse for exchanging information, and the launch of our collective endeavor to articulate and operationalize for academic investigation what we meant by the use of the concept *Black Experience.* There was a broad consensus that the field of Africana Studies is a teaching and research enterprise "that is committed to the interpretation and explication of the total phenomenon called the Black Experience." We delineated four basic tasks for the Black Studies scholar: (1) to *defend* (legitimize) against racism and intellectual chauvinism the fundamental right and necessity of Africana Studies, at all levels of American education, for all people, but most especially for African American people; (2) to *disseminate* (teach and publish) Black Studies social theory and analysis, criticism, and historiography, and to reference the work of pioneering black scholars; (3) to *generate* (new) knowledge (research) and codify existing information and predicate contemporary study upon the truths formulated by our mentors; (4) to *preserve* the acknowledged value of rare and classical texts in the field (archival and library collections), and maintain the scholarly tradition and rich heritage of African peoples and their descendants.

The reader has undoubtedly noticed at this point that I use "Africana Studies" and "Black Studies" interchangeably. Africana Studies is the more formal and proper terminology, while Black Studies is the more common usage. On this matter I agree with Professor John Henrik Clarke:

> I prefer to use the phrase "Africana Studies" to "Black Studies." Black is an honorable word, and I am glad to see so many people lose their fear of using it, but it has its limitations. Black, or Blackness, tells you how you look without telling you who you are, whereas Africa, or Africana, relates you to land, history, and culture. No people is spiritually and culturally secure until it answers only to a name of its own choosing—a name that instantaneously relates that people to the past, present, and future. As the Caribbean writer Richard B. Moore has said in his book *The Name 'Negro': Its Origin and Evil Use,* "Slaves and dogs are named by their masters. Free men name themselves."[1]

Africana Studies is essentially about renaming self in the world of knowledge and human relations.

The conference organized by the Africana Studies and Research Center at Cornell University was the nexus and logical sequence to the IBW meeting. Some of the key figures from the first meeting were participants at this conference, such as Lerone Bennett, Vincent Harding, William Strickland, Stephen Henderson, and Howard Dotson.

An introductory essay to a topic as large as the subject of Black Studies will inevitably be selective and representative of the perspective of the writer. However, this book of selected articles is reflective of our continuing intellectual and pedagogical interest in the vitally important task of assessing the progress of the field. The tenth anniversary was certainly a milestone in the life of the Africana Studies and Research Center. It rather naturally occurred to us that this would be a very appropriate occasion to assemble an interdisciplinary group of prominent scholars in Africana Studies, as well as colleagues from other departments and programs from universities across the country, and a selection of some of our best students over the past decade, to exchange ideas about research and teaching experiences. The gathering surpassed our most optimistic expectations and has been widely hailed as the most significant coming together of Africana Studies scholars since the Institute of the Black World meeting.

The development of the Africana Studies and Research Center is quite indicative of the typical pattern generally associated with the concept of the modern Black Studies movement. We trace our origins to the second Black Renaissance of this century during the 1965–75 period, a time of extraordinary intellectual and social ferment and artistic creativity in the African American community. This period has been generally referred to as the high point of the black (arts) consciousness/black power movement. Black students at predominantly white campuses were most often (though not exclusively, as Howard, Jackson State, Fisk, North Carolina A&T, and Atlanta Universities and others were significant) catalysts for promoting the Black Studies proposition at the university and college levels. Black students joined concerned educators and intellectuals in pointing out "the urgent necessity for including the study of African-American experience." Though we refer to a modern stage in Black Studies, we must hasten to point out the fact that, contrary to a broad popularly held belief, Africana Studies is not a recent development. As the author of the preface has explained in a previous monograph, the field has a rich intellectual legacy extending from at least the early nineteenth century, based on the works of such people as Edward Wilmont Blyden, Martin Delaney, Francis Harper, Benjamin Brawley, and Casely Hayford, and from the beginning of this century, with W.E.B. DuBois, Carter G. Woodson, Leo Hansbury, Arthur Schomburg, Charles S. Johnson, J.A. Rogers, and Ida B. Wells, to name a few. We shall discuss this point further later on in this preface.

There is a unique character to this contemporary stage in the intellectual history of the study of people of African descent. Our social roots (fertilized as they were by the challenges for change of the 1960s) gave rise to an intellectual perspective that proposed that Black Studies would supersede the traditional disciplines by pursuing a holistic structural interpretation in its research and teaching methodology of the Black Experience. Essentially this means a commitment to an interdisciplinary approach in the construction of both social theories and research paradigms of the various dimensions (i.e., social, cultural, political-economic) of African American societies.

The concept *Africana* is derived from the philosophy of the "African continuum and African consociation," which posits fundamental interconnections in the global Black Experience. Consequently, curriculum is predicated upon a model of Black Studies that begins with the African background and, next, the transformation—slavery—into the African diaspora, from which the African American experience derives textual meaning. The *black world* is perceived as patterns within a trilateral relationship between Africa, the African Caribbean, and the African Americas with, understandably, primary concentration on African America. Moreover, all segments of the black world population live under social conditions directly related to the international political economy of advanced industrial capitalism. Africana as a construct is congruent with James Stewart's theory of an "Expansive Model of Black Studies." His paradigm is based on a methodology of Black Studies that transcends and transforms the boundaries of the traditional disciplines into a new *interdiscipline*. An expansive model in Black Studies constitutes an investigative emphasis with an ethnographic orientation. Philosophically its argument is that a more accurate understanding of African American sociocultural and politico economic realities is achieved "if the research concerns emanate from their [African Americans'] experience and phenomenological frame of reference."[2] If it is true, and I certainly contend it is, that Anglocentric (or so-called mainstream) scholarship on the Black Experience is biased towards person-centered variables and *internal* causal contingencies, and attributional schemes with person (group) change implications, then Africana Studies is an "alternative presuppositional perspective"[3] that gives at least as much investigative emphasis to systemic institutional-centered variables and external causal contingencies that impact the life chances and social conditions of black people. Africana research "which attempts to emanate from the perception and experience of those under study is more apt to illuminate the fact that psychological and behavioral and cultural processes are inextricably linked to their economic-political, social, and situational contexts. Such considerations move the research away from ethnocentric analysis and more toward (systemic) and ethnographic ones,"[4] which is a far more socially useful research on black people in American society. Stewart's concept *expansive* also assumes a "historical tradition of the linkage between scholarship and activism while simultaneously reflecting the constraints imposed by the contemporary social knowledge and the application of knowledge to promote black liberation and human dignity."[5]

This is a specifically Black Studies conceptualization of the role for black intellectuals in terms of their active relationship to the ongoing institutional and organizational process of the African American community and the oppression and racist inequality that it confronts. An expansive approach to Black Studies assumes that education is based on a philosophy of history. Alkalimat and Bailey, *et al.*, refer to the criticality of a historical focus that elucidates qualitative developments in the dynamic human process; that is, the interpretation of history as social analysis, in order to provide an analytical paradigm for the assessment of significant events and quantitative changes in the configuration of society. They posit, particularly in their text *Introduction to Afro-American Studies*, a philosophy of history that associates events with specific time frames, which reflects continuities and discontinuities in the complex of forces that shape the configuration of society. This process is commonly referred to as periodization of the Black Experience. However, to achieve an expansive model in Black Studies the purpose of history must be for higher intellectual exposition than recording and describing the facts of events. Evidentiary statements in historical documentation must give more than a chronicle and should present instead an interpretation that penetrates the social meaning, in human terms, of the important *stages* in the movements of history.

As a methodology, history, in Black Studies, constitutes the foundation for theoretical construction of an analysis of the fundamental relationship between the political economy of societal developments and the racial divisions of labor and privilege, and the common patterns of life chances peculiar to the social conditions of black people. Basic to the teleology of Africana Studies is the application of knowledge to promote social change. This primary tenet has been the focus of some controversy. The basis of controversy concerning Africana Studies is related directly to an extant perception that Black Studies is at variance with the societal zeitgeist. Though the expansive model subsumes the traditional academic approach, it nonetheless conflicts with the reigning ideological premise that knowledge should be pursued for the sake of knowledge per se. The assumption is that scientific investigation is a value-free process. This argument ignores what some scholars have identified as the "unscientific nature of the scientific enterprise." Research is a social product, and the values and assumptions of the investigator are, more usually than not, congruent with the dominant ideas and prevailing forces that govern the status quo. In the real world, virtually all scientific research is geared to one sort of problem or another that changes society progressively. Funded research in the sciences is concentrated, for the most part, on such concerns as military weaponry, food and animal production, reclamation of marine life and water resources, transportation and communication technology, industrial and farm productivity, and medical cures. Knowledge is pursued for enlightenment of social experiences. Art is contemplated more for abstract existential properties. Even the deliberations on aesthetics are not without social purpose. The humanities are all too frequently the bastion of white racism-national/cultural chauvinism, as they serve to perpetuate a basic Eurocentric philosophy of history, language/literature, music/creative production, and sociology of society by essentially omitting and derogating non–European people and their projects.

In his discussion of the relationship of Africana Studies to traditional disciplines, James Stewart states that "it is important to keep in mind that it [Black Studies] seeks to (a) fill a wide gap in the existing intellectual arena and (b) to resurrect a formal linkage between the academic and social formations. The intellectual task is not then simply to pick or choose among the conceptual and methodological toys of traditional disciplines but to reconceptualize the social fabric and rename the world in a way that obliterates the voids that have inevitably occurred as a result of artificial disciplinary demarcations. It is by renaming the world, that is, by employing linguistic conventions that specifically meet the needs of Black Studies per se, as opposed to imitating the conventions of traditional disciplines, that the power of forgotten voices to speak to the living can be restored. This latter claim implies that *history* has a preeminent hierarchical position in the context of the academic project of Black Studies, with insights from other foci of inquiry serving to clarify patterns of historical continuity and change."[6] Pedagogically and intellectually, Africana philosophy seeks to "rename the world" and broaden the knowledge base for all of us through the concept of Afrocentricity in Black Studies.

The Black Studies proposition at the empirical and conceptual levels relates to fundamental methods of acquiring knowledge and organizing curriculum from which we all receive education. In recent years, black educators have criticized with growing intensity the limitations in Anglocentric assumptions and, particularly, the notion that there are ultimate or absolute truths derived from universal research. The process of accepting new theories in the academic community is not simply a matter of adopting explanations of experimentally verified empirical observations but of accepting competing conceptions of reality and dissimilarities of reference language. Moreover, a scientific theory is more likely to be a conceptually relative entity in the sense that the language of one theory may not be translatable into the language of its predecessor in the same field of research. The major propositions characterizing the mainstream of academic research conclude that empirical laws of social regularity should be the basis of predictions; that social scientists should be disinterested, objective observers of social phenomena and their works (value) free of normative content; that all expressions or normative judgments are reducible to emotive expressions and thus of limited theoretical worth or, at least, open to suspect. However, the major disciplines have a primal tendency to reduce all problems of understanding to technical problems of information gathering and gauging variables.

The dominant fields of knowledge thus surreptitiously support the status quo, because the *normative judgments* germane to its technical procedures, and applications of their findings, are generally ignored and do not face the test of critical examination or empirical verification. Indeed, the normative principles are so ensconced in the conceptual orientation that they are not even recognized as such. For all the contention and support lent by American intellectuals and educators to the possibility of, and need for, value-neutral social theory, the product of the mainstream too often "turns out to be disguised ideology." This is not necessarily a condemnation; the essential point being made here is summed up in the following proposition: If there are grounds for holding that facts of nature are seen through a paradigmatic scheme, in effect there are grounds for believing social facts are not independent of conceptual paradigms used to investigate them. Dr. Lorenzo Morris is particularly poignant on this point: "When social statistics are perceived as meaningful in America, it is because they relate to values in American society. Conversely, when the conditions of Black and White Americans ... are compared, no social statistic can be completely neutral unless it is also completely meaningless."[7]

The theoreticians of Black Studies use the basic social science concept of the sociology of knowledge to explain the legitimacy of the idea that the position of black people in the social structure not only offers peculiar insights but also represents a specific meaning about social truth. Furthermore, all knowledge is a perspective on shared experience.

A. Olomenji argues, in a manuscript soon to be published, that one's point of origin, the place from which one looks out at the world, will largely determine what and how one perceives. A collective perception acts as a filter through which all reality is screened and transformed into a practical belief system. The collective perception and belief system define a people's reality, as well as what that reality means. The collective worldview provides a basic framework for viewing what exists in the world, as well as a basic supposition of how the world operates. A belief system reinforces the common assumptions of a collective perception. It is the practical and central reference for all action.

Professor Wade Boykin has pointed out that "there is inherent subjectivity and bias in the research enterprise.... One's assumptions are actually so critical in determining the nature of one's research enterprise."[8] We have come to realize with increasing clarity that presupposition effectively modifies perspectives and is the source of *a priori* bias. Boykin explains that "'truth' in science is based considerably on a social-cultural-consensual reality."[9] This "consensual reality," vis-à-vis the Black Experience, actually translates into ideational hegemony of Anglocentric presuppositions and perspective. To be sure, ethnocentrism, prejudice, and ignorance are factors that influence the intellectual tone of many white educators, particularly in terms of their attitudes towards Africana Studies. However, Boykin has made an even more salient observation of common Anglocentric bias. He postulates what he calls the Law of Personal Presuppositions:

> You will rarely find a researcher-scholar concluding anything in his or her research that is inconsistent, contradictory, or threatening to his or her own self-definition, self-sustenance and value system.[10]

In as much as the raison d'etre of Africana Studies, at least partially, is to critically redefine significant aspects of conventional knowledge both in social theory and social values, proponents of Black Studies have had to contend, and continue to do so, with long-standing bias in education, especially in curriculum, that is widespread at virtually all levels and institutions in American academia. Professor Sterling Stuckey, a prominent black historian at Northwestern University, has commented: "Black people have met with as great injustices from American scholarship as they have from American life. In fact, colleges and universities have long paved the way for confusion and ignorance, arrogance and presumptuousness ... in Black-White relations."[11]

With the beginning of substantial desegregation of public schools and larger numbers of black young people at predominantly non-black campuses, the concern for how young black people were being socialized by their (new) educational environment became a serious "sociology of knowledge" issue throughout Afro-America. Harold Cruse, a Black Studies professor at the University of Michigan and a distinguished social historian and political theorist, offered a poignant comment on this issue: "The further the Negro gets from his historical antecedents in time, the more tenuous become his conceptual ties, the emptier his social connections, the more superficial his visions. His one great and present hope is to know and understand his African-American realities in the United States more profoundly. Failing that, and failing to crate a new synthesis in history and the humanities and a new social theory, he will suffer the historical fate of intellectual subterfuge."[12] This very same issue was the focus of Harvard-trained African American historian Dr. Carter G. Woodson's seminal study, *The Mis-education of the Negro*, 35 years earlier. Woodson observed:

> The "educated Negroes" have the attitude of contempt towards their own people because in their own schools as well as in their mixed schools Negroes are taught to admire the Hebrew, the Greek, the Latin and the Teuton and to despise the African. These "educated" people, however, decry any such thing as race consciousness.... They do not like to hear such expressions as "Negro Literature," "Negro Poetry," "African Art," or thinking (B)lack.[13]

This matter of identity and educational socialization—in all its interrelated social and individual aspects—is central to the concerns of black educators over serious omissions in established knowledge and commission of distortions in the major intellectual enterprises because of exaggerations of Euro-American particularism and it ontological bias. The importance of this point was expressed in the writing of an exceptionally insightful and honest anthropologist, Charles Valentine: "Social issues and political movements have been intertwined with the search for valid knowledge and expressions of the Black Experience in the United States ever since early precursors of modern Afro-American Studies."[14] The dean of African American social science, Dr. St. Clair Drake, social anthropologist and professor emeritus at Stanford University, reports in a significant study recently published in the respected journal *The New York University Education Quarterly*, that since 1974 "Black Studies grew steadily and became entrenched (during) the next five years, though there were some erroneous reports in newspapers and magazines during 1974 that such programs were in decline."[15] In fact, he contends that "The Black Studies field has become institutionalized in the sense that some of its values are being accepted by the educational system."[16] One of these was the concept that "an ideal university community would be multi-ethnic with ethnicity permitted some institutional expression and with Black Studies being one of the sanctioned forms"[17] as the caste structure in American higher education slowly transforms into an emerging form of pluralism. But there is continuing resistance, based largely upon ideological and theoretical bias, academic nationalism and competitive interests, and some behavior where motivation can only be explained as racist. In this respect it is important to realize that "at least 250 programs devoted to the study of the Black Experience in the United States exist today. Half of these have been operating since 1970, and of the sixty-four that were granting degrees in 1971, all except four have continued to develop. All give some attention to the implications of an African origin for Black people in the New World, and increasingly a "diaspora" frame of reference focuses some attention upon the Caribbean and Latin America for comparison with the United States."[18]

Sociologist Wilson Record, of Portland State University, conducted a study in 1972 and 1973 of Black Studies on 50 campuses across the country for the purpose of assessing their impact on university procedures for curricular innovation and faculty recruitment. He suggests that the effect of the dynamic development of Black Studies in postsecondary education has effected changes such that "colleges and universities would never be quite the same again."

The establishment of numerous departments of African American Studies is generally viewed as a recent phenomenon originating in the last ten years. Though it is true that the field of Black Studies is very new in its present development, its legacy extends to the earliest beginnings of black intellectual history over two centuries ago. Though one can argue that the concept of Black Studies does predate the twentieth century, its recent emergence as an academic field is much more related to the endeavors of black intellectuals during the past 50 years. The proper interpretation and inclusion of the historical role, cultural creation, and social circumstance of black people in America has been of major concern, especially to black scholars in the humanities and social sciences. The development of African American Studies in this century can be traced through several stages.

The origins of the modern movement can be traced to the ferment that began between 1918 and 1929. It was during this period that black scholars actively participated in the mass awakening of the general black population that was precipitated by the social and cultural renaissance of the era. The second phase of the development of Black Studies was ushered in by the Great Depression and marked by the forced parochialization of many black concerns. By the mid–1930s the question of Afro-American Studies was almost entirely the domain of black urban intelligentsia, but is was also during this period that the idea of Black Studies as a separate academic field began to emerge. In 1940 the advent of World War II began a period of dormancy that lasted until roughly 1960. There was a lull that was caused by the war and a gap in the generational shift of black scholars that was accentuated by the changing of priorities by many postwar academicians. The 1960s witnessed the rejuvenation of the civil rights movement, which provided the atmosphere for the question of Black Studies to become a major innovation in higher education. Campus protests created the subsequent pressure for the recognition and proliferation of Afro-American Studies programs throughout the nation. However, once these programs were established, they were confronted with the essential task of academic construction—of organizing curriculum and developing pedagogical methodology. Essential to this task was the selection of source materials as reference and texts for classroom instruction. The teaching function was to be the foundation for most of the programs. As a "new" field there was the immediate challenge of developing prototypical courses that could serve as beginning models for standardization and cross-reference of courses between the various departments and programs. Each instructor was responsible for developing his or her own individual syllabi. But if the program was to grow and become effectively institutionalized and regularized, there was going to have to be coordination between instructors in a given program in order to achieve a reasonable degree of systematic organization of courses for effective interface and a logical symmetry in intellectual focus. There had to be a meaningful division of academic endeavors that would provide a basis for integrated learning from one course to another in a program.

There are specific functions common to all disciplines, and they are in two dimensions. First, the intellectual parameters of the field must be relatively clearly established with rather apparent theoretical configuration. Second, the ideational and analytical "meanings" of the discipline—that is, what characterizes what we do as different, and significantly, from what is done in other disciplines—must be delineated. In sum, a fairly commonly adhered-to definition of the raison d'être of the field must emerge: for example, what is the consequence of "Afro-centric" perspective for the pursuit of truth? This difference must not be different for difference's sake; moreover, it must comprise a *significant* difference in the social construction of knowledge. It should challenge and enrich the learning process and provide a *particular* symbolic ethos of the discipline. This means that Black Studies would (and should) not serve as a secondary appendage or an intellectual afterthought to another established discipline (what would be essentially a modicum of black content in an erstwhile "Europerspective" subject). This raises the question of whether African American Studies composes a discipline in its own right and could contribute academically to the development of new knowledge. Other related questions are: Can the field generate new theory? Does Black Studies have a viable intellectual tradition of research investigation and scholarly literature?

There is a great deal of discussion among scholars and educators about what constitutes a discipline. For instance, is a course on biology and society, biology or sociology?; Is art history, art or history?; Is history a science or an orientation to factual information within the humanities? What about social psychology; is it an academic bastard without sufficient specific identity and legitimate claim to a parent discipline, or is it on the frontier of theory as a consequence of cross-fertilization between and within traditional structures of knowledge? If political science is a discipline, what is its cogent theoretical definition and a characteristic explanation or description of its methodology?

The point is, we think, that knowledge is being packaged with new labels and in different arrangements, representing the realities of modern society. Though the initial questions may seem important, they may not be relevant or germane. Nonetheless, these questions about Black Studies as knowledge reveal a complex argument couched in and implied by theoretical development stemming from dominant mainstream criteria concerning adequate theory (empirical, interpretive, critical) and converging trends and opinions among the most institutionalized and professionally prestigious academic disciplines concerning self-referential evidence supportive of the Black Studies criteria.

The fact that most of the major arguments in history, social science, anthropology, arts, literature, and the humanities derive from Euro-American particularism in experiences that have been held to be generalizable to the universe reflects a dialectic historicism operative in modern Western theoretical development. Black Studies represents a disillusionment and critique of "certified knowledge," and the historical currents of disillusionment with the mainstream and also a current of progressive contribution towards a more adequate social analysis and public policy. Therefore Black Studies is a "reconstruction discipline," as a synthesis of what its criticisms imply, convergence with theories reviewed, and the philosophic methods of its pedagogical emphasis. If the reconstruction method is, itself a workable procedure, we have in Black Studies a way of arriving at new theory. Black Studies is a conceptual paradigm that principally tells us, like other academic discourse, what counts as a fact and what problems of explanation exist. It is commonly accepted among social scientists that "what we take to be an action, and even its proper description, is internally related to the interpretations that are intrinsically constitutive of it." But an action, to some extent, can be judged according to the linguistic and conceptual structure through which that action is filtered. A social science bereft of an analysis of the interchange between the subjective and the objective is thus a social science orientation that condones a tendency of "uncritical acceptance of ideological bias" of both a cultural and moral sort. Thus, conclusions about what constitutes a significant contribution to knowledge reveal that a similar filtering process is operative in such evaluation.

This debate, I am sure, will continue to go on and, in my judgment, should go on, because of its intellectual importance and significance in redefining and reformulating issues of theory and methodology. Undoubtedly we can expect continued contentious relations with many non-black educators and even with neoconservative black intellectuals who have gained a sort of prominence as clients of the new-right (and, for that matter, the old right-wing) thrust directed at all institutions of American society—education notwithstanding. I suspect that we will have to come to grips with the reality that ours is not just a protracted contention, but that, as is true in most other arenas of race relations, the difficulties Black Studies scholars will confront, because of the prevailing institutional forces in American education, are endemic. Nonetheless, there has been an impressive degree of "settling in" that provides a firmer foundation for the next decade. Many of our colleagues who began a decade ago in Africana Studies have been able to achieve relatively permanent, tenured positions at a cross section of colleges and universities in the country.

A recent catalog by Greenwood Press indicates that there are approximately 20 serious academic journals and magazines devoted to Africana Studies. There are better than a half dozen professional associations whose central purpose is the support and advancement of Africana Studies as an academic discipline and the cultivation of scholars. There has been a sound basis in the development of conceptual and theoretical clarity. Though there has been some want in funding resources for research and a falloff in interest by major publishing houses in recent years, the productivity of scholarship in the field has been steady, evidenced by a discernible increase in the quality and in the quantity of published manuscripts. In spite of the obstacles there have been some major publications in the past few years worthy of note: *The Shaping of Black America*, Lerone Bennett; *The Harder We Run*, William Harris; *Survival and Progress: Afro-American Experience*, Alex Swan; *Black Americans and the Political System*, L. Barker and Jesse McCorry; *Langston Hughes: Before and After Harlem*, Edith Berry; *There Is a River*, Vincent Harding; *Black Women Novelists*, Barbara Christian; *The Slave Community*, John Blassingame; *How Europe Underdeveloped Africa*, Walter Rodney; *When and Where We Enter*, Paula Giddings; and the recently published *The Principles of Black Political Economy*, Lloyd Hogan.

This list could be much longer; it is not meant to be exhaustive. My intention is to give a representative sample of the scope and caliber of scholarship characteristic of the field. Perhaps most significant of all has been the publication of two widely used introductory texts in Africana Studies. The two-volume set *Introduction to Afro-American Studies*, an edited collection by Peoples College, and the more recent, first single-authored text, *Introduction to Black Studies*, by Maulana Karenga, have made critical contributions to the standardization of the Black Studies curriculum. These introductory texts are vitally important to conveying a coherent definition and common identity to the discipline. Ultimately, the consolidation of Africana Studies will be predicated upon a foundation of an integrated, standardized curriculum.

While we have good reasons to enjoy a reasonable sense of satisfaction at this stage, the path ahead will not necessarily be unobstructed. The conservative mood in the country is impacting educational policy. Dr. Faustine Jones, of Howard University, has identified definite patterns of erosion in commitment to inclusion of formally neglected and oppressed national *minority* groups in the educational system. With the election of the Reagan administration there have emerged neoconservative political action groups that are targeting public sources of information and public education for political assault as part of their version of a "holy" war to safeguard the "soul" of the republic from what they perceived to be unwelcome ideas. Prominent among these self-initiated guardians of society are organizations like the Committee for a Free World, which began in 1981 and issued the following statement: "We are persuaded that the struggle for freedom may in the end be won not on the battlefields but in books, newspapers, broadcasts, classrooms, and in all public institutions."[19]

Their rallying cry is for an ideological war to control America's mind. We can expect that such political chicanery will enduce encounters, at the institutional level, that will challenge us to stand firm on the ground we have achieved thus far. It is precisely because of this kind of raging conservatism, which is being mobilized as a retrogressive social movement, that Africana Studies is all the more essential to the preservation of the modest gains made by African Americans over the last decade. There will very likely be those who will ask, with the transformations of society toward greater technological concentration in the scientific and computer age of the 1980s and 1990s, is Black Studies feasible or necessary? Stewart has pointed out in this regard that "the current socialization of students prior to entry into higher education is undeniably generating a careerist mentality. This trend has its counterpart among Black Studies faculty, many of whom face continuing subtle and overt harassment by non–Black Studies colleagues. Many of the first faculty in the field are gradually de-emphasizing involvement in community activities as they have succumbed to (or have been seduced by) the orthodox norms of academic traditionalism in their pursuit of careerist aspirations for legitimacy and acceptability for purposes of job stability and security. Younger faculty have not been quite as engaged by commitment to community outreach and the wedding of intellectual and social activism on behalf of the liberation of the black community.

This phenomenon is denying Black Studies both a critical bridge to the potential beneficiaries of applied scholarship, that is, the external community, and a source of power to facilitate the continuation of innovative projects in the face of renewed opposition. Dr. Robert C. Johnson, writing on "Why Colleges and Students Need Black Studies" in the *Chronicle of Higher Education*, states that academically and vocationally Black Studies are important for a variety of reasons. Some of his reasons are as follows: one-third of all children born in this country are black, Hispanic, Asian, American Indian, etc.; 25 percent of the population consists of racial ethnic groups; many regions (particularly urban centers) and institutions (that is, urban public schools) are rapidly approaching a black and Hispanic majority; and the vast majority of the people in this world are racial ethnic groups of non–Anglo linkage. He concludes that "for the most part, the majority of the students in American institutions of higher education are being grossly underprepared to function in a multiethnic, multiracial, multicultural world."[20] Dr. Eleanor Traylor indicates a similar point when she states: "Moreover, in a country as culturally plural as the United States, we enjoy the large opportunity to educate our children multi-culturally and multi-linguistically. And because of the nature of our world today, nothing is more desirable than multi-literate citizens whose respect for one another transforms old enmities or superstitions threatening the very existence of the planet itself."[21]

The research department of the New York Urban League recently conducted a tri-state study of New York, Pennsylvania, and New Jersey to ascertain the kind of mentor relationships black students have in graduate schools. Their findings revealed that for most of these students there was no significant mentor relationship to encourage and guide them in their study. This is due, in part, to too few black faculty in American higher education. In the *Chronicle of Higher Education*, Charles Farrell reports that "virtually no gains are being made in increasing minority representation in the faculties and administrations of predominantly white colleges, according to many educators familiar with academic recruiting."[22]

This observation is supported by a special investigative study of the shortage of black professors by the *Wall Street Journal*. The *Journal* found: "In few industries today are Blacks as scarce as in higher education. In predominantly white schools, Blacks usually make up only about 1 percent of the tenured and non-tenured faculty. Princeton University has only 9 Black faculty out of a total staff of 581. The University of Michigan has 20 out of a total of 684—and that's the highest percentage of Blacks in the Big 10."[23] The University of Pennsylvania had 31 black faculty in 1972 and it has 31 black faculty in 1984. The situation is getting worse because the potential pool is getting smaller. For the past five years, the number of blacks applying to arts and sciences graduate schools has steadily declined. Between 1975 and 1980, Harvard, Yale, and Princeton each produced a total of 10 or fewer black undergraduates who went on to earn their doctorates; Howard University produced 275. Institutions such as Morehouse College in Atlanta have been far more successful than most white institutions in encouraging black students to go on to graduate school. Black colleges educate only about a quarter of the black undergraduates, but over half the blacks with new Ph.D.'s got their undergraduate education there.

The vice provost and dean of graduate studies at Stanford University, Gerald Lieberman, says, "Part of the problem is a national climate of indifference and even suspicion toward affirmative action. Many colleges seem to have developed a "plateau mentality" that does nothing more than maintain present ratios of minorities and white."[24] As associate director of the American Council on Education's office of minority affairs, Sarah Melendez, says, "It is very clear that there is an underrepresentation of minorities on faculties and administrations."[25]

The future prospects are not good, as there is little, if any, expectation of improvement. The prognosis is that the situation will get worse as minority faculty are terminated by denial of tenure and through the syndrome of "last hired, first fired" during programs of retrenchment and fiscal austerity. Currently the proportion of black faculty in American higher education is 4.0 percent. Lorenzo Morris points out, "The data on the status of Blacks from 1975 through 1977, however, show that progress in all areas of higher education has slowed down and in areas like professional education, it has come to a standstill."[26] In a special report, "Participation of black students in Higher Education. A Statistical Profile from 1970-71 to 1980-81," prepared by the National Center for Educational Statistics and released November 1983 by the U.S. Department of Education, the following summaries were offered:

During the first half of the 1970s:

The large increase in Black enrollment coincided with the expansion in both federal legislation and federal policies aimed at reducing barriers to higher education for minorities and low-income students.

By 1975 the percentage of Black high school graduates who enrolled in college was the same as that for whites (although high school graduation rates were still lower for Blacks than whites).

During the last half of the 1970s:

Black participation in higher education stabilized in most areas.

The number of Blacks who enrolled in college remained about the same, in spite of the fact that the number of Black youth eligible for college increased by almost 20 percent.

The number and proportion of degrees awarded to Blacks remained about the same at the bachelor's, doctor's, and first professional levels, while there were substantial declines at the master's level.

The number of Blacks receiving master's degrees declined 16 percent, four times greater than the decline for non-Blacks.

Doctoral degrees awarded to black students for the years 1976, 1979, and 1981 were 3.6, 3.9, and 3.9, respectively. Though the data are not firm for the past three years, there is evidence that indicates trends of decline in black student enrollment in both undergraduate and graduate schools. Professors Laurie Hatch and Kent Mommsen, from their study of racial gaps in education, report that "from this analysis two major points emerge. The substantial and widening racial gap in American higher education is accounted for primarily by remaining inequities among males."[27] The pattern seems to be significantly related to the Reagan administration's cutbacks and changes in federal aid to higher education, particularly the government's support for need-based financial assistance to students and guaranteed low-interest loans. The shift has been especially severe among indigenous black males.

These trends appear to have some rather direct implications for the progress of Black Studies, in the long term if not immediately. Fewer African American faculty would mean that there is a lessened likelihood that students will have mentors who will introduce them to Africana Studies and encourage them to seriously consider academic careers in the field. There will also be a diminishing potential source of new colleagues necessary to further the field. Relatively fewer black students in American higher education will reduce the natural constituency and bridge of support for the field. How these problems are resolved or transcended will impact as much, critically, upon the future of Africana Studies as will the ongoing discourse on questions related to ontology and epistemology.

NOTES

1. John H. Clarke, "Africana Studies: A Decade of Change, Challenge, and Conflict" (paper presented at the conference "Consolidating Africana Studies: Bonding African Linkages" on the occasion of the tenth anniversary of the Africana Studies and Research Center, Cornell University, September 26–28, 1980), p. 1.

2. A. Wade Boykin, "Black Psychology and the Research Process" (unpublished manuscript), p. 14.

3. *Ibid.*, p. 15.

4. *Ibid.*, p. 16.

5. James B. Stewart, *Toward Operationalization of an "Expansive" Model of Black Studies* (Atlanta: Institute of the Black World, 1983), p. 1.

6. *Ibid.*, p. 5.

7. Lorenzo Morris, *Elusive Equality* (Washington, D.C.: Howard University Press, 1980), p. 18.

8. Boykin, *op. cit,* p. 1.

9. *Ibid.*, p. 8.

10. *Ibid.*, p. 7.

11. Sterling Stuckey, comments made during a lecture at a symposium on Black Studies at the Institute of the Black World, Atlanta, 1970.

12. Harold Cruse, comments from a paper presented at a conference sponsored by the University of Michigan on African American Studies, Ann Arbor, April, 1978.

13. Carter G. Woodson, *Mis-education of the Negro,* (Washington, D.C.: The Associated Publishers, 1969), p. 7.

14. Charles Valentine, *Afro-American Studies: An Intellectual Tradition* (New York: Bobbs Merrill Reprint Series, 1980), p. 9.

15. St. Clair Drake, "Black Studies in Higher Education," *New York University Education Quarterly* 21, no. 3: p. 2.

16. *Ibid.*, p. 4.

17. *Ibid.*, p. 5.

18. *Ibid.*, p. 12.

19. Richard Goldstein, "The War for America's Mind," *The Village Voice,* 8 June 1982, p.1.

20. Robert Johnson, "Why Colleges and Students Need Black Studies," *Chronicle of Higher Education,* 17 November 1980, p. 24.

21. Eleanor Traylor, letter to the director of the National Endowment for the Humanities, Washington, D.C., July 1984.

22. Charles Farrell, "Minorities Seen Making No Gains in Campus Jobs," *Chronicle of Higher Education,* 13 June 1984, p.1.

23. Anne MacKay Smith, "Large Shortage of Black Professors in Higher Education Grows Worse," *Wall Street Journal,* July 10, 1984, p.2.

24. Farrell, *loc. cit.*

25. *Ibid.*

26. Morris, *op. cit.*, p. 18.

27. Laurie R. Hatch and Kent Mommsen, "The Widening Racial Gap in American Higher Education," *Journal of Black Studies* 14: 4 (June 1984): p. 470.

9. Reaching for Higher Ground: Toward an Understanding of Black/Africana Studies

James B. Stewart, Ph.D.
Vice Provost
Pennsylvania State University

Introduction

This chapter explores two issues that are central to assessing the current developmental trajectory of Black/Africana Studies. The issues of particular concern are (a) the nature of the linkage between traditional disciplines/approaches to inquiry and Africana Studies, and (b) the concept of Afrocentricity and its impact on the current status and future development of the field.

The first issue has been discussed and debated extensively over the last two decades. The debate has intensified recently, in part due to the visibility afforded to writings by literary critics and historians who, although they identify primarily with traditional disciplines, assert connections to Black Studies [Baker (1984); Gates (1988); Harris, Hine, and McKay (1990); Huggins (1985)]. This turf battle has re-energized discussions about the nature of Black Studies, i.e., is it a self-contained and distinct body of knowledge or simply an adjunct to traditional disciplines?

The second issue is of more recent origin. The work of Asante (1980, 1987, 1990) and other prominent figures who employ complementary approaches, e.g., Maulana Karenga (1982, 1988, 1990), have popularized the concept of Afrocentricity both within and outside academe. Their contributions and those of an older generation of "scholarly/community griots" (John Henrik Clarke and Josef Ben-Jochannon) have spurred commentators outside of academe to develop popularized "Afrocentric" analyses. These popular treatments have been integrated into various media, including music and film. Unfortunately, the analytical precision of the academic conceptions is typically lacking, with accuracy sometimes sacrificed for the sake of art.

"Popular Afrocentrism" is being confused increasingly with systematic intellectual approaches in the field. This confusion has contributed to a distorted view of the state of the field and is fueling uneasiness in some circles about the intellectual credibility of Black/Africana Studies.

The context outlined above grounds the present discussion. First, an overview of evolving conceptions of the field over the last two decades and the rationales used to support those conceptions is presented. That discussion serves to explicate why the disjunction persists between discipline-linked and stand-alone models. It also attempts to establish the general limitations of traditional disciplines to inform modern Black/Africana Studies. The focus is on the general linkage between traditional disciplines in the aggregate and Black/Africana Studies. The third section examines the field's specific linkages to the subject areas of history, literature/literary criticism, and psychology.

The significance of the concept of Afrocentricity for Black/Africana Studies is explored in the fourth section. The concept is first defined and critiqued. Its use in three systems of thought identified with the field is then examined.

The final section suggests possible directions for future development that can address the problems identified in the preceding sections. A synthesis of elements of the field's three major systems of thought is proposed as a foundation for future efforts.

In Search of a Philosophical Base

Conceptions of Black/Africana Studies. The general academic and non-academic conceptions of the field are first discussed. Attention is then focused specifically on academic conceptions of Africana Studies. Five distinct rationales used to support various academic conceptions of the field are explored.

Allen (1974) provides a useful classification of modern conceptions of Black Studies that emerged during the formative stage of the late 1960s and early 1970s. Three conceptions were identified: (1) an *academic conception* that treats the mission of Black Studies as researching black history and illuminating the contributions of blacks; (2) an *ideological conception* that identifies Black Studies as an instrument of cultural nationalism; and (3) an *instrumental conception* whereby the role of Black Studies is to serve as a vehicle for social change within black communities.

Allen's scheme is a useful reminder that discussion of the relationship between Black/Africana Studies and traditional disciplines cannot ignore the historical symbiotic relationship between academic and political conceptions of Black Studies. However, throughout the formative period and subsequently there have been efforts to de-emphasize the linkage between scholarship and social activism. As a consequence, care must be taken in discussing the relationship between Black/Africana Studies and traditional disciplines to avoid misrepresentation of the multifaceted character of the enterprise.

These concepts require modifications to accommodate both the Marxist school of thought and the emergent Africana Women's Studies movement. The Marxist approach rejects cultural nationalism as the appropriate ideological orientation and simultaneously denies the usefulness of traditional disciplinary demarcations. This approach is consistent with the view of Karl Marx (1971, p. 44) who wrote, "we know only of a single science, the science of history." Marxist scholars, of course, have advocated aggressively for strong linkages between academic inquiry and political struggle. They are, in fact, responsible for institutionalizing this value by coining the slogan, "Academic Excellence and Social Responsibility." This phrase has been adopted as the official motto of the National Council for Black Studies.

The Africana Women's Studies movement is challenging traditional patterns of male chauvinism in the field. Two intellectual tendencies exist within this movement. One school of thought embraces the field's long standing cultural nationalist ideology. It urges the forging of a new partnership between Africana men and women in pursuit of previously articulated intellectual and political objectives (see Henry and Foster, 1982). The second school of thought elevates feminism to a higher ideological status than cultural nationalism (see Hull, Scott, and Smith, 1982). Advocates of the second approach tend to be more directly connected to traditional academic disciplines than are their counterparts and, more specifically, they are clustered in the areas of literary criticism and creative writing. The specific disciplinary linkages and the visibility afforded those advocating priority to feminist perspectives have reinforced the misperception that the principal bases of activity in Black/Africana Studies are in the humanities or outside academe.

Although the historical precedents of the field were clearly forged outside of academe, the locus of development during the modern era has been and remains solidly inside the academy. Moreover, as emphasized in the next section, within the academic arena the social sciences, rather than the arts and humanities, have come to provide the major models that have shaped conceptions of the field.

Disentangling Academic Conceptions. The extreme version of Allen's academic conception is exemplified by the comments of Blassingame (1969), who argued that Black Studies programs were inappropriate vehicles for promoting development in black communities. Ford (1974, p. 224) defines the field almost exclusively as an academic venture: "The term Black Studies refers to educational courses concerned with the study of research in various aspects of the experience, attitudes, and cultural artifacts of peoples of African origin.... Black Studies is concerned primarily with the history, literature, art, music, religion, cultural patterns and lifestyles developed in America by a race of people cut off completely from all contact with the land of their origin." Russell (1975, p. 185) takes a similar approach arguing that Black Studies "...has a respectable body of knowledge and researchable content with the Black humanities and social sciences comprising its core curriculum..."

General descriptions of this type spawned five more specific approaches to justifying the existence of a distinct body of knowledge: (1) the value-added rationale, (2) rationale by negation, (3) multidisciplinary rationales, (4) rationales based on applications of Western philosophies of science, and (5) rationales based on historical precedent.

> *Value-Added Rationales:* The language used by Allen in describing the academic conception of Black Studies and the specifications of Ford and Russell are useful for establishing a baseline position regarding the linkages between Black/Africana Studies and traditional disciplines. All three statements ascribe a special status to the humanities and the social and behavioral sciences. In addition, all three implicitly employ what can be described as a "value added" rationale for the existence of the field. In other words, Black Studies has a legitimate role in academe because it extends the explanatory power of traditional disciplines. Significantly, the issue of whether the theories and methods utilized in traditional disciplines are directly applicable without modification to the study of the experiences of peoples of African descent is not addressed. As a consequence, this line of argument can support either a model of "black studies" as a subset of the knowledge base of traditional disciplines or a model identifying "Black Studies" as a self-contained and distinct body of knowledge.
>
> In recognition of this problem, another strategy used to differentiate between Black/Africana Studies and traditional disciplines is rationale by negation.
>
> *Rationale by Negation:* This approach both critiques the limitations of traditional theories and methods and defines the distinct nature of Black/Africana Studies analyses. This unique aspect of the field is said to emanate from the synthesis of either the academic and ideological or the academic and instrumental sub-missions. To illustrate, Alkalimat (1973, pp. 187-188) argues that "the conceptual approach of white social science is only useful on the analytical level of classification since for each term the social content must be specified.

The concepts presented for a Black social science clearly suggest a specific socio-political content to be understood as the race problem." In a complementary vein, McClendon (1974, p. 18) asserts that "Black Studies will insist that students examine and comprehend a multitude of theories and teachings. The relevance of each body of knowledge to black liberation can be determined only through obtaining an understanding of the substantive content."

Jackson (1970, p. 132) claims that Black Studies scholarship should be geared toward improving life in the black community, an approach that would be accomplished by creating a closer symbiosis "between pure and applied roles of science with a greater stress on application of knowledge."

These approaches to synthesis do not introduce any particular conceptual difficulty in linking social-scientific and humanistic approaches in a self-contained model of Black/Africana Studies. This is true, in part, because the concept of a "black aesthetic" provides a parallel in the humanities and the arts to the idea of a unique "black" value orientation and observational language in the social sciences of the type suggested by Alkalimat (1973) and McClendon (1974). Potential problems do arise, however, in reconciling an "arts for arts' sake" philosophy with the notion of instrumental knowledge. In addition, the disjunction between social scientific and humanistic approaches has contributed to a gradual decline in the frequency of formal statements about the role of humanistic scholarship and the creative arts as integral components of Black/Africana Studies.

The social sciences increasingly have become the senior partner in the social science/humanities/creative arts nexus of Black/Africana Studies. It is from that vantage point that Karenga (1982, p. 32) asserts that "Black Studies, as both an investigative and applied social science, poses the paradigm of theory and practice merging into active self-knowledge which leads to positive social change. In a word, it is a discipline dedicated not only to understanding self, society and the world but also to them in a positive developmental way in the interest of human history and advancement."

If, as Karenga argues, Black Studies is a discipline, then how does it relate to other disciplines? One approach to answering this question involves attempts to define the field as a combination of existing disciplines, i.e., articulation of a *multidisciplinary rationale.*

Multidisciplinary Rationales: Distinctions can be drawn between weak and strong multidisciplinary rationales. *Weak multi/interdisciplinary rationales* take the existing disciplinary structure as given but argue that Black/Africana Studies provides unique added value because it develops knowledge that represents disciplinary synthe- ses. Most advocates of this position simply assume that because Black/ Africana Studies examines aspects of life experience that cut across traditional disciplinary boundaries, the resultant analyses are by definition interdisciplinary. However, virtually no attention is devoted to the examination of the underlying theoretical constructs neces- sary for "interdisciplinarity" or "multidisciplinary" to be manifested.

The weak multidisciplinary rationale can be contrasted to what can be described as the *strong multidisciplinary rationale*. The prin- cipal distinctions between the two are (a) the efforts of advocates of the strong rationale to ground their arguments in the philosophy of science, and (b) the emphasis on subject areas rather than disciplines as the unit analysis. One important statement of this position is found in Karenga (1982, pp. 35-36): "Black Studies ... as an inter- disciplinary discipline has seven basic subject areas. These intradis- ciplinary foci which at first seem to be disciplines themselves are, in fact, separate disciplines when they are outside the discipline of Black Studies, but inside, they become and are essentially subject areas which contribute to a holistic picture and approach to the Black Experience. Moreover, the qualifier Black, attached to each area in an explicit or implicit way, suggests a more specialized and delim- ited focus which of necessity transforms a broad discipline into a particular subject area. The seven basic subject areas of Black Stud- ies then are: Black History; Black Religion; Black Social Organiza- tion; Black Politics; Black Economics; Black Creative Production (Black Art, Music and Literature); and Black Psychology."

In particular, several critical questions can be raised regarding Karenga's assertions, including (1) does the transformation from dis- cipline to subject area involve the transformation of the underlying disciplinary constructs, (2) how can affixing the prefix "black" pro- duce the hypothesized transformation, and (3) if Black/Africana Studies is a social science how exactly are the subject areas of black history, black religion, and black creative production integrated into the enterprise?

Questions of the type proposed above are typically within the province of the philosophy of science. And, in fact, some proponents have turned to this field to generate a fourth approach to establish- ing the case for the intellectual legitimacy of Black/Africana Stud- ies.

Western Philosophy of Science-Based Rationales: Various scholars includ- ing Karenga (1988); Stewart (1979, 1982a, 1982b); and Turner (1984) have used this approach to clarify the intellectual project of

Black/Africana Studies. The most popular framework used is that of Kuhn (1970), although selected analyses draw upon the writings of other philosophers including, Lehrer (1975) and Toulmin (1972) [*see* Stewart (1982a)]. Even members of the Marxist school of thought have adapted Kuhn's basic constructs to explicate their approach to the field [*see* Alkalimat (1990)].

In contrast to the use of Western philosophies of science as a means to generate analogies, Asante (1987) has used the work of critical theorists as a foil to differentiate their project from that which he ascribes to "Africalogy." This thrust is understandable given the neo–Marxist overlay associated with the constructs of most critical theorists. Asante's commitment to cultural nationalism thus engenders an approach to critical theory that is a variant of the rationale of negation.

In general, the use of Western philosophies of science to define Black/Africana Studies has further removed the humanities and the arts from center stage. Philosophies of science are just that—philosophies designed to examine intellectual processes in scientific disciplines, not intellectual processes associated with other areas of inquiry. In fact, even the range of applicability across different scientific fields is restricted. Generally, philosophy of science models have been fashioned to examine intellectual processes in the physical and natural sciences. Thus, even the extension of the models to the social and behavioral sciences requires relaxation of some critical assumptions. The role of the humanities and the arts in Black/Africana Studies further complicates matters. Moreover, as described in Stewart (1982a), there remains the problem of how to handle the activist mission of Black/Africana Studies within a philosophy of science framework.

Toulmin's (1972) specification of the necessary conditions for disciplinary status highlights the nature of the problem. For Toulmin (1972, p. 133) an area of inquiry develops into a scientific discipline when it has "one and only one set of well-defined goals at a time (that is explanation of phenomena falling within the scope of the disciplinary inquiry), and one set of selection-criteria." Reconciling this notion of discipline with Karenga's specification of Black Studies as a discipline presented previously is a major intellectual task.

While acknowledging these caveats regarding the applicability of philosophy of science models to describe Black/Africana Studies, experimentation with such models has added substantial precision to the discussion of many important topics. As a means of illustration, Kuhn (1970) introduces the use of the term "research paradigm" to characterize the specific application of the scientific method within an area of inquiry. The term "disciplinary matrix" was later offered as an alternative to "paradigm." Disciplinary matrices are said to be comprised of four components: (a) a metaphysical component; (b) values shared by practitioners; (c) symbolic generalizations, observational language, and research methods, and (d) exemplars (concrete examples of the application of the theoretical and empirical framework).

The metaphysical component of disciplinary matrices consists, in part, of beliefs about the explanatory power of particular models.

One metaphysical component that could be used to differentiate Black/Africana Studies analyses from other investigations is the model of peoples of African descent as actors continuously striving to achieve sufficient power to maintain their cultural identity and define their collective destiny. This model contrasts with alternative "metaphysical" orientations that either treat blacks as perpetual victims or as a population of individuals in the process of assimilating Euro-American culture. Other beliefs that differentiate Black/Africana Studies from competing orientations include the preference for collectives rather than individuals as the unit of analysis and the emphasis on modeling social processes as cyclical rather than linear phenomena.

In Kuhn's model, the second component of the disciplinary matrix values actually has two sub-categories: macro- and micro-order values. Kuhn (1970) uses the example of beliefs in whether or not "science should or need not be socially useful" as an example of a macro-order value, and indicates that scientists in a field may disagree about this issue. This observation has clear relevance for the earlier discussion of the disagreement between those committed to a more detached academic conception of Black/Africana Studies and those advocating for a more applied research focus. The operative point is that Kuhn's framework provides a means for incorporating such discussions in a way that reaffirms the "scientific" character of Black/Africana Studies. Micro-order values are beliefs about the nature of the scientific enterprise that guide the behaviors and judgments of practitioners. For example, some micro-order values specify how the relative merit of competing theories is to be judged. Again, the relevance to the earlier discussions about differences among the academic conceptions of Black/Africana Studies Occasional Papers are obvious. Black/Africana Studies analyst/activists who support a standalone conception of the field place more weight on the applicability of knowledge to guide social change than on esoteric explanatory power measured, for example, by statistical robustness. In addition,

there are potential tradeoffs among judging criteria. In Black/
Africana Studies, theories and applied analyses are judged on the
bases of "beauty," "functionality," "rhythm," and "compatibility with
folk wisdom," in addition to "precision." Consequently, precision
could be self-consciously sacrificed to achieve other objectives in
some cases.

Micro-order values also address how information generated by
practitioners in the discipline is to be disseminated. In traditional
disciplines, there is typically a stated preference between articles in
referred journals and monographs. In the case of Black/Africana
Studies, the multiple missions have led to emphasis on monographs
and on another mode of dissemination, i.e., public speeches. The
controversy surrounding a speech given by Leonard Jeffries in July
1991 is instructive regarding the strengths and weaknesses associated
with this medium.

Rationale by Exemplar: The generation of a body of exemplars to support the documentation of an intellectual history of Black/Africana
Studies is consistent with the metaphysical belief in cyclical social
processes. Intellectual production is also a social process. This means
that historical theory and praxis can serve as a means of gauging the
degree of compatibility between contemporary scholarship/activism
and long term cultural trends in these arenas.

Since many traditional disciplines are largely products of the twentieth century, Black/Africana Studies predecessors were not saddled
with the ideological baggage associated with twentieth century disciplines. In addition, prior to the affirmation of the social values of
disciplinary specialization and detachment of academics from the
public sphere, it was much more likely that scholars would be
engaged in a wide range of activities in addition to intellectual
inquiry.

The multiple missions of Black/Africana Studies necessitate the
generation of a much wider variety of exemplars than envisioned by
Kuhn. In particular, the expectation that practitioners will not be
simply scholars but scholar/activists suggests the importance of
examples of historical figures who combined scholarly activity and
social activism in ways comparable to that advocated for contemporary Black/Africana Studies scholar/activists. Thus, there is a need
for a collection of biographies of figures whose value orientation mirrors that of the contemporary Black/Africana Studies community.
Strengthening the instrumental and nationalist dimensions of the
field will require examples of how quasi-autonomous African and
African American societies organized social relations. Conversely,

examples of failed attempts would facilitate identification of ineffective strategies that should not be replicated.

In the cases of both individual "intellectual/activist autobiographies" and "community development models," "pure" cases of unambiguous correspondence to contemporary values will not be found. The reality of the historical experiences of peoples of African descent and the pattern of domination of the intellectual landscape by traditional disciplines will cause most case studies to exhibit significant ambiguity. Consequently, the most useful exemplars are likely to be composites of several examples rather than distinct individual cases.

In some cases, the generation of exemplars involves the wresting of "heroes" and "heroines" from the clutches of other fields. To illustrate, Stewart (1984) has provided an interpretation of the life, career, and writings of W.E.B. DuBois that clearly defines him as a predecessor of modern Black/Africana Studies. Earlier interpretations either linked DuBois' writings to specific disciplines or subject areas, or examined his political movements in isolation from his scholarly activity. These approaches necessitated the use of edited volumes in an attempt to capture the complexity of his life and writings [See, for example, Clarke, Jackson, Kaiser, and O'Dell, eds., (1970)]. This "shotgun" approach mirrors the attempt through individual traditional disciplines to capture the complexity of the experiences of peoples of African descent.

From this vantage point, Stewart's Black/Africana Studies interpretation of DuBois eliminates the clumsiness and fragmentation of discipline-oriented interpretations. It can serve, then, as an exemplar for a general approach that could be usefully applied to examine a variety of historical figures, including Maria Stewart, Martin Delany, Edward Blyden, Alaine Locke, and Zora Neale Hurston. In the case of Locke and Hurston, efforts to graft simplistic discipline-oriented interpretations or topical treatments have been undertaken by scholars outside of Black/Africana Studies, comparable to those applied to DuBois (See Linneman, 1982 and Wallace, 1990).

There are a number of African American societies that would be appropriate subjects for the type of historical community studies advocated above. These include the various maroon societies—communities founded as a result of the Exoduster movement: Mound Bayou, Mississippi; Durham, North Carolina; and Promiseland, South Carolina (See Painter, 1977; Bethel, 1981; Herman, 1981; and DuBois, 1912).

Unfortunately, only limited attention is currently directed at developing the types of exemplars described above. Current attention is focused disproportionately on classical African civilizations, and in particular on ancient Egypt or Kemet. The thrust of interest in this area in general has been to identify the African origins of Egyptian civilization and, more specifically, to document the extensive presence and impact of peoples of sub–Saharan African origin in various dynasties. This research is necessary and important for several reasons. It provides the ammunition to mount a direct attack on traditional interpretations of ancient Egyptian society as a pseudo–European civilization. The Europeanization of Egypt has facilitated the efforts of historians of Western thought to project the notion of a continuous intellectual history of strictly European lineage. Current research that debunks this interpretation can provide a foundation for reconstructing a continuous intellectual history of African thought that can connect to modern Black/Africana Studies.

The examination of value systems in classical African civilizations prior to the emergence of Western political domination can provide exemplars that can clarify the metaphysical and values components of the Black/Africana Studies disciplinary matrix. In such societies, peoples of African descent were rulers rather than subjects. As a consequence, their world views were not shaped by the history of domination that has conditioned much of the thought of peoples of African descent who were kidnapped and transplanted to the West. Studies of classical civilizations have also identified individual figures who can serve as exemplars for contemporary Black/Africana Studies scholar/activists, e.g., Imhotep.

Despite the potential benefits associated with the study of classical African civilizations, there are drawbacks to such an emphasis. Unfortunately, the vast majority of the scholarship to date is contributionist in orientation, rather than undertaking systematic investigation of the degree of applicability of classical ideas and social formations for the present and future. Most of these studies have embodied a "rationale by negation," with the goal of disputing traditional claims that ancient Egyptian civilization bore little connection to sub–Saharan Africa. Little effort has been made to shape these studies in ways that contribute to the generation of the continuous intellectual history advocated previously. Finally, the focus on Kemetic studies needs to be balanced with comparable levels of scrutiny of other classical African civilizations and societies/communities in the Western Hemisphere.

Summary: In this section five general approaches to establishing the intellectual credibility of Black/Africana Studies have been explored. The discussion has examined the relationship between the field and traditional disciplines. Although no effort was made to establish a temporal progression in the development of the various rationales, the different approaches could be loosely grouped into "early" and "contemporary" rationales. The first category would encompass the value added, negation, and multidisciplinary rationales, while the philosophy of science and exemplar rationales constitute more contemporary approaches. The intellectual ground established by the contemporary approaches is generally more solid than that associated with the earlier lines of argumentation.

Recognition of the evolutionary path of academic justifications used in promoting the field is helpful in approaching the examination of the confluence of specific disciplines or areas of inquiry with contemporary Black/Africana Studies.

Afrocentricity and the Ontology of Black/Africana Studies

The principal thrust in this section is to explicate how the concept of Afrocentricity is affecting efforts to refine the Black/Africana Studies disciplinary matrix. That discussion first requires critical examination of the concept of Afrocentricity. Some definitions or specifications of "Afrocentricity" have created the perception that the concept reflects a closed and homogeneous ideology. However, as emphasized in the introduction to this chapter, there are critical distinctions between academic and popular conceptions. Further, there are also subtle but important differences among various academic conceptions.

Afrocentricity. Two distinct claims are generally identified with the concept of Afrocentricity. What will be termed the "strong claim" is the assertion that the liberation of peoples of African descent requires a psychological reorientation that focuses on reconstructing selected aspects of traditional African psychology, values and behaviors in the present. The "weak claim" entails the position that liberation requires that top priority be assigned to the interests of peoples of African descent in social and political intercourse with other collectives.

Most of the criticisms directed at Afrocentricity have relevance only with respect to the strong claim. Three specific criticisms will be considered for clarification. One criticism suggests that predetermined models of society and individual behavior are attached to the concept that adherents seek to impose on all peoples of African descent. A related criticism alleges that the models of society and individual behavior celebrated by Afrocentrists are drawn from epochs long past and are largely irrelevant to the modern world. A third criticism suggests that the concept encourages racial chauvinism and inter-group conflict by asserting the superiority of peoples of African descent relative to other populations.

There is no question that the most "radical" formulations of Afrocentricity are vulnerable to the criticisms cited above. However, as implied above, these radical formulations are grounded in the strong rather than the weak claim. Some formulations, for example, reject the possibility that non–Africans can generate authentically Afrocentric analyses through application of some type of biological notion of race and culture. One line of reasoning identifies the chemical melanin as the source of unique powers inherent in African peoples. Another position makes the case for racial/cultural distinctiveness among groups using evolutionary models. As an example, Nichols (1990) uses a quasi-geographical/biological evolutionary model to argue that different survival imperatives in diverse climates generated systematic and continuing variation in the world views, axiologies, epistemologies, and logics employed by different groups.

This latter approach establishes a foundation for the existence of multiple and parallel centrisms. However, some Afrocentrists who acknowledge plural centrisms generally also aggressively attempt to distinguish Afrocentricism from Eurocentrism. Advocates of this view argue that Eurocentrism is plagued by an inherent predisposition toward control and domination that produces attempts to create hierarchical rather than cooperative relationships with other peoples. It is argued that this predisposition is absent in other centrisms.

There are obviously a number of critical issues that require further discussion in respect of the nature of, and relationship among, centrisms. Space does not permit such a discussion. For present purposes, however, the most critical question is the extent to which specific groups have maintained culturally conditioned or biologically determined privileged access to certain types of knowledge or ways of knowing over time. This question is problematic because, as noted previously, the treatment of the phenomenon of "race consciousness" among African Americans in the historical scholarship focuses on the problem of "psychic duality" or "double consciousness." This concept invokes imagery of the bifurcation of the African American psyche. The general conclusion reached by historical writers is that the optimal solution to this dichotomy is achieving a balance between the two components of the psyche with the African/African American component providing the core structure. In contrast, as discussed earlier, the radical school of African American psychologists generally argues that it is necessary to eradicate totally all non–African constructs from the psyche for Africans and African Americans to attain mental health and pursue liberation effectively.

One of the implications of psychic duality is that it will (a) generally increase the degree of disjunction between expressed ideology and observed behavior, and (b) reduce self-efficacy. To illustrate, DuBois (1979) argued that "incessant self-questioning and the hesitation that arises from it ... is making the present period a time of vacillation and contradiction for the American

Negro; combined race action is stifled, race responsibility is shirked, race enterprises languish, and the best blood, the best talent, the best energy of the Negro people cannot be marshalled to do the bidding of the race."

Further clarification can result from examining a specific form of the strong claim that reflects the type of psychological dynamics implied above. For the sake of argument, let Afrocentricity refer to the degree of overlap between an idealized model of thought and behavior generated from an interpretation of traditional African thought and practice and an individual's actual thought and behavior. The process of becoming Afrocentric, then, can be disaggregated into three components: (a) increasing the causal connection between an individual's expressed ideology and observed behavior; (b) increasing the degree of overlap between an individual's expressed ideology and observed behavior and the modal thought and behavior of African Americans (or Africans depending on the selected reference group); and (c) increasing the degree of overlap between an individual's current expressed ideology and behavior and the ideology and behavioral patterns advocated by "strong claim" Afrocentrists.

The foregoing suggests that systematic intervention strategies will be required to facilitate the Afrocentric transformation of individuals. But this is a project that is more compatible with the mission of those trained in psychology than that of Black/Africana Studies grand theorists. The normal inquiry of the field's generalists is not likely to affect individual psyches directly.

Asante (1987, p. 6) suggests that Afrocentricity entails "placing African ideals at the center of any analysis that involves African culture and behavior." Karenga (1990, p. 1) suggests that Afrocentricity entails thought and practice "in the cultural image and human interests of African Americans." Within the context of these "weak claim" specifications, two general guidelines can be offered regarding the praxis of Black/Africana Studies scholar/activists. First, the field's disciplinary matrix must incorporate provisions for a collective process to determine "the cultural image and human interests of African Americans" rather than allowing special interests to dominate dialogue and impose a set of artificial strictures. Second, the intellectual leaders in the field must advocate simultaneously for the necessity of "placing African ideals at the center of analyses involving African culture and behavior" and the right of individuals and collectives to determine the course of their own intellectual production and personal development.

These suggested guidelines are designed to recognize that individual and collective psychology are both developmental and cyclical in character. They seek to minimize unproductive labeling and conflicts over ascriptive status rather than intellectual coherency. Although these definitions allow for cultural exchange, they do not specifically define the boundaries of race and culture as they relate to scholarly inquiry. To illustrate, Asante (1990, p. 40)

suggests that as a theory, Afrocentricity "is not, nor can it be, based on biological determinism. Anyone willing to submit to the discipline of learning
the concepts and methods may acquire the knowledge necessary for analysis." The specifics of the linkage between Afrocentricity and selected stand-
alone paradigms are examined in more detail below.

Afrocentricity and the Black/Africana Studies Disciplinary Matrix.
The focus of this discussion is how the concept of Afrocentricity is linked to
the disciplinary matrix of Black/Africana Studies. A comparison of the use
of the concept in different systems of thought is undertaken. The frameworks
examined are those of Asante, Karenga, and a collective of Marxist-oriented
scholars (*See* Alkalimat and Associates, 1986).

Figure 1 presents a classification scheme that clarifies the conceptions of
the field discussed to this point. The contributions of Asante and Karenga are
identified with a conception of the field as a "Disciplinary Matrix Driven
Enterprise." The Marxist collective's "Paradigm of Unity" is identified with
a view of the field as an "Adjunct to Traditional Metatheories." Figure 1 characterizes various other conceptions including syntheses of traditional disciplinary perspectives, adjuncts to traditional disciplines, and selective Afrocentric foci. These other conceptions are peripheral to efforts to generate a
fully developed disciplinary matrix.

Specific components of the systems of thought developed by Asante,
Karenga, and the Marxist collective are compared in Figure 2.

Focusing first on the function concept of Afrocentricity, per se, it is critical to note that in Karenga's system, the concept is derived from a model of
culture based on the Nguzo Saba. From this vantage point, the term "Afrocentricity" simply renames a focus that was inherent in the values expressed
by the Nguzo Saba. These values constitute a synthesis of various African
traditions rather than being culled from the examination of classical African
civilizations per se, although the usefulness of the value framework has been
reinforced by Karenga's research examining classical African civilizations [*See*,
for example, Karenga (1990)].

Figure 1
Categorization of Alternative Conceptions
of Black/Africana Studies

1. Black/Africana Studies as a Disciplinary Matrix Driven Enterprise

   Kawaida Theory (Karenga)
   Africalogy (Asante)

2. Black/Africana Studies as a Discipline constituting syntheses of Traditional Disciplines

Multidisciplinists
Non-disciplinists

3. Black/Africana Studies as an adjunct to Eurocentric Metatheories

   Marxism—Paradigm of Unity (Alkalimat and Associates)
   Feminism

4. Black/Africana Studies as a sub-component of Individual Disciplines

   History
   Literature
   Sociology

5. Black/Africana Studies as a Component of Non-Disciplinary Aggregates

   African Studies
   American Studies
   Ethnic Studies
   Multi-Cultural Studies

6. Black/Africana Studies as expressions of selective emphases

   Kemetologists
   Melanists
   Generalized Folk Approaches

Asante's contribution is a theory of inquiry for the discipline of Africalogy built upon the concept of Afrocentricity. Africalogy is defined as "the Afrocentric study of African concepts, issues, and behaviors" [Asante (1987, p. 16)]. Asante (1990, p. 141) asserts, in the spirit of Karenga (1982), that "Africalogy is a separate and distinct field of study from the composite sum of its initial founding disciplines," i.e., seven subject fields comparable to those specified by Karenga [Asante (1990, p. 12)]. In addition, the geographical locus of the field is defined as the African world, i.e. "Wherever people declare themselves as African, despite the distance from the continent or the recentness of their outmigration" a concept that "includes Africa, the Americas, the Caribbean, various regions of Asia and the Pacific" [Asante (1990, p. 15)].

Asante's concept of Afrocentricity is generated from the general concept of centrism. According to Asante (1990, p. 12) "Centrism, the groundedness of observation and behavior in one's own historical experiences, shapes the concepts, paradigms, theories, and methods of Africalogy." Africalogy is said to incorporate three paradigmatic approaches: functional, categorical, and etymological [Asante (1990, pp. 12–13)]. According to Asante (1990, p. 6) "The Afrocentrist seeks to uncover and use codes, paradigms, symbols, motifs,

Comparative Criteria	Kawaida Theory	Systematic Africology	Paradigm of Unity
Concept of Afrocentricity	"In the cultural image and human interests of African Americans"	"placing African ideals at the center of any analysis that involves African culture and behavior"	Unspecified
Treatment of Gender	In the context of male/female relationships	Unspecified	As a biological category
Theoretical Focus	Theory of Culture	Theory of Inquiry	Theory of Social Change
Theoretical Emphasis	Social Organization Cultural Authenticity	Authenticity of Knowledge and Culture	Social Dynamics Class Relations
Key Constructs	Nguzo Saba	Afrocentricity Nommo	Social Cohesion Social Disruption
Treatment of Race	Cultural (Emphasis on Consciousness)	Cultural (Emphasis on Language and Symbols)	Biological
Observational Language (Degree of Transformation)	Partial	Complete	Standard Marxist)
Subject Areas	History, Religion, Social Organization, Economic Organization, Political Organization, Creative Production, Ethos	Society, Communication, Historical, Culture, Politics, Economics, Psychology	Consciousness, Society, Economy, Biology
Periodization Scheme	Unspecified	Unspecified	Two-stage cycle
African Emphasis	Classical Civilizations	Classical Civilizations	Traditional Pre-slave trade
General Methodology for Assessing Research	Determine if a study can be incorporated into a theoretical	Locate study in an Africalogi-Grid synthesis	Locate study in a Temporal/Structural Grid
Special Data Sources	Classical Texts	Oral and Visual Data	Collections of Primary Source Materials
Central Crises Threatening Africana Peoples	Cultural Amnesia Eurocentrism	Dislocation Eurocentrism	Capitalism Racism
Resistance Strategies	Creation of a National Culture	Centering	Class Consciousness

myths, and circles of discussion that reinforce the centrality of African ideals and values as a valid frame of reference for acquiring and examining data."

Although Asante's definitional grounding appears at first glance to be holistic and comprehensive, more detailed scrutiny reveals the continuing influence of his earlier training in the field of communication. He asserts that the effort is to "bring the consciousness of rhetorical structure to the study of African communication" and "set a conceptual field for exploring the Afro-centric perspective on discourse where *nommo* as word-force is a central concept [Asante (1987, p. 17)]. This focus on language undergirds a notion of social dynamics whereby "social or political change is nothing more than the transmitting of information as an act of power" [Asante (1987, p. 35)]. It is from this value framework that Asante (1987, p. 16) defines Africalogy as "systematic exploration of relationships, social codes, cultural and commercial customs, and oral traditions and proverbs, although interpretation of communicative behaviors, as expressed in discourse, spoken or written, and techniques found in jazz studies and urban street-vernacular signifying, is also included."

One of the interesting characteristics of Asante's formulations is that it overlaps significantly with the perspective advanced by Gates (1988) discussed previously. Specifically, both scholars focus on communication and language as the foundational frame of reference. For Gates, "signifying" becomes the dominant mode of discourse because it reflects cultural powers in conflict. This notion is similar to the imagery invoked by Asante in discussing the concept of "Nommo." The point is that Asante's concepts are very much discipline-tied and area specific and that in many respects he and Gates stand on the same ground. The question is whether the field can reach higher ground by synthesizing multiple foci. As noted previously, the contributions of Karenga and the Marxist collective provide alternative foci.

Focusing again on Figure 2, it is critical to understand that the extent to which a system of thought is Afrocentric is only one of many criteria that are relevant for judging the overall usefulness of a conceptual framework. A comparative examination can facilitate refinement of the field's composite disciplinary matrix by identifying the collective strengths and weaknesses of its major systems of thought. As an example, none of the frameworks address the issue of gender adequately and the collective treatment of history is weak.

Ameliorating the collective weaknesses in the self-contained systems of thought under discussion is a strategy that can guide efforts to refine the collective disciplinary matrix in a manner that can help Black/Africana Studies scholar/activists to reach higher ground. This requires a foundation in the form of a synthesis that reflects the strengths of each system of thought, i.e., a theory of history (Marxists), a theory of society (Karenga), and a theory of inquiry (Asante). The beginnings of such a synthesis are outlined below.

Reaching for Higher Ground

Several directions for the continuing development of the Black/Africana Studies disciplinary matrix can be gleaned from the preceding discussions. In particular, seven developmental thrusts can contribute significantly to the project: (1) generation of a theory of history, (2) articulation of a theory of knowledge and social change, (3) delineation of a theory of race and culture, (4) expansion of the scope of inquiry encompassed by the disciplinary matrix, (5) expanded examination of the historical precedents to modern Black/Africana Studies, (6) increased emphasis on applications of theoretical work, and (7) strengthened linkages to interests outside academe to minimize misappropriation of knowledge and improve information dissemination. Space does not permit a detailed discussion of each point, but an effort is made below to suggest possible directions in each area.

DuBois (1953) warned that "there is ... on the part of the overwhelming majority of the people in the world, a feeling that the Anglo-Saxon type of cultural organization has failed and that new cultural patterns should be tried, and that for the trial of these new cultural patterns there is demand for cultural democracy and intercultural tolerance. That without this, civilization in its present form is doomed." In this spirit, the refinement of the Black/Africana disciplinary matrix is critical for the salvation of human civilization and for ushering in the multicultural world that DuBois envisioned. This chapter has attempted to establish the ground upon which Black/Africana Studies scholar/activists can stand to meet this challenge.

REFERENCES

Airhihenbuwa, C. "Race and Health Care in America." *The Western Journal of Black Studies* 9, 4 (1985): 204–211.

Alkalimat, A. "The Ideology of Black Social Science." In J. Ladner, ed., *The Death of White Sociology*. New York: Random House, 1973.

Alkalimat, A., and Associates. *Introduction to Afro-American Studies: A Peoples College Primer*. Chicago: Twenty First Century Books and Publications, 1986.

Alkalimat, A., ed. *Paradigms in Black Studies*. Chicago: Twenty-First Century Books and Publications, 1990.

Allen, R. "Politics of the Attack on Black Studies." *The Black Scholar* 6, 1 (September 1974): 2–7.

Asante, M. *The Afrocentric Idea*. Philadelphia: Temple University Press, 1987.

_____. *Afrocentricity: The Theory of Social Change*. Buffalo: Amulefi Publishing Co., 1990.

_____. *Kemet, Afrocentricity and Knowledge*. Trenton, N.J.: Africa World Press, 1990.

Baker, H. *Blues, Ideology and African-American Literature*. Chicago: University of Chicago Press, 1984.

Baldwin, J. "The Psychology of Oppression," in M. Asante and A. Vandi, eds., *Contemporary Black Thought*. Beverly Hills, Calif.: Sage Publications, 1980; pp. 95–100.

Bethel, E. *Promiseland; A Century of Life in a Negro Community*. Philadelphia: Temple University Press, 1981.

Blassingame, J. "Black Studies: An Intellectual Crisis." *The American Scholar* (1969): 38.

Boyi, H. "From the Sixties to the Nineties: The Problematics of Canon Formation in Afro-American Literature" (June 1991). Paper prepared for the NCBS Summer Faculty Institute, Ohio State University.

Brossard, C. "Classifying Black Studies Programs." *The Journal of Negro Education* 53 (1984): 278–295.

Bullard, R. *Dumping in Dixie: Race, Class, and Environmental Quality.* Boulder, Colo.: Westview Press, 1990.

Cheatham, H., and Stewart, J., eds. *Black Families, Interdisciplinary Perspectives.* New Brunswick, N.J.: Transaction Publishers.

Clarke, J.H., Jackson, E., Kaiser, E., and O'Dell, J.H., eds. *Black Titan: W.E.B. DuBois.* Boston: Beacon Press, 1970.

Coulburn, Rushton, and DuBois, W.E.B. "Mr. Sorokin's Systems." *Journal of Modern History* 14 (1942): 500–521.

Cross, W. The Negro-to-Black Conversion Experience." *Black World* (July 1971): 13–27.

____. "The Thomas and Cross Models on Psychological Nigrescence: A Literature Review." *Journal of Black Psychology* 4 (1978): 13.

____. *Shades of Black Diversity in African-American Identity.* Philadelphia: Temple University Press, 1991.

Diop, C.A. *African Origins of Civilization, Myth or Reality.* M. Cook, ed. & trans. Westport, Conn.: Lawrence Hill, 1974.

____. *The Cultural Unity of Black Africa.* Chicago: Third World Press 1990.

DuBois, W.E.B. "The Beginnings of Slavery." *Voice of the Negro* 2 (1905): 104–106.

____. "The Evolution of the Race Problem." *Proceedings of the National Negro Conference* (1970): 142–158.

____. "The Upbuilding of Black Durham." *World's Work* 13 (1912): 334–338.

____. [Review of *History of the Negro Church*]. *The Freeman* 6 (1922).

____. "The Social Origins of Negro Art." *Modern Quarterly* 3 (1925).

____. "Negroes and the Crisis of Capitalism." *Monthly Review* 12, 4 (1953): 478–485.

____. "Race Relations: 1917–1947." *Phylon* 9 (1948): 245–249.

____. "The Field and Function of the Negro College" (Alumni Reunion Address, Fisk University, 1933). Reprinted in H. Aptheker, 2 ed., *W.E.B. DuBois: The Education of Black People, Ten Critiques 1900–1960.* Amherst: University of Massachusetts Press, 1973.

____. "Postscript." *The Ordeal of Mansart.* Millwood, N.Y.: Kraus Thomson, 1976. Reprinted from Mainstream Publishers, 1957.

____. "The Conservation of Races." In P. Foner, ed., *W.E.B. DuBois Speaks: Speeches and Addresses 1890–1919.* New York: Pathfinder Press, 1979. (Originally published as Occasional Paper No. 2, American Academy Occasional Papers, 1897.)

Ford, N. "Black Studies Programs." *Current History* (November 1974).

Gayle, Addison, ed. *Black Aesthetic.* Garden City, N.J.: Doubleday, 1971.

Gates, H. *The Signifying Monkey: A Theory of Afro-American Literary Criticism.* New York: Oxford University Press, 1988.

Hanson, A., and Martin, R. "The Problem of Other Cultures." *Philosophy of the Social Sciences,* 3 (1973): 191–208.

Herman, J. *The Pursuit of a Dream.* New York: Oxford University Press, 1981.

Harris, R., Hine, D., and McKay, N. *Three Essays, Black Studies in the United States.* New York: Ford Foundation, 1990.

Hendrix, M., Bracey, J., Davis, J., and Herron, M. "Computers and Black Studies: Toward the Cognitive Revolution." *The Journal of Negro Education* 53 (1984): 341–350.

Henry, C., and Foster, F. "Black Women's Studies: Threat or Challenge?" *The Western Journal of Black Studies* 6, 1 (1982): 15–21.

Huggins, N. *Report to the Ford Foundation on Afro-American Studies.* New York: Ford Foundation, 1985.

Hull, G., Scott, P.B. and Smith, B. *All the Women Are White, All the Blacks Are Men, But Some of Us Are Brave: Black Women's Studies.* Old Westbury, N.Y.: Feminist Press, 1982.

Jackson, M. "Towards a Sociology of Black Studies." *Journal of Black Studies* 1, 2 (December 1970): 131–140.

Jaynes, G. and Williams, R., eds. *A Common Destiny: Blacks and American Society.* Washington, D.C.: National Academy Press, 1989.

Karenga, M. *Kawaida Theory: An Introductory Outline.* Inglewood, Calif.: Kawaida Publications, 1980.
_____. *Introduction to Black Studies.* Los Angeles: University of Sankore Press, 1982.
_____. "Black Studies and the Problematic of Paradigm." *Journal of Black Studies* 18, 4 (1988): 395–414.
_____. "The Challenge of Culture: A Kawaida Analysis." An Outline of a presentation delivered as part of the Summer Faculty Institute organized by the National Council for Black Studies, Ohio State University, Columbus, Ohio (June 1990).
_____. "Towards a Sociology of Maatian Ethics: Literature and Context." In *Reconstructing Kemetic Culture* (1989), pp. 66–96.
Kuhn, T. *The Structure of Scientific Revolutions,* 2nd ed. Chicago: University of Chicago Press, 1970.
Lehrer, K. "Social Consensus and Rational Agniology." *Synthese* (1975): 23.
Linnemann, R., ed. *Alain Locke, Reflections on a Modern Renaissance Man.* Baton Rouge: Louisiana State University Press, 1982.
Marable, M. "The Modern Miseducation of the Negro: Critiques of Black History Curricula." In *Institute of the Black World, Black Studies Curriculum Development Course Evaluations.* Conference I. Atlanta: Institute of the Black World, 1981; pp. C1-C28.
Marx, K. Reprinted in A. Schmidt, *The Concept of Nature in Marx.* London: NLB, 1971. (Originally printed in *Marx-Engels Gesamtsausgabe, V, Part I.* Berlin: 1932.)
McClendon, W. "Black Studies: Education for Liberation." *The Black Scholar,* (September 1974).
Nobles, W. "African Philosophy: Foundations for Black Psychology." In R. Jones, ed., *Black Psychology.* New York: Harper & Row, 1980; pp. 23–36.
Painter, N. *Exodusters: Black Migration to Kansas After Reconstruction.* New York: Knopf, 1977.
Russell, J. "Afro-American Studies: From Chaos to Consolidation." *The Negro Education Review* (1975): 25.
Sorokin, P. *Social and Cultural Dynamics,* volumes 1-4. New York: Bedminster Press, 1937–41.
Stewart, J. "Black Studies and Black People in the Future." *Black Books Bulletin* 4 (1976): 21–25.
_____. "Introducing Black Studies: A Critical Examination of Some Textual Materials." *UMOJA* 3 (1979): 5–18.
_____. "Alternative Models of Black Studies." *UMOJA* 8 (1982): 17–39.
_____. *Toward Operationalization of an Expansive Model of.* An analysis prepared for the Black Studies Curriculum Development Project, Institute of the Black World, Atlanta, Georgia, 1982.
_____. "Factors Affecting Variation in Published Black Studies Articles Across Institutions." *The New England Journal of Black Studies* 4 (1983): 72–83.
_____. "Psychic Duality of Afro-Americans in the Novels of W.E.B. DuBois." *Phylon* 44 (June 2, 1983): 93–108.
_____. [Review of *An Introduction to Black Studies*]. *The Western Journal of Black Studies* 7 (1983): 113–117.
_____. "The Legacy of W.E.B. DuBois for Contemporary Black Studies." *The Journal of Negro Education* 53 (1984): 296–311.
_____. "Kondratieff Cycles and the Political-Economic Status of Blacks in the United States" (1985 mimeo).
_____. "Toward a Black Studies—S-STS Interface." An analysis prepared for the project "Improving the quality of secondary science and technology instruction for urban and minority students through science/technology/society," STS Urban Education Project, U.S. Department of Education, 1987–88. Leonard Waks, Principal Investigator.
Toulmin, S. *Human Understanding,* vol. 1. Princeton, N.J.: Princeton University Press, 1972.
Turner, J. "Africana Studies and Epistemology, A Discourse in the Sociology of Knowledge." In J. Turner, ed., *The Next Decade: Theoretical and Research Issues in Africana Studies.* Ithaca, N.Y.: Africana Studies and Research Center, 1984; pp. 23–36.
_____, and McGann, C.S. "Black Studies as an Integral Tradition in African-American Intellectual History." *Issue* (1976): 73–78.
Upton, J. "Applied Black Studies: Adult Education in the Black Community—A Case Study." *The Journal of Negro Education* 53 (1984): 322–333.

Wallace, Michele "Who Owns Zora Neale Hurston? Critics Carve Up the Legend." *Invisibility Blues*. London: Vengo, 1990.

Willie, C., Garibaldi, A., and Reed, W. *The Education of African-Americans*. New York: Auburn House, 1991.

Woodson, C. *The History of the Negro Church*. Washington, D.C.: Associated Publishers, 1922.

Wright, R., ed. *African Philosophy; An Introduction*, 3rd ed. Lanham, Md.: University Press of America, 1984.

Young, C., and Martin, G. "The Paradox of Separate and Unequal: African Studies and Afro-American Studies." *The Journal of Negro Education* 53 (1984): 257–267.

10. African American Studies: Locating a Niche in the Public Sphere of Higher Education

James L. Conyers, Ph.D.
Associate Professor of Black Studies
Chair, Department of Black Studies
The University of Nebraska at Omaha

Introduction

The intellectual tradition of African American Studies has its roots in the mid–1800s. Scholars such as W.E.B. DuBois, Carter G. Woodson, Charles Harris Wesley and others made significant contributions to the study of African diasporic phenomena within the academy of higher learning. Their valor and quest to examine black life and history demonstrated their scholarly commitment to the upliftment of the race. Of course, all of these scholars were trained in traditional disciplines, yet they consistently struggled with the analysis of locating African American history and culture on the margins of Western civilization.

From their efforts and the body of scholarship they produced, thus, came the intellectual idea of autonomizing the study of African diasporic phenomena within the academy of higher education. Although in the 1960s, there was a social, political, and economic movement toward the organizational structure of African American Studies.

During the sixties, America was in an uproar over the rebellion and radical stance taken by African Americans, Latin Americans, Asian Americans, and Euro-Americans for justice and civil rights. College students played an integral part of this movement and protested across the United States by using tactics such as sit-ins, freedom rides, and protest marches. Maulana Karenga identifies the student movement in four initial thrusts:

1. Break down the barriers of legal segregation in public accommodations.
2. Achieve equality and justice for Blacks.
3. Organizing Blacks into self-conscious social force capable of defining, defending, and advancing their interests.
4. Demanding and achieving Black Studies.[1]

James Banks adds, "A major goal of the ethnic revival movements of the 1960s and 1970s was not only to include more information about the culture and history of ethnic groups in the social studies curriculum but also to infuse the curriculum with new perspectives, frames of reference, and values."[2]

The movement for establishment of Black Studies existed in institutions of higher education across the United States. Many of the institutions that engaged in the early struggle for a Black Studies curriculum were institutions such as Howard University, Ohio State University, Cornell University, the University of Pennsylvania, San Francisco State College, Yale University, UCLA, the University of Wisconsin/Madison, Harvard University and Wesleyan College. It was during this era that African American students began to critically question administrative officials and faculty about the type of education they were receiving. Interestingly, Huggins mentions that "black students and scholars thus began to challenge the 'objectivity' of mainstream social science. In most scientific discussions of problems, a norm was assumed, that of the white middle class; the social scientist, himself, was at the center defining all variation as deviation and blaming the victim, as critics liked to say."[3] Consequently, African American students recognized they were receiving a Eurocentric hegemonic education. As a result, they took a pro–African position. Taking a pro–African position meant they wanted to see African culture—then on the periphery—studied within the contours of humanity. However, due to the insensitivity of institutional administrators, their mission was to consistently endorse a Eurocentric curriculum.

Huggins correlates the movements for African American Studies and civil rights when he said: "To understand Afro-American Studies, a product of that period and of the interaction of those spheres, it is thus necessary to consider both American higher education and the American civil rights Movement."[4]

Rationale and Context

The status of Black Studies in contemporary times is at an ideological and intellectual crossroads. Propaganda, discourse and debate about this academic enterprise has revolved around issues such as:

1. The re-naming of Black Studies as a discipline (i.e., African American Studies, Africology, Africana Studies, Afro-American Studies, etc.);

Figure 3
Conceptual Framework of Black Studies

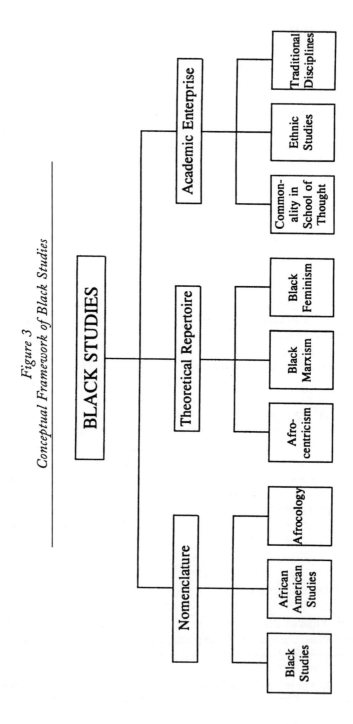

2. Theoretical repertoire and commonality in the school of thought among Africana Studies scholars;
3. Curriculum structure and development;
4. Organization structure of units, promoting the idea of Africana Studies as a holistic discipline.

James Stewart adds,

> The debate has intensified recently, in part due to the visibility afforded to writings by literary critics and historians who, although they identify primarily with traditional disciplines, assert connections to Black Studies [Baker (1984); Gates (1988); Harris, Hine, and McKay (1990); Huggins (1985)]. This turf battle has re-energized discussions about the nature of Black Studies, i.e., is it a self-contained and distinct body of knowledge or simply an adjunct to traditional disciplines?[5]

Figure 3 provides the conceptual schematic framework of this essay. It attempts to describe and evaluate issues and schemea that focus on nomenclature, ideology, and the basic constitutes of an academic disciplinary enterprise.

Ironically, Houston Baker points out that by the 1970s, Black Studies was encountering conflict within the academy. Perhaps the reason for this conflict can be attributed to Black Studies scholars' attempt to provide an alternative epistemology of examining African phenomena.[6] Stewart points out that this movement toward curriculum standardization, while intuitively attractive, assumes that sufficient consensus exists about the definition and structure of Black Studies to allow such an effort to be successful.[7]

The significance and relevance of this essay is two-fold: (1) to examine African American Studies from a disciplinary lens; and (2) to examine the theoretical, methodological, contextual, and interpretative analysis of Black Studies scholars. Throughout this review, I will use the terms "African American Studies," "Black Studies," and "Afrocology" interchangeably, referring to the study of African phenomena from an Afrocentric perspective.

Transformation of Language

Culture, language, and motifs are essential to the ontology of an academic discipline. Historically, the transformative process of nomenclature in African American Studies illustrates the political and social mandates in African American history and culture throughout the diaspora. As such, Africana Studies has been referred to as Negro History, Black American Studies, Black Studies, Pan-African Studies, Afro-American Studies, African American Studies, Africana Studies, Africanology, and Afrocology. Abdul Alkalimat proposes that the rationale for diversity in names can be ascribed to the historical and social context of the Black Experience in America.[8] Robert Harris adds critical analysis on the transition of name changes of African Americans, citing:

The group appellations employed by black people in this country reflect their status and perspective at different times, as revealed to some extent in this pamphlet. Sterling Stuckey, in *Slave Culture: Nationalist Theory and the Foundations of Black America* (page 244), has astutely observed that, "The names controversy reveals important attitudes toward Africa, contending strategies of black liberation in America, and the place of black people and institutions in American life. From African to Colored, to Afro-American to Negro, to Black to Afro-American, and now African American, the black population has grappled with its identity, culture, heritage, and history, both in Africa and the United States."[9]

These name changes are reflective of the social collective consciousness of African Americans, describing space and time of the black experience. These lexicons described the authentic representations of African diasporic history and culture. Thus, the state of formation in African American Studies begins with continental African history and culture.

The key component of an academic discipline is the axiological parameters to infuse theory to praxis. Paradigms are essential to disciplinary development whereas the construct prisms are a set of rules, boundaries, language, and ethos to quantify or qualify a scientific approach to examining phenomena. Unfortunately, traditional disciplines have fallen short in their aim and objective to examine African phenomena because of the employ of a Eurocentric hegemonic perspective. Africology presents a corrective and alternative to the orientation of traditional disciplines; this discipline intellectually transforms an epistemology of "sciences" from a geocentric position to a holistic convergence. Consequently, such challenges are labeled as dysfunctionalism or demagogy studies by transgressors who employ a Eurocentric hegemonic perspective.

In contemporary times, the name Afrocology has been registered by scholars in Black Studies for two reasons: (1) theory development; and (2) ideological location concerning commonality in the state of mind. Nomenclature and theory development acknowledge a cohort of scholars who appear committed to the transformation and transcendence of the intellectual history of Africana Studies. Paradoxically, this scholar/activism advances American higher education in two ways: (1) recentering an epistemological base concerning the notion of science; and (2) presenting a pluralist perspective that is nonhegemonic to examine human phenomena.

Ideological Repertoire and School of Thought

Ideological repertoire and commonality in school of thought is one of the critical issues of discourse concerning the status of Africana Studies in contemporary times. Cultural Nationalism, Pan Africanism, and Afrocentricism are some of the prevailing ideologies in Black Studies. On the other hand, post-modernism, deconstruction, essentialism, and Black Marxism are some ideologies that are sustained in traditional disciplines, yet seeking to infuse themselves into Black Studies. In *Newsweek* of September 23, 1991, there were seven pages devoted to various topics on African American Studies and Afrocentricism. Molefi K. Asante explained Afrocentricity as, "both theory and practice of interpretation and analysis from the perspective of African people as subjects rather than objects."[10] Karenga amply addresses the intellectual concept of Afrocentricity:

> Afrocentric theory is based on the assumption that if an African-centered approach is incorrect or of little value, then so is the discipline of Black Studies which is based on an equally important assumption that the African experience is both a valid and valuable subject of study.[11]

Moreover, the relevance of Afrocentricism is that it presents a cosmology, holistic perspective and representation of African phenomena as having culture and a classical civilization.

Scholars outside the disciplinary have labeled African American Studies as an adjunct discipline and Afrocentricity as a form of "dogmatism." Stewart's analysis is prolific and straightforward:

> "Popular Afrocentrism" is being confused increasingly with systematic intellectual approaches in the field. This confusion has contributed to a distorted view of the state of the field and is fueling uneasiness in some circles about the intellectual credibility of Black/Africana Studies.[12]

I contend that, methodically, research is conducted in two ways, quantitatively and qualitatively. Hard data and primary sources illustrate rigor, intellectualism, and craftsmanship of original research. Thus, the Afrocentric perspective seeks to provide hard data that examines the African diasporic experience. From this particular worldview, Black Studies scholars focus on authentic representations of African diasporic history, ethos, and motifs. My query is, how does this equate to "dogmatism" or "demagogy"? Simply put, double standards and labeling are defenseless in the arena of intellectual discourse.

Labeling theory has been applied to denote the scholarship and intellectualism of Afrocentric scholars. Of course, a majority of this critique has been coming from individuals who are outside the discipline of Black Studies. Black Studies' interdisciplinary core curriculum speaks to the failure of traditional education. Melville Herskovits acknowledged that one of the outstanding characteristics of Afro-American Studies is the interdisciplinary and inter-continental treatment of Africans throughout the diaspora.[13] These allegations dismiss theory development, culture, language, ideological repertoire, and the concept of formation of African diasporic history and culture.

In an aesthetic sense, Afrocentric scholarship is a breath of fresh air to corridors of the academy.

Two general allegations about African American Studies are (1) there is no common state of mind that organizes or identifies scholars in the field; and (2) the study of African phenomena could be studied more objectively in the traditional discipline. Stewart concludes that "the critical issue which divides the Marxist and Nationalist camps of Black Studies analysts is the perpetual disagreement about the relationship between race and class. The resolution of this conflict requires serious attention to important works in the areas of Black Psychology and the nature of racism."[14] Located within the contours of traditional discipline, African American Studies is dislocated, whereas African phenomena are studied from the margins. The intellectual tradition of African American studies demonstrates a philosophy of social activism, with emphasis on theory and praxis.

Nick Nelson cites Tanenhaus and Somit by writing,

> A learned discipline is characterized by a common state of mind. This means that in order for a discipline to exist, the members of the discipline must think of themselves as belonging to a distinct and functioning profession.[15]

In Figure 2 (p. 124), James B. Stewart outlines some of the comparative criteria of ideologies in Black Studies. Thus from these data, he provides a synthesis to locate the deep structural analysis of Black Studies paradigms. Of course, there are several ideological hues among Afrocentric scholars, but the common state of mind is African-centered. The tools of analysis in describing, evaluating, and presenting interpretative analysis are grounded in the historical experiences, ethos, and motif of African people. These are the ontological grounds that shape and format this academic enterprise.

Curriculum Emphasis/Text Selection

Language, common state of mind, and organizational structure are key components of Black Studies. Advancement in these variables shape and format the structure of scholarship and curriculum in the discipline.

Curriculum establishes the operative axiology in theory, methods, research designs, and pedagogy. The National Council of Black Studies produced two monographs describing and evaluating Afrocology. Their analysis locates Afrocology on the cutting edge, renovating subject areas such as Urban Studies, Black History, Multicultural Studies, Women Studies, and Minority Studies. NCBS data findings provide an Afrocentric worldview to establishing an alternative epistemology within in the academy of higher education. Alkalimat contends that the two objectives of Afro-American Studies are (1) to rewrite American history and reconceptualize the essential features of

American society; and (2) to establish the intellectual and academic space for Black people to tell their own story.[16]

Talmadge Anderson addresses the rationale and purpose of the enterprise, stating:

> African American studies warrants particular academic interest because it is a branch of knowledge that was deliberately slighted or expunged from the American scheme of education. Critical issues pertaining to its development and social problems between black and white Americans will continue as long as the field of study is treated outside the main sphere of the educational process. In fact, the ignoble and deplorable history and contemporary state of race relations in the United States might be attributed to the failure of the educational system to reveal and to treat with integrity the African experience in America.[17]

Thus, an intellectual movement as such requires a transformation of the traditional scientific canon. Introductory curriculum in African American Studies encompasses an array of texts such as:

Alkalimat, Abdul. *Introduction to Afro-American Studies: A Peoples College Primer*. Chicago: Twenty-First Century Books, 1986.

Anderson, Talmadge. *Introduction to African American Studies*. Dubuque, Iowa: Kendall Hunt, 1993.

Asante, Molefi Kete. *Kemet, Afrocentricity and Knowledge*. Trenton, N.J.: Africa World Press, 1990.

Conyers, James L., Jr. *The Evolution of African American Studies*. Lanham, Md.: University Press of America, 1995.

Franklin, John Hope. *From Slavery to Freedom*. New York: Random House, 1994.

Harding, Vincent. *There Is a River*. New York: Vintage Books, 1983.

Karenga, Maulana. *Introduction to Black Studies*. Los Angeles: University of Sankore Press, 1994.

These are but a few of the growing number of texts that are attempting to examine the human experience from a black prism; they serve a vital function as research tools to the intellectual transcendence of the discipline. Banks provides critical analysis by stating, "Other reasons often given for the lack of progress since the 1960s in substantially reforming the curriculum to reflect ethnic and cultural diversity include the lack of effective teaching materials, ambivalent teacher attitudes toward ethnic diversity, and lack of administrative support."[18]

Niche/Qualification in the Academy

Russell Adams discusses Afro-American Studies emergence in the academy by writing:

> Afro-American Studies bears the mark of its early stages. Unlike the estab-
> lished disciplines, this area of interest has not had time to evolve through all
> of the stages characteristic of traditional and relatively settled disciplines. As
> with the appearance of significant numbers of minority students in institu-
> tions of higher learning in modern times, the presence of Afro-American
> Studies and its accompanying professionals represent enlargement of diver-
> sity and of conceptions of the academically useful. The contents of Afro-
> American Studies as a movement and intellectual concern constitute an
> interdisciplinary enlargement of interest and perception which implicitly and
> often explicitly go to the roots of values, social structure, and societal dynam-
> ics.[19]

The issue of whether a discipline qualifies to exist deserves a scholarly and
common-sense approach. Yosef ben-Jochannan once raised the query, "Did
the first man to award a degree, have one?" This query has always left me in
awe, in awe of re-defining the ontology of the humanities and social sciences.
Western intellectualism has proved to be hegemonic for the most part; such
a rigid and linear world-view deserves critique and reconstruction.

Thus, this chapter reflects my narrative, theoretical philosophy, and opti-
mism concerning the state of African American Studies for the next decade.
Routine competence and pedestrian modes of pedagogy will eventually lead
to academic dysfunctionalism. American historiography illustrates a pattern
of traditional disciplines subordinating the study of black history and culture. On the other hand, Darlene Clark Hine provides an optimistic view concerning the status and function of the discipline by saying:

> Black studies has opened up vast and exciting new areas of scholarship, espe-
> cially in American history and literature, and has spurred intellectual inquiry
> into diverse social problems affecting the lives of significant portions of the
> total population.[20]

Earl Thorpe wrote about this paradoxical dilemma, concerning the enterprise
of Black history.

> Black history is American history with the accent and emphasis on the point
> of view, attitude, and spirit of Afro-Americans, as well as on the events in
> which they have been either the actors or the objects of action. Because black
> people have been forcibly kept in a subordinate status, their portion of Amer-
> ica's wealth and power has been smaller than their numbers would command.
> This necessarily means that their point of view, attitude, and spirit are
> different from those of white Americans.... Black history is that American
> history which, until the 1960s, was viewed by white America with contempt
> and disdain or ignored altogether, just as black people themselves were viewed
> and treated. Men tend either to deny or force out of consciousness the evil
> that they do. Much of black history, then, is the story of the cruelties and in-
> humanities which a powerful white majority has inflicted on a defenseless
> black minority.[21]

The Eurocentric hegemonic perspective in education has proved to be "inept"; these problems illustrate the abortion of an alternative epistemology to examine African phenomena from an interdisciplinary perspective.

NOTES

1. Maulana Karenga, *Introduction to Black Studies*, Los Angeles: Kawaida Publications, 1983, p. 18.
2. James A. Banks, *Search for New Perspectives*, p. 133.
3. Nathan Huggins, *A Report to the Ford Foundation on Afro-American Studies*, New York: Ford Foundation, 1985, p. 15.
4. Nathan Huggins, *A Report to the Ford Foundation on Afro-American Studies*, New York: Ford Foundation, 1985, p. 5.
5. James B. Stewart, "Reaching for Higher Ground: Toward an Understanding of Black/Africana Studies," *The Afrocentric Scholar* 1, 1 (May 1992): 1.
6. Houston Baker, *Black Studies, Rap, and the Academy*, Chicago: University of Chicago Press, 1993, p. 17.
7. James B. Stewart, "Introducing Black Studies: A Critical Examination of Some Textual Materials," *UMOJA* ns. 3, 1 (spring 1979): 5.
8. Abdul Alkalimat, *Introduction to Afro-American Studies: A Peoples College Primer*, Chicago: Twenty-First Century Books and Publications, 1986, pp. 3-4.
9. Robert L. Harris, *Teaching African American History*, Washington, D.C.: American Historical Association, 1992, p. x.
10. Molefi Kete Asante, "Putting Africa at the Center," *Newsweek*, September 23, 1991, p. 46.
11. Maulana Karenga, *Introduction to Black Studies*, Los Angeles: University of Sankore Press, 1994, p. 37.
12. James B. Stewart, "Reaching for Higher Ground: Toward An Understanding of Black/Africana Studies," *The Afrocentric Scholar* 1, 1 (May 1992): 2.
13. Melville J. Herskovits, "Problem, Method, and Theory in Afroamerican Studies," *Phylon*, vol. 7, 1946, p. 337.
14. James B. Stewart, "Introducing Black Studies: A Critical Examination of Some Textual Materials," *UMOJA* ns. 3, 1 (spring 1979): 5.
15. Nick Nelson, *Africology from Social Movement to Academic Discipline*, Columbus, Ohio: Center for Research and Public Policy of the Ohio State University Black Studies Community Extension Center, Black Studies Research Series, 1990, p. 8.
16. Abdul Alkalimat, *Introduction to Afro-American Studies*, pp. 4-5.
17. Talmadge Anderson, *Introduction to African American Studies*, Dubuque, Iowa: Kendall/Hunt Publishing Company, 1993, p. 6.
18. James A. Banks, "Social Studies, Ethnic Diversity, and Social Change," in Charles V. Willie, Antoine M. Garibaldi, and Wornie L. Reed, eds., *The Education of African Americans*, Westport, Conn.: Auburn House, 1991, p. 137.
19. Russell L. Adams, "Evaluating Professionalism in the Context of Afro-American Studies," *Western Journal of Black Studies* 4, 2 (1980): 140–141.
20. Darlene Clark Hine, "Black Studies: An Overview," in Hine, Robert L. Harris and Nellie McKay, *Black Studies in the United States*, New York: Ford Foundation, 1990, p. 18.
21. Earl E. Thorpe, *Black Historians: A Critique*, New York: William Morrow, 1971, pp. 3-4.

Part Three:
Africana Womanism

11. Womanist Issues in Black Studies: Towards Integrating Africana Womanism Into Africana Studies[*]

Delores P. Aldridge, Ph.D.
Grace Towns Hamilton Professor
of Sociology and African American Studies,
Emory University

Two of the most significant reforms in American higher education over the past two decades have emerged from the Africana (Black Studies) and Women's Studies movements.[1] Black or Africana Studies began as a field of study in the 1960s in the wake of the civil rights movement and in the midst of pervasive campus unrest. From the outset it had both an academic and social mission. Though contemporary Black Studies as an interdisciplinary enterprise is a product of the sixties, it draws much of its academic content from earlier times.

Students of the sixties were confronted with an absence or distortion of the Black Experience in the higher education curriculum and a sense of cultural alienation generated by the predominantly white colleges and universities they entered. First they demanded black recognition in any form, such as black faculty and staff, black programs, more black students, necessary financial aid, and black history courses. But, it quickly became clear that black history was simply a beginning and that a broader demand would and did emerge for a comprehensive interdisciplinary curriculum with history at its center.

Women's Studies sought to introduce the study of women as a means of providing her story and to eradicate many of the myths and distortions surrounding the lives of women. The Women's Liberation movement following

[*]*A revised version of the earlier work which appeared in* The Afrocentric Scholar *vol. 1, no. 1 (May 1992).*

on the heels of the civil rights movement served as a catalyst for conscious-raising on women's issues. And, though much controversy has surrounded the movement with the opposition from both men and women, whites and non-whites, its effects have pervaded the society at all levels, including the university, where women faculty and staff have led attempts to bring equity to gender issues. For the most part, white women benefiting from and modeling after the efforts of the civil rights and Black Studies movements have fostered an explosion of new approaches and content in the academy. Their increasing numbers and continuity have played heavily into their institutionalization in American higher education. Whereas Africana students, who are transient but in larger numbers than Africana faculty, have been a mainstay in pecking away at institutional barriers to the incorporation and perpetuation of Africana Studies, Women's Studies has enjoyed the growing critical mass of women faculty and staff with real access to structural change.

While both movements addressed some very real inadequacies such as paucity of faculty, absence and distortion of curriculum content and programmatic resources in the academy, neither has been particularly sensitive to the unique experiences of women of African descent in America, on the continent or through the diaspora.

Some Africana women intellectuals have viewed the struggles of women of African descent in America as part of a wider struggle for human dignity and empowerment. As early as 1893, Anna Julia Cooper, in a speech to women, provided this perspective:

> We take our stand on the solidarity of humanity, the oneness of life, and the unnaturalness and injustice of all special favoritisms, whether of sex, race, country, or condition.... The colored woman feels that woman's cause is one and universal; and that ... not till race, color, sex, and condition are seen as accidents, and not the substance of life; not till the universal title of humanity to life, liberty, and the pursuit of happiness is conceded to be inalienable to all; not till then is woman's lesson taught and woman's cause won—not the white woman's nor the black woman's, not the red woman's but the cause of every man and of every woman who has writhed silently under a mighty wrong.[2]

This humanist vision led Alice Walker to identify with the term womanist, of which she says "womanist is to feminist as purple is to lavender," addressing the notion of the solidarity of humanity. She defines "womanist" in *In Search of Our Mother's Gardens: Womanist Prose*. For Walker, a "womanist" is one who is "committed to the survival and wholeness of an entire people." Clinora Hudson-Weems (1993) enlarges upon this notion grounding us in Africana Womanism. The term "Africana" refers not only to continental Africans but also to people of African descent worldwide. In *Africana Womanism: Reclaiming Ourselves*, Hudson-Weems explores the dynamics of the conflict between the mainstream feminist, the black feminist, and the Africana womanist. In the book, she names and defines traits that characterize an Africana woman. According to Hudson-Weems, Africana Womanism is neither an outgrowth nor an addendum to mainstream feminism but rather a concept grounded in the culture and focuses on the experiences, needs and desires of Africana women. Africana womanists and feminists have separate agendas. Feminism is female centered; Africana Womanism is family centered. Feminism is concerned primarily with riding society of sexism; Africana Womanism is concerned with ridding society of racism first, then classism and sexism. Many feminists say their number one enemy is the male; Africana womanists welcome and encourage male participation in their struggle. Feminism, Hudson-Weems says, is incompatible with Africana women, as it was designed to meet the needs of white women. In fact, the history of feminism reveals a blatant, racist background. For example, in reaction to the ratification of the 15th Amendment to the Constitution in 1870, which granted Africana men voting rights, suffragist leader Carrie Chapman Catt asserted that middle-class white men recognize "the usefulness of woman suffrage as a counterbalance to the foreign vote, and as a means of legally preserving white supremacy in the South." And, so it is from the perspective of Africana Womanism that this discourse is developed.

The civil rights movement, which stressed liberation in the late sixties, marked the first time Africana people engaged in a struggle to resist racism, whereby distinct boundaries were established which separated the role of women and men. Africana male activists publicly acknowledged expectations that women involved in the movement conform to a subservient role pattern. This sexist expectation was expressed as women were admonished to manage household needs and breed warriors for the revolution. Toni Cade (1970) elaborated on the issue of roles which prevailed in black organizations during the sixties:

> It would seem that every organization you can name has had to struggle at one time or another with seemingly mutinous cadres of women getting salty about having to man the telephones or fix the coffee while the men wrote the position papers and decided on policy. Some groups condescendingly allotted two or three slots in the executive order to women. Others encouraged the sisters to form a separate caucus and work out something that wouldn't split the organization. Others got nasty and forced the women to storm out to organize separate workshops. Over the years, things have sort of been cooled out. But I have yet to hear a coolheaded analysis of just what any particular group's stand is on the question. Invariably, I hear from some dude that Black women must be supportive and patient so that Black men can regain their manhood. The notion of womanhood, they argue—and only if pressed to address themselves to the notion do they think of it or argue—is dependent on his defining his manhood. So the shit goes on.[3]

Though many black women activists did not succumb to the attempts of black men to reduce them to a secondary role in the movement, many did. Bell Hooks writes:

> Black women questioning and/or rejecting a patriarchal black movement found little solace in the contemporary women's movement. For while it drew attention to the victimization of black women by racist and sexist oppression, white feminists tended to romanticize the black female experience rather than discuss the negative impact of oppression. When feminists acknowledge in one breath that black women are victimized and in the same breath emphasize their strength, they imply that though black women are oppressed they manage to circumvent that damaging impact of oppression by being strong—and that is simply not the case. Usually, when people talk about the "strength" of black women they are referring to the way in which they perceive black women coping with oppression, that endurance is not to be confused with transformation.[4]

Thus, to be an activist in the liberation of black people or women did not necessarily mean there was sensitivity for Africana women.

In *All the Women Are White, All the Blacks Are Men, But Some of Us Are Brave,* three Africana women scholars wrote:

> Women's Studies ... focused almost exclusively upon the lives of white women. Black Studies, which was much too often male-dominated, also ignored Black women.... Because of white women's racism and Black men's sexism, there was no room in either area for a serious consideration of the lives of Black women. And even when they have considered black women, white women usually have not had the capacity to analyze racial politics and Black culture, and Black men have remained blind or resistant to the implications of sexual politics in Black women's lives.[5]

The above characterization has seemingly been acknowledged, for within the last several years there has been increasing advocacy for recognition and correction of this failure to deal equitably with Africana women in scholarship and the academy. Throughout the country, Africana men and women speak to the existence of racism in Women's Studies and sexism in Africana Studies in courses on campuses, in associations, and in scholarly publications. It would seem to follow, then, that there are a number of critical areas for attention: Africana women and scholarship, Africana women and the academy, and Africana women and professional organizations.

Scholarship, Africana Studies and Africana Women

The increased number of Africana women scholars in the academy has yielded an increase in scholarly research about them. Prior to their significant presence, Africana men and others had largely written from their own interests and perspectives—excluding, minimizing or distorting the reality of Africana women. This, then, has been a major factor in the absence of Africana women in Africana Studies curriculum—the lack of a critical mass of Africana women scholars equipped to write about Africana women. Even with a growing number of Africana women scholars, it has been difficult for them to publish. Though it has not been easy to publish the works of Africana women scholars in general, Africana women have seen the doors closed more often on their publishing interests. But in spite of obstacles pertaining to the relevance and seriousness of Africana women's issues, there has been considerable scholarship over the last two or three decades. The seventies and eighties—which witnessed the rise and institutionalization of both Africana and Women's Studies—have surfaced much previous work and added to the continued productivity. There were various pioneering works in the seventies and eighties which included Toni Cade's *The Black Woman* (1970), the first anthology of its kind on Africana women in America with the focus on the voices of Africana women themselves who analyzed contemporary issues.

    In 1972 Gerda Lerner provided *Black Women in White America: A Documentary History* demonstrating the importance of examining the experiences of women of African descent as distinct from those of non–Africana women and Africana men. Following on the heels of these two works was the first anthology by two Africana historians, Rosalyn Terborg-Penn and Sharon Harley. Their work, *The Afro-American Woman: Struggles and Images* (1978), is a collection of original essays from a historical perspective. A single-authored historical volume by Deborah Gray White, entitled *Ar'n't I a Woman?* (1985), provided some new insights into the lives of slave women. And, at the beginning of the decade of the eighties, two social science anthologies were developed by LaFrances Rodges-Rose and Filomina Chioma Steady entitled respectively, *The Black Woman* and *The Black Woman Crossculturally*. The former work was and remains the first edited, definitive volume of original research by African American women social scientists on African American women. The latter volume was an outstanding accomplishment in arraying a wide range of work focusing on women of color throughout the world.

    A single-authored volume of significance in the 1980s was by Lena Wright Myers, entitled *Black Women: Do They Cope Better?* This sociological work provided a new framework for understanding how women of African descent in America viewed themselves positively in spite of a racist, sexist, classist society. Another sociological work which has not received the exposure it deserves, *Black Women, Feminism, and Black Liberation: Which Way?* was published by Vivian Gordon (1985). This work places in perspective the critical issues facing Africana women and Africana Studies if the field of Africana Studies is to fully realize its potential. A trailblazing work of the nineties was authored by the writer. It attempted for the first time to theoretically conceptualize black male-female relationships in America. Aldridge (1991) in

Focusing: Black Male-Female Relationships provided a foundation for understanding relationships with strategies for developing healthy ones. Earlier in 1989, she had laid the groundwork with *Black Male-Female Relationships: A Resource Book of Selected Materials* which was an edited volume comprising the most comprehensive collection of scholarly work available written by social scientists. Another work of significance for the nineties was authored by sociologist Patricia Collins, *Black Feminist Thought: Knowledge, Consciousness, and the Politics of Empowerment.* It encompasses most of the relevant work on Africana women and will probably serve as a point of departure for research for many on the subject in the future, notwithstanding the even more revolutionary work on Africana Womanism by Clinora Hudson-Weems. Hudson's work has no parallel as a new way of understanding Africana women.

Dozens of books and articles in the literary humanist tradition were authored over the last two decades. And, perhaps the most visible work to emerge in the nineties is the huge encyclopedia volumes on black women edited by Darlene Clark Hine. Other earlier works included: Mary Helen Washington's *Black-Eyed Susans: Classic Stories by and about Black Women* (1975) and *Sturdy Black Bridges: Visions of Black Women in Literature* edited by Roseann Bell, Betty Parker, and Beverly Guy-Sheftall (1979). In the decade of the eighties, a number of valuable works were set forth on feminist literary criticism for Africana women. Among these notable works were Barbara Christian's *Black Women Novelists: The Development of a Tradition 1892–1976* (1981) and Gloria Wade-Gayle's *No Crystal Stair, Visions of Race and Sex in Women's Fiction* (1984). A controversial, but valuable, piece for illuminating the complexity of Africana womanhood is the interdisciplinary work of Bell Hooks' *Ain't I a Woman: Black Women and Feminism* (1981).

This growing scholarship is necessary to move toward integrating Africana women into Africana Studies in the academy. If there continues to be this flowering of scholarly products, the future in encouraging for the institutionalization of Africana women throughout curriculum, programming and academic appointments at all levels.

The Academy, Africana Studies and Africana Women

Presently, entrenchment in the academy in terms of formal courses has been far less observable than the scholarship developed over the last two decades. Significantly, the *Core Curriculum Guide* developed by the National Council for Black Studies (1981) did not address the issue of inclusion of women as a distinct focus for study. And, Colon's particularly crucial work, "Critical Issues in Black Studies: A Selective Analysis," (1984) failed to devote attention to the lack of inclusion of women in curriculum in any significant way as an area of concern. These omissions were addressed a decade later in the revised *Core Curriculum Guide of the Council for Black Studies* and the subsequent works by visible male Africana Studies scholars as well as female Africana Studies scholars.

A cursory examination of curricula in Africana Studies or Women's Studies units reflects very few, if any, courses that treat Africana women in their own right. And, when they do, most often the courses are in literature and occasionally tied to a family course. There are some exceptions, usually where courses are jointly listed in Africana and Women's Studies with titles such as "The Black Woman in America" or "The Black Woman in History." Notably where proactive Africana Women's scholars are located, there are generally one or two courses in the course listings.

The above tenuous assessment is based on an examination of a limited sample of schools with both Africana and Women's Studies academic units. It should also be noted that institutions that have white women scholars who are sensitive to Africana women's issues and are politically astute enough to recognize the fertile terrain for research are more likely to have courses that give attention to issues of importance for Africana women. But, it is necessary to bear in mind the struggle which exists to control curricula on Africana women as well as to gain and maintain loyalty and commitment to Africana Studies by Africana women on campuses where strong Women's Studies programs exist. In *But Some of Us Are Brave,* there are course descriptions of African American Women's Studies. Some of these courses may prove to be useful as a point of departure for developing courses on Africana women in programs where they are nonexistent.

Beyond the courses on campuses, the campus cultural arena must be examined to determine the extent to which it fosters educational enlightenment on issues of relevance to Africana women. How many lectures by and about Africana women occur during the academic year? What kinds of audiences turn out for these occasions? What accounts appear in campus media on Africana women: Who or what units are the promoters of Africana women on campuses? Data has to be systematically gathered to respond to these kinds of questions to get a handle on the extent to which Africana women are being incorporated into Africana Studies, specifically, and on campus in general. Again, the data from the dozen or so campuses are not very impressive. The list of women as speakers is much more limited than men in numbers as well as in the subfields of Africana Studies.

Very few women emerge as "famous people" to bring to campus outside of the political activists, entertainers or the popular novelists such as Maya Angelou, Alice Walker, Toni Morrison, etc. Virtually no Africana women theoreticians among the social and behavioral science scholars, or, for that matter, humanists such as historians surface immediately for student groups or faculty to bring to campus except when brochures from speakers bureaus are consulted. The point is that we have virtually no highly visible "giants" among

Africana women who are committed to and who are doing significant work on Africana women within the field of Africana Studies.

Most of those who are visible view themselves as part of a traditional discipline or as part of a newly emerging discipline of Black Women's Studies and as such are not an integral part of the promotion and development of Africana Studies as a discipline. They seek to emphasize issues of women while minimizing the experiences of people of African decent as a totality. The overriding issue today is: do we need an Africana Women's Studies movement separate from the general movement or will Africana Studies be able to incorporate the experiences of black women?

It must be borne in mind that, until recently, an overwhelming majority of Africana Studies units were administered by Africana males who controlled curriculum development and cultural programming activities and were guilty, even if unintentionally, of treating Africana women as whites had treated both men and women of African descent in the academy—distorting or dismissing them and their experiences. And, where women were administrators their faculties were usually still heavily male—probably sensitive but unequipped to teach courses. This suggests the dual need for sensitivity and necessary resources. The decade of the nineties is witnessing positive changes in both of the aforementioned.

There are growing numbers of scholars with interest in women's issues as well as an increasing number of Africana administrators, both male and female, who are sensitive to women's issues, realizing the need to incorporate significantly curriculum and experiences of students both male and female. For example, the Emory University African American and African Studies program, under it founding Africana woman director, inaugurated an endowed lecture series in the name of an African American woman and subsequently created a distinguished chair in the name of an Africana woman with an African American woman as the first individual to hold the chair. Both incidents were firsts at a major institution in this country. But significantly there has never been a strong presence of Africana women in the curriculum in this institution for a variety of reasons, including most importantly the lack of continuity of faculty equipped to teach these courses.

Professional Organizations, Africana Studies and Africana Women

Just as scholarship and the academy have been largely void of a significant Africana women's presence and skill in "directing traffic," such has been the case for Africana Studies professional organizations until the late eighties and nineties. It is in these very organizations that Africana women have begun to have their presence felt—not simply by being the leaders or presidents but through drawing more women into all levels of the organizations.

Organizations must have infrastructures which develop their character and form.

The National Council for Black Studies (NCBS), The African Heritage Studies Association (AHSA), and the African American Life and History Association (ASALH) have contributed to professionalizing the field of African American Studies. They have taken steps to move towards parity among women and men with respect to key positions throughout the organizations; integration of women's issues and experience in the annual conference programs; recognition of women with awards; and special projects devoted to them.

Much of this movement came about due to efforts of women as they have gained in numbers but also because some men have come to see the injustice and the waste of talent in not fully actualizing the wealth of resources which abound when men and women come together in enlightening the world. But, it probably has been easier to integrate women in the professional organizations than in the curriculum because of the nature of political machinery in organizations, as opposed to garnering resources for faculty positions to staff courses on Africana women. All too often, these courses are seen as frills rather than staples, not only, and perhaps, not even as much by Africana scholars as by central administrators who control budgets.

Toward Integrating Africana Women into Africana Studies

Integrating Africana women into Africana Studies should not need to be a topic for dialogue. For the incorporation of Africana women should be as natural to the field as breathing is to living. This is particularly true if those in the field share a fundamental womanist perspective as mentioned earlier in this chapter and which more recently has been summarized by Gordon (1985) and Hudson-Weems (1993). In *Black Women, Feminism and Black Liberation: Which Way?* Gordon contends black liberation represents freedom from racism and sexism, and as such black women should not have to compartmentalize themselves into segments of race versus gender. Both black men's and black women's central goal is to be liberated, and it can happen only if both are fairly treated.[6] Hudson-Weems points out specifically what encompasses a liberated people as she details the characteristics of the Africana woman. She lists 18 features: (1) a self-namer, (2) a self-definer, (3) family-centered, (4) genuine in sisterhood, (5) strong, (6) in concert with male in struggle, (7) whole, (8) authentic, (9) a flexible role player, (10) respected, (11) recognized, (12) spiritual, (13) male compatible, (14) respectful of elders, (15) adaptable, (16) ambitious, (17) mothering and (18) nurturing.[7]

Guided by an Africana Womanist perspective, then, and by way of summary and emphasis, the following points are offered for consideration as challenges or opportunities for integrating Africana women into Africana Studies:

1. Continued development of scholarship by and about Africana women, particularly with increased focus in the social and behavioral sciences, the natural sciences, professions and policy studies.

2. Increased contributions by women to conceptualization of theoretical and empirical issues of the field in general. Women are invisible for the most part in framing central issues of the discipline of Africana Studies. Two notable exceptions are Young (1984) and Aldridge (1988), who guest edited special issues of the *Journal of Negro Education* and *Phylon: Review of Race and Culture.* Earlier in 1972, Young had edited the significant and widely used *Black Experience: Analysis and Synthesis.* More recently, Marimba Ani (1994) has emerged with what may well be the major theoretical piece for Africana Studies produced by male or female in this century.

3. Continued involvement of Africana women with womanist perspectives in leadership positions in the professional bodies for Africana Studies so that programs and policies reflect their perspectives.

4. Increased attention to developing new and restructuring old curricula to reflect a balance that is inclusive of Africana women.

5. Increased balancing of speakers and cultural activities on campuses that draw upon both men and women not only from the literary tradition but other orientations. Much more effort will have to be exerted to draw upon talent among the less famous but no less substantive than some of the famous.

6. Concentrated efforts to search out and quote the work of both Africana women and men in the field as scholars of other fields do.

While by no means exhaustive, the aforementioned points are offered as challenges or opportunities for integrating Africana women into Africana Studies. Thus, Integration would foreclose on any needs for Africana Women scholars to abandon the discipline—a discipline which can only grow stronger and richer with the full treatment of both its men and women.

NOTES*

For a comprehensive examination of women's studies generally, see Marilyn J. Boxer, "For and About Women: The Theory and Practice of Women's Studies in the United States," *SIGNS,* 7 (1982): 660–95. For an overview of Africana Studies refer to James E. Turner (ed.), *The Next Decade: Theoretical and Research Issues.* Ithaca, N.Y.: Cornell University, 1984.

1. Bert J. Loewenberg and Ruth Bogin, eds., *Black Women in Nineteenth-Century American Life.* University Park: Pennsylvania State University Press, 1976.

2. Bell Hooks, *Ain't I a Woman: Black Women and Feminism.* Boston: South End Press, 1981, p. 6.

*The author appreciates the discussion of the original draft of this work with LaFrances Rodgers-Rose who provided valuable insights.

3. Toni Cade, ed., *The Black Woman: An Anthology.* New York: New American Library, 1970, pp. 107–108.
4. Bell Hooks, *op cit.*, p. 6.
5. Gloria T. Hull, Patricia Bell Scott, and Barbara Smith, eds., *All the Women Are White. All the Blacks Are Men, But Some of Us Are Brave: Black Women's Studies.* Old Westbury, N.Y.: Feminist Press, 1981: pp. xx–xxi.
6. Vivian V. Gordon, *Black Women, Feminism, Black Liberation: Which Way?* Chicago: Third World Press, 1985, pp. 68–69.
7. Clinora Hudson-Weems, *Africana Womanism: Reclaiming Ourselves.* Troy, Mich.: Bedford Publishers, 1993, p. 179.

BIBLIOGRAPHY

Aldridge, Delores P., ed. "New Perspectives on Black Studies," Special issue, *Phylon: Review of Race and Culture* 49, 1 (Spring 1988).
_____. *Black Male-Female Relationships: A Resource Book.* Dubuque, Iowa: Kendall-Hunt, 1989.
_____. *Focusing: Institutional and Interpersonal Perspectives on Black Male-Female Relations.* Chicago: Third World Press, 1991.
Ani, Marimba. *Yurugu: An African-Centered Critique of European Cultural Thought and Behavior.* Trenton, N.J.: Africa World Press, 1994.
Bell, Roseann P., Bettye J. Parker and Beverly Guy-Sheftall, eds., *Sturdy Black Bridges: Visions of Black Women in Literature.* New York: Anchor Books, 1979.
Boxer, Marilyn J., "For and About Women: The Theory and Practice of Women's Studies in the United States," *Signs* 7 (1981): 660–695.
Cade, Toni, ed. *The Black Woman: An Anthology.* New York: New American Library, 1970.
Christian, Barbara. *Black Women Novelists: The Development of a Tradition 1892–1976.* Westport, Conn.: Greenwood Press, 1981.
Collins, Patricia H. *Black Feminist Thought: Knowledge, Consciousness, and the Politics of Empowerment.* London: Harper Collins Academic, 1990.
Colon, Alan K. "Critical Issues in Black Studies: A Selective Analysis," *The Journal of Negro Education* 53 (1984): 268–277.
Gordon, Vivian V. *Black Women, Feminism, Black Liberation: Which Way?* Chicago: Third World Press, 1991.
Harley, Sharon, and Terborg-Penn, Rosalyn, eds. *The Afro-American Woman: Struggles and Images.* Port Washington, N.Y.: Kennikat Press, 1978.
Hooks, Bell. *Ain't I a Woman: Black Women and Feminism.* Boston: South End Press, 1981.
Hudson-Weems, Clinora. *Africana Womanism: Reclaiming Ourselves.* Detroit: Dunlap Press, 1993.
Hull, Gloria T., Scott, Patricia Bell, and Smith, Barbara, eds., *All the Women Are White, All the Men Are Black, But Some of Us Are Brave: Black Women's Studies.* Old Westbury, N.Y.: Feminist Press, 1982.
Ladner, Joyce. *Tomorrow's Tomorrow.* Garden City, N.Y.: Doubleday, 1971.
Lerner, Gerda, ed. *Black Women in White America: A Documentary History.* New York: Pantheon Books, 1972.
Loewenberg, Bert J., and Bogin, Ruth, eds. *Black Women in Nineteenth-Century American Life.* University Park: Pennsylvania State Press, 1976.
Myers, Lena Wright. *Black Women: Do They Cope Better?* New York: Prentice-Hall, 1980.
National Council for Black Studies. *Black Studies Core Curriculum.* Bloomington, Ind.: National Council for Black Studies, 1981.
Rodgers-Rose, LaFrances. *The Black Woman.* Beverly Hills, Calif.: Sage Publications, 1980.
Steady, Filomina, ed. *The Black Woman Cross-Culturally.* Cambridge, Mass.: Schenkman, 1981.
Turner, James E., ed. *The Next Decade: Theoretical and Research Issues.* Ithaca, N.Y.: Africana Studies and Research Center, Cornell University, 1984.
Wade-Gayles, Gloria. *No Crystal Stair, Visions of Race and Sex in Women's Fiction.* New York: Pilgrim Press, 1984.

Walker, Alice. *The Color Purple*. New York: Washington Square Press, 1982.
_____. *In Search of Our Mother's Gardens: Womanist Prose*. New York: Harcourt Brace Jovanovich, 1983.
Washington, Mary Helen. *Black-Eyed Susans: Classic Stories by and About Black Woman*. Garden City, N.Y.: Doubleday, 1975.
White, Deborah Gray. *Ar'n't I a Woman? Female Slaves in the Plantation South*. New York: W.W. Norton, 1985.
Young, Carlene. "An Assessment of Black Studies Programs in American Higher Education," special issue of *The Journal of Negro Education* 53 (1984).
_____. *Black Experience: Analysis and Synthesis*. San Rafael, Calif.: Leswing Press, 1972.

12. Black Women, Feminism, and Black Liberation: Which Way?

Vivian Gordon, Ph.D.
Professor of Africana Studies
State University of New York at Albany

The purpose of this chapter is to review briefly the difference in the nature of the oppression of African American women and Euro-American women who again call to black women for full participation in the movement popularly known as Women's Liberation. The position presented here is that a black woman's coalition with a white woman-dominated movement centered around an Eurocentric focus holds the potential for an isolation of black women from the promised rewards of the coalition as well as an isolation from their historic identity and efforts in behalf of the liberation of the African American community.

In support of this contention, we shall consider: (1) traditional coalition theory, (2) the emergence of Women's Studies programs, (3) the black woman as a victim of a trilogy of oppression, (4) the socio-historic record of black/white female relationships, (5) status and color conflict among black women, (6) feminism and imposed definitions for black female/male relationships, (7) economic inequality by race and sex, (8) black women's organized efforts against racism and sexism, (9) the present and future struggle: a typology of attitudes, (10) directions for change in black female/male relationships, and (11) some conclusion.

The position presented here will no doubt be loudly condemned by some who point to a so-called common oppression of all women and thereby proclaim that this oppression is the basis for a black/white women's coalition. This group considers gender to be the salient issue. Others will view this work to present an anti-white posture that will only contribute to a greater conflict between black and white women. However, that is because such people do not understand that the motivation for this work reaches beyond the potential for further cleavage in an already highly polarized racist society to other concerns which permits a clear focus upon the issue of the viability of a black/white women's coalition as a means for socio-political and economic gains for black women and the black community.

Many black Americans are increasingly distressed by the obvious surrender of much within the black community to a promise of a "better situation" through integration—which, for the dominant group, usually means movement from a black culture into white conformity—and which has often failed in its rewards to black people even where reported to have taken place. Moreover, it would appear that the integrative process provides little hope for real changes in the immediate future, but encourages the additional losses of vital African American talent and resources.

Social change must begin with self definition, especially among the youth who must establish firm roots if they are to sustain in the battle that seeks to render them powerless. From this perspective, it becomes apparent that black women and the black community must carefully scrutinize appeals from white dominated movements with Eurocentric underpinnings. Black women who identify with the women's liberation movement will internalize the rhetoric and perspective of that movement and become alienated from themselves (self-hate), and alienated from the race, as well as from a splendid record of activities against racism. It is important, therefore, that any focus on African American women be evaluated to determine the collective benefits or losses to the African American community, even when the short-range goals might hold obvious benefits for black women.

Traditional Coalition Perspectives and Black/White Women's Issues

Traditional coalition theory underscores the necessity for a strategic evaluation of the basic power in the *reward phase* of the effort as a requirement for partnership, if there would be a meaningful and nondestructive achievement for the component with the *lesser power*. When one considers the relative posture of black and white women, and the accompanying dynamics of their linkages, one clearly must view the direct white female/male power linkages as they have historically existed and as they continue to exist today. Such linkages result from ethnicity, marriage and a shared "othergroup" philosophy. As the coalition schema illustrates (see page 157), a black/white female coalition represents an ill-fitted choice for African American women.

The more obvious coalition dynamic would be between the various nonwhite American "Third World" women. That such a coalition is fraught with difficulties is a further indication of the extent to which minority women have, all too often, internalized the white-good/black-bad self-associations which represent the religio-political ideologies of the dominant group. The inability of American non-white women to establish long-term and mean-ingful coalitions is a complex topic to be addressed by a different paper.

The schema assumes the following situations to exist in the nation: (1) dominant economic and socio-political power concentrated within white America (the collective white ethnic) with the white male holding the monopoly; (2) a sharing in that white male power by his primary group, i.e., the family and its relationships; (3) power by white women either independently or by virtue of their linkages to white men; (4) international economic and socio-political power linkages between white American males and females resulting from historic conditions of war conquests, colonialization, economic investments, and various contemporary manifestations of a philosophy of manifest destiny.

The limited linkages, where such exist, between African Americans in general and black women in particular, are dramatized by broken lines in the schema. These relatively weak socio-economic and political linkages between non-white people in general, African and American black women, may be viewed to be supported by the following: (1) the absence of any continuous, clearly defined linkages between the African American and non-white international communities; (2) within the nation, an ongoing denial of African origins and the accompanying kinship between African Americans and Africans; (3) limited contemporary and historic support for pan–Africanism; (4) limited focus on the African diaspora in studies about the African American experience; (5) limited dialogue and association between Africans in America and African Americans, especially among students and faculty in higher education; and (6) the manipulated or orchestrated conflict between African American and other non-white minorities who continue to compete with each other for limited economic and socio-political resources.

Non-White/White Power Relationships
by Selected Categories

Figure 4

A. *Economic Domination*

	A^1	A	B	C	D	E	F	G		
A^1	—	0	1	1	1	1	1	1	|	6
A	1	—	1	1	1	1	1	1	|	7
B	0	0	—	1	1	1	1	0	|	4
C	0	0	0	—	0	0	0	0	|	0
D	0	0	0	1	—	1	0	0	|	2
E	0	0	0	0	0	—	0	0	|	0
F	0	0	0	1	1	1	—	0	|	3
G	?	0	1	1	1	1	1	—	|	5

C and E represent the most economically dominated, and thus, powerless groups.

Key:

A¹-International Eurocentric White Male
    Power
A-Euro-American White Men
B-Euro-American White Women
C-African American Women

D-African American Men
E-Other Non-White American Women
F-Other Non-White American Men
G-International Non-White/Non-Eurocen-
    tric Male Power

Figure 5

B. *Political Dominance*

	A¹	A	B	C	D	E	F	G		
A¹	—	0	1	1	1	1	1	0	|	5
A	0	—	1	1	1	1	1	0	|	5
B	0	0	—	1	1	1	1	0	|	4
C	0	0	0	—	0	0	0	0	|	0
D	0	0	1/2	1	1	—	0	0	|	2 1/2
E	0	0	0	0	0	—	0	0	|	0
F	0	0	1/2	1/2	0	1/2	1/2	—	|	2
G	0	0	1/2	1/2	0	1/2	1/2	—	|	2

C and D represent the most politically dominated groups. D's limited political strength reflects the greater total number of black male elected officials compared to C and E.

Figure 6

C. *Cultural Domination*

Control over education, the media, and primary institutional values

	A¹	A	B	C	D	E	F	G		
A¹	—	0	0	1	1	1	1	0	|	4
A	1	—	—	1	1	1	1	0	|	6
B	—	—	—	1	1	1	1	0	|	4
C	0	0	0	—	0	0	0	0	|	0
D	0	0	0	—	—	0	0	0	|	0
E	0	0	0	0	0	—	—	0	|	0
F	0	0	0	0	0	—	—	0	|	0
G	0	0	0	0	0	0	0	—	|	0

A maintains the highest level of cultural domination through control over education, the media and primary institutional values. B shares the culture of A^1 and A. None of the non-white groups are in a dominant culture position. They do not control the media and their own educational programs.

Figure 7

D. *Physical Domination*

The potential for body abuse.

	A^1	A	B	C	D	E	F	G		
A^1	—	0	1	1	1/2	1	1/2		|	4
A	0	—	1	1	1/2	1	1/2		|	4
B	0	0	—	1/2	1/2	1/2	1/2		|	4
C	0	0	0	—	0	0	0	0	|	0
D	0	0	1/4	1	—	1/2	0		|	1 3/4
E	0	0	0	0	0	—	0		|	0
F	0	0	1/4	1	0	1	—		|	2 1/4
G	non salient								|	

The fear of reprisal by A^1 and A limits the potential for D and F to exercise power over B. D and F are not able to provide equal protection for C and E from A^1 or A or B as B may impart upon A or A^1 against C and E, or as B may be guilty through complicity, as was the case during slavery.

Key:
A1-International Eurocentric White Male Power
A-Euro-American White Men
B-Euro-American White Women
C-African American Women

D-African American Men
E-Other Non-White American Women
F-Other Non-White American Men
G-International Non-White/Non-Eurocentric Male Power

Figure 8

E. *Military Power*

Control by para-military or military forces within the nation.

	A^1	A	B	C	D	E	F	G		
A^1	—	0	1	1	1	1	1		|	5
A	0	—	1	1	1	1	1		|	5

B	0	0	—	1/2	1/2	1/2	1/2			2
C	0	0	0	—	0	0	0	0		0
D	0	0	0	0	—	0	0			0
E	0	0	0	0	0	—	0			0
F	0	0	0	0	0	0	0			0
G	non salient									

In this situation G is again not salient. In the sense that B shares in or benefits from the control A^1 and A are able to exercise, B has the potential for strength in this arena. Although C D E and F are represented in the military structure they have limited control.

Note: The most frequent comment about the coalition schematic and the power diagrams is that the representation for G (Figure 4) should be much smaller in proportion to A^1 and that the non-white women's power within G should be about one-half the strength represented. Even if these changes were to be made, the basic contention would be sustained. In fact, the basic thought would be enhanced.

Given this situation, traditional coalition theory would presume linkages between C and B, advocated by C who has less power than both B and A. However, what traditional coalition theory does not consider is that although B reports domination by A and a desire to loosen the A-B linkage, in fact, B is bound to A as a result of shared economic and socio-political benefits through marriage, social and intimate relationships as well as a shared belief system; in particular, a shared belief about C. B's linkages with A result from the role complex of wife, mother, sister, daughter and primary sex partner. It could be argued that in these traditional sex-linked roles, B as primary socializer of the children perpetuates the belief system of A and B about C.

There is no viable coalition between B and C, or A and C. Traditional theory might underscore that for C some small gains resulting from a C-B coalition would be better than no gains. However, this perspective does not consider the nature of C's caste by virtue of color. Nor does such a perspective give attention to the *nature* of the power dimension in black/white relationships in America. Power concedes to power and only to the extent necessary to maintain power. Moreover, power extracts a heavy toll for small concessions. For example, to achieve limited economic and socio-political gains from B, and especially from A, C is required to surrender important linkages of identity, self-group value, and traditions, as well as positive social and intimate relationships with African American men, D. C would be required to become a further victim of Anglo conformity (cultural imperialism). Such conformity would ultimately result in the destruction of the African American community and culture, especially since for that culture C is the primary transmitter and socializer.

In decisions about the ultimate outcome of a B-C or A-C coalition (though A-C would be unlikely), C must maintain an awareness of the extent to which, in America, race remains a caste/class stigma which limits upward mobility for non-whites. There is limited equal interaction even for those persons presumed to have accomplished upward mobility through socio-economic achievements.

> If minorities are not in mutual contact, have very diverse cultures and economic interests, and have a previous history of intense competition of conflict with one another, then one may expect that the degree of mutual trust and communication among them will be too low to overcome the normal resistances to cooperation.... Closely related to previous minority contact and competition is the question of how the minorities are ranked along some relatively distinct hierarchy of prestige of power. This, too, is likely to be linked to whatever are the predominant lines of social cleavage within the society.... Degree of similarity to the dominant group is also likely to be a strong correlate of position in the hierarchy. If C is more similar to A and B than is D, C will have a vested interest in emphasizing its differences with D and its similarity to A. A, in turn, is likely to differentiate itself from all three minorities unless, of course, it finds it necessary from time to time to form a conservative coalition with B against C and D, or with B and C against D....
>
> Most important, perhaps, is the extent to which the minorities perceive themselves to be in a 'zero-sum' competition in which the gains of one group must always be made at the expense of another. On the other hand, minorities may perceive themselves as being in a 'positive-sum' situation in which the gains of one add to the gains of all, making a coalition more desirable.[1]

The contemporary literature which addresses social movements tends to move away from the traditional coalition thinking represented by the Gordon schematic and places a focus upon the mobilization of resources to bring about change. From this perspective, we could consider it reasonable for African American women to form *time-limited, issue-specific* coalitions with white women. It is *only* within these parameters that a black/white women's coalition, such as that required by Jesse Jackson through his "Rainbow Coalition" could be accomplished. Emphasis is given to the time-limited, issue-specific nature of such a white/non-white women's coalition, for many black women of today remember the extent to which a similar "rainbow-type" coalition in the 1960s resulted in the displacement of black women by white women from key positions in the movement. Jackson stated that he would consider the selection of a woman vice presidential running mate. Hopefully, he would have selected a Third World American woman. Black male leadership must recognize the extent to which they often extend to white women in political coalitions and show themselves to be insensitive to black women—the very women from whose wombs and nurturing they emerged.

As is established later in this chapter, white women have historically and consistently *welcomed* black men into organizational efforts while at the same time *excluding* black women. Had his support been more extensive, Jackson would have been in a unique position to reverse past trends and to make a statement to all people about the recognized abilities, activities and political acumen of African American women, and other women of color so often neglected by the political world.

After a look at the life conditions of black women and those of the general black community, exchange with dynamic and concerned black women from a range of socio-economic backgrounds, and exchange with black women scholars contributing to research and the historic evaluation of the black woman's experience, one can only conclude that there are some dynamic incompatibilities between African American women and feminism as advocated by the Women's Liberation movement.

African American women are one of the most victimized and understatus groups in the nation. It is important that the gains which have been so painfully accomplished not be put into jeopardy through a scattering of talents and energies to contextual appeals which hold considerable potential for destruction of the black community. It is appropriate that we now consider the more recent phase of the women's movement: programs for Women's Studies.

Civil Rights in the 1960s
and the Emergence of Women's Studies

One of the newest programs within higher education is Women's Studies, which followed the path cleared by black college students in the 1960s when they demanded representation, participation and relevance in higher education through classes and then programs of Afro-American studies.

The primary focus of Women's Studies has been upon gender-specific discrimination and the inattention to, as well as the lack of analyses of, women's roles in the development of the nation. The first Women's Studies class was taught in the late 1960s and based on the model set by Afro-American Studies. Presenting themselves as "woman as nigger," predominantly white groups of women in higher education spoke of their oppression as analogous to that of the black American.

In some instances, the initiation of Women's Studies presented a direct threat to the already established degree-granting programs for Afro-American Studies because of the increased demand that was placed on "minority study dollars" that were to be further stretched. The scenario of "minority" competition for limited economic resources is well known. Thus, we can see how in some situations the emergence of Women's Studies was viewed with serious concern by black women committed to African American Studies and to the philosophy of black liberation as the means through which sexism and racism would be equally attacked.

Black women in Black Studies watched the emergence of Women's Studies and at the same time heard an appeal by faculty and students for the recruitment to higher education of increased numbers of "minorities," i.e., women and black faculty. Black women in higher education, well aware of the need for a critical mass of black faculty, listened to the administrative appeals for "black faculty and women" and tried to determine where their already scattered energies should be concentrated.

More importantly, black women in higher education were aware of the more extensive resource pool from which white women faculty could emerge compared to a shrinking pool—due to decreases in financial aid—of black scholars. Already, white women faculty, although very much in the minority, considerably outnumbered black faculty, both male and female. Even in their oppression, white women have been able to obtain those credentials which make them more readily available when there is a push for "minority" recruitment. It may be documented, for example, that white males in higher education reportedly losing their jobs to black women are actually losing their jobs to white women.

With few exceptions, Women's Studies follows in the tradition of the Eurocentric perspective of higher education, only with a gender-specific theme. Most often the curriculum does not include a significant number of courses, if any, about non-white women. Where such courses are present, the black female experience is cast into a "traditional" course in which the black female/black male pathology model emerges. In those instances where this traditional literature has been abandoned, and, in particular, where there is some specific curriculum representation of black women, the perspective which usually dominates is that of the radical feminist and the radical feminist lesbian who certainly present valid issues of oppression but do not represent the primary experiences of the pluralistic majority of black women.

Moreover, the perspective of most Women's Studies programs is that black and white women have suffered a common experience of oppression which is gender specific. There is a pervasive unwillingness to acknowledge the distinctively *different nature* of oppression for white and non-white women. Seldom is attention given to the extent to which white women have benefited from the oppression of black women or have been active participants in racism.

Black Women as Victims of a Trilogy of Oppressions

Because racism, sexism and economic oppression are so pervasively entwined in America, black women might reasonably be expected to have difficulty identifying which negative experience is the primary cause of their oppression at any given time. Indeed, most often, these three oppressive forces impact upon black women simultaneously with a relentlessness that leaves them drained of both creativity and vision. Without a doubt, a by-product of the most minimal resistance to this relentless attack is exhaustion. Our observation has been that most black women at any given moment will first and foremost report themselves to be tired and exhausted. "Lord, I am weary" is a recurring theme.

In too many instances, what results from this three-pronged attack is a "survival" mentality that can give only limited thought to aggressive strategies and long-term planning. Tragically, one is frequently able to view destructive patterns of escape from the attacks such as: (1) a religious fanaticism which becomes a substitute for personal interactions and gratifying self-giving; (2) a pattern of "other" blaming which allows the victim to suspect the "ill-intentions" of *everyone*; or (3) at the other extreme, a self-doubt and self-blame which results in total dependency upon others for validation, in particular, a dependency upon male validation that often allows for extreme abuse, both physical and psychological. In many instances, such abuse is perceived to be their "just due" by black women thinking themselves worthy of little else. Moreover, because of the limited potential for a long-term monogamous relationship, many women accept abuse in exchange for secure sexual relationships. Clearly, the "victim" mentality emerges from and contributes to the three-pronged attack of racism, sexism and economic exploitation of black women.

It is appropriate to define these oppressive forces before we consider how Black women have been able to respond:

RACISM—a condition of control over the means for both the life chances and lifestyles of the subordinated other through the use of stigma, pejorative treatment, and discrimination resulting in differential opportunities and highly differentiated sharing in the rewards of society. The precondition for racism is the *power* to control and manipulate the major societal forces, and the ability to define for the "other" the requirements for participation. Fundamental to racism is a belief system that places a supremacy focus upon one group over the other. In the Western world, this racial supremacy has been translated to mean Anglo-Saxon male.

SEXISM—the use by males of the power of gender through both legal and nonlegal means to dominate through pejorative treatment people of the opposite gender (females). Such power is most often the result of superiority attitudes manifested through the rules of society that are both determined and enforced by the control group—men. The dictates for sexism may be observed to emerge through physical dominance, through a religious belief system which promotes the view of a divine order which mandates male power, or through the skillful use of sexual politics.

ECONOMIC OPPRESSION—subjugation and exploitation of the "other" through differential opportunities maintained through discrimination seated in racism. Limited access to the rewards of the system. The earning and purchasing power of groups is limited by those in power through a control over the means for production and distribution of the rewards. This control usually emerges from an internalized system of privilege and hierarchy based upon race and male gender which justifies consolidations and coalitions which block out others. There is, as well, the ability to maintain people control through local, state and federal military. A popular participation in consumerism enhances the power of those in economic control.

Given the fact that race and sex are ascribed characteristics and since in American society these two characteristics relegate non-whites to a caste group with limited influence and economic opportunity, it might be argued that the African American female is born into a trilogy of oppression from which there are very limited opportunities for escape. Survival under these conditions is at best tenuous. It is small wonder that those black women who do survive under such conditions, and who also manage to fight back and maintain a positive sense of self, find themselves sanctioned and labeled by three power groups who are: (1) the board members of the white male club, (2) those of the structure who aspire to (top) board membership in the club (other white males), and (3) those who receive some fringe benefits because of gender identity (black males).

We are all familiar with the denigrating labels which confront the black woman who strikes out and dares to maintain a valued self; such women are variously viewed to be domineering, aggressive, probably non-threatening to the man, bad-looking/bad-acting woman that no man wants. More recently, they are also presumed to be man-hating homosexuals. A small group of black women escape from those labels only to find that they must confront other labels which identify them as: (1) harmless types who know their proper place; (2) sexless matronly family heads who contentedly rock on the front porch to the tune of "The Lord Will Provide"; (3) the modern day nanny whose functioning enhances the power of the dominant group; (4) the young survivalist who is allowed to manipulate within limitations under the control of "her man"; (5) the blue collar to white collar educated and trained woman who is legitimized by the power group and allowed to receive limited rewards as long as she is a supporter of the established order; and finally (6) the talented black woman who entertains us all and is often compromised and nonthreatening because of financial co-optation or interracial marriage.

These are the most familiar stereotypes used to represent black women. Such images are presented and reinforced through every means for education and communication within the society, from the all-powerful television, to movies, to radio, to award-winning books praised by culturally selective white critics. Each generation of black women has grown up with its version of the Beulah, the Sapphire, the tragic semi-precious mulatto, the long-suffering abused survivalist, the so-called bourgeois college woman snob. The tragedy is the extent to which many black women have interalized these stereotypes and have eventually assumed such roles—thus, participating in a self-fulfilling prophecy as well as the process of victim blaming.

In spite of a long history of the manipulation of these stigmas which enhance the control and power of the major perpetrators of racism, sexism and economic oppression, the majority of black women have managed to maintain positive self-identities, and to experience some levels of success as mothers, wives, sisters and daughters; as leaders, activists, women working outside of the home; and as women generally contributing to the quality of life within the African American community. Traditional history, and in large measure African American Studies and Women's Studies, have most often excluded any focus upon the experiences of these black women.

However, more recent socio-historic research evidences positive self-perceptions by black women in America since the time of the sprinkling of the diaspora on this continent through chattel slavery. Clearly, the various forms of female slave resistance, the anti-racism and anti-sexism activities of black women's organizations, their partnership with black men in the women's organizations, and their partnership with black men in the struggle against oppression are all evidences of collective positive consciousness among African American women.

Regrettably, many African American women do not know their own history, nor do they know of the cultural linkages between themselves and other women of the African diaspora. African American women of today must learn that they are a part of the continuity between African women and women of the diaspora. They must embrace that heritage with praise and love.

A Brief Look at the Socio-Historic Record

Excellent historical research and Afrocentric sociological studies have more recently extricated the black woman from obscurity and falsely reported limited roles and replaced these with a more correct view of her dynamic and forceful presence in the struggle against oppression. The socio-historic record is presented in excellent scholarly form by a number of works, including those by Angela Davis, Gerda Lerner, Darlene Clarke Hine, Jeanne Noble, Sharon Harley, Rosalyn Terborg-Penn, LaFrances Rodgers-Rose, Joyce Ladner, Jacquelin Jackson, and Linda Perkins, to name a few women scholars concerned with black women's issues.

These works report through either historic chronicle or sociological analyses the positive self-perceptions of black women who, in addition to maintaining responsibilities to family, have devoted presence and talent to the liberation continuum. Of particular importance to us at this time is the extent to which such works highlight the difference in the nature of oppression experience by black and white women, and the difference in organizational as well as personal responses to such oppression. As Gerda Lerner, a white woman historian and author of one of the more popular black women's histories, writes:

> Black women have always been more conscious of and more handicapped by race oppressions than by sex oppressions. They have been subject to all of the restrictions against blacks and to those against women. In no area of life have they been permitted to attain higher levels of status than White women. Additionally, ever since slavery, they have been sexually exploited by White men through rape or in forced sexual services. These sexual mores, which are characteristic of the relationship of colonializers to the women of the conquered group, function not only symbolically but actually to fasten the badge of inferiority onto the enslaved group. The black man was degraded by being deprived of the power and the right to protect his women from white men. The black woman was directly degraded by the sexual attack and, more profoundly, by being deprived of a strong black man on whom she could rely for protection....[2]
>
> Black women have had an ambiguous role in relation to white society. Because they were women, white society has considered them more docile, less than a threat than black men. It has "rewarded" them by allowing—or forcing—black women into service in the white family. Black women, ever since slavery, have nursed and raised white children, attended white people in sickness and kept white homes running smoothly. Their intimate contact with white people has made them interpreters and intermediaries of the white culture in the black home. They have consistently had the lowest status in society—the economic and social—political status ranking order consisting of white men, white women, black men, black women. Black women's wages, even today, are lowest of all groups.

To the extent that white female leaders and scholars refuse to acknowledge this difference in the nature of the oppressive experiences of black and white women in America, it is certain that there can never be a viable coalition between African American and Euro-American women. As is evident from these very terms, we are speaking about two historically different cultural orientations. Black women can not negate their Afrocentricity just as white women cannot negate their Eurocentricisms.

Status and Color Conflict among Black Women

Much has been written about the patterns of stratification within the ranks of black womanhood as well as the black community. Such stratification patterns have primarily emerged as a result of "white owner" validations of "better than" for those of their acknowledged biological paternity. It is most often stated that such "fair skinned women" were privileged by close contact with white owners as house slaves compared to those who were the field slaves during the time of chattel slavery in America. However, when we review the contemporary research about slave women, especially the research by black women scholars, we learn that for the mulatto female the position as house slave was seldom one of privilege. Those female house slaves served both as beasts of burden, with no lessened physical labor, and, in addition to that role, the mulatto was especially selected for sexual exploitation by white men and their appointed studs. They were "selected" for white male owner profits for prostitution. White males were the initial "pimps" of African American women whose bodies they owned, and whose sexual exploitation was accepted as a part of the master-owner mentality that pervaded.

Moreover, the mulatto female slave was also faced with the wrath of the plantation mistress who was forced daily to confront this symbol of white male (father, husband, son) lust. Atrocities were perpetuated upon black slave women and, in particular, the female mulatto house slave resulting from the rage and jealousies of white women who often both resented and envied the collective strengths of slave women. It has been suggested, for example, that the ultimate pain of having one's child sold away was a primary threat practiced by white women against their black slave women.

We know, also, from studies of the plantation records and personal diaries of plantation mistresses, by Angela Davis, Darlene Clark Hine, Kate Willenstein, and others, that the daily abuse as laborer as well as the sexual abuse and exploitation of black women slaves was most often dismissed or ignored by white women who refused to make a gender association. For example, the white plantation mistress usually avoided making any identification with female slaves as women, for to have used such a term would have been to acknowledge a shared gender relationship by them and the slave women. It is reported that in times of sympathy, plantation mistresses often viewed slave women paternalistically, as did white men, referring to them as "poor creatures," "wretched creatures," "the suffering females of their kind." In times of anger and revenge, those same white women referred to black slave women as "wenches," "libidinous whores," or "apt breeders." Thus, the stratification of slave women by skin color and the so-called privileged position of the "fair skinned" among those same women was imposed upon the slave community.

Skin color divisions among women within the African American community have been promoted because of *dominant other* evaluations of value and worth. Such divisions are ultimately incredulous, for no matter how overtly rewarded by the dominant group, no individual black woman is immune to the darts of oppression for those who step out of their appointed (anointed) roles—whether that role is based upon skin color, athletic ability, income, education or other factors. That black women continue to allow unity and sisterhood to be interrupted by divisions based upon color and status is a testimony to the incredible extent to which an oppressed people who do not control the means for their own education are subject to indoctrination, which often results in an identification with the oppressor.

The black woman who is on the lowest economic, status and prestige rung, barely surviving and not knowing from time to time how she will provide for her children or herself, and her black sister (who because of *relative* opportunity, education or luck has been able to be upwardly mobile within the allowed limitations) are inextricably linked by their common oppression, whether it takes the form of the overt daily hassle of the street or the covert sugar-coated arsenic of higher education. The sister struggling to feed her family and the sister of more fortunate economic circumstance (no matter how hostile they may be to each other at one level) know, that on the other level, they have *both* been called "black bitch" with equal venom. The more pervasive tragedy is that they are seldom aware of their bond—sisterhood—other than through the factors of oppression.

> The codification of Blackness and femaleness by whites and males is seen in terms of "thinking like a woman" and "acting like a nigger" which are based on the premise that there are typically Black and female ways of acting and thinking. Therefore, the most pejorative concept in the white/male world view would be that of thinking and acting like a "nigger woman."[3]

These two groups of black women who function on different levels of stratification could learn much from each other. They are historically linked to the Motherland and they are linked in the struggle in America to raise whole and decent children; the struggle to maintain meaningful relationships with black men, etc. At different levels they fight the same battle, which equally exhausts and often destroys them, through different means; however, destruction is destruction.

African American women must reconstruct their supportive linkages, many of which have been severed because of their rejection of each other. This rejection will be increased by a women's movement based upon a strictly gender definition of oppression and for whom the primary participant is middle and upper-middle income women. The division promoted by such a movement could be devastating. It is a division which allows for an additional blow to the often shaky foundations of unity among black women of a range of hues, and socioeconomic circumstances. Therefore, existing black women's organizations, whether they be community-based or select small groups, must focus upon the issues which the feminist movement so readily identifies, but fails to embrace with any real solutions: abortion, sexual harassment on the job, rape, childcare, medical abuse, and limited opportunities for education and training, to name some of the more salient issues.

White feminists who point to a so-called lack of involvement by black women in women's issues reflect a lack of awareness of the historic role of black women. Such feminists also fail to realize the extent to which they accept and continue to be influenced by the white male-dominated record of women's history and African American events. Moreover, such persons must realize that historically and contemporarily, African American women have been and are involved in activities which have directly confronted sexism and racism. That resistance has taken them into many dangerous situations in which they have frequently sought, but more often did not receive, the alliance of white feminist advocates.

African slave women were the initiators of feminism in America. It was their struggle for the humanity of womanhood that first made white women aware of white male paternalism which limited their development, but idolized their status. As Paula Giddings reports in her very recent work:[4]

> The White wife was hoisted on a pedestal so high that she was beyond the sensual reach of her own husband. Black women were consigned to the other end of the scale, as mistresses, whores, or breeders. Thus, in the nineteenth century, Black women's resistance to slavery took on an added dimension. With the diminution of overt rebellion, their resistance became more covert and internalized. The focus of the struggle was no longer against the notion that they were less human, ... but that they were different kinds of humans. For women this meant spurning their morally inferior roles of mistresses, whore and breeder—though under the "new" slavery they were "rewarded" for acquiescing in them. It was the factor of reward that made this resistance a fundamentally feminist one, for at its base was a rejection of the notion that they were the master's property. So Black women had a double challenge under the new slavery: They had to resist the property relation (which was different in form, if not in nature, to that of White women) and they had to inculcate the same values into succeeding generations.

Repeatedly, white feminists have been unwilling to acknowledge the extent to which they have participated, either overtly or through complicity, in the oppression and destruction of black women. Also, such women have not been willing to admit their privileged position of control over the immediate lives of most *contemporary* black women. For example, how many white women feminists provide security for their domestics through (1) minimum wages, (2) a retirement plan, (3) sick leave with pay, (4) maternity leave, or (5) a confrontation with their fathers, husbands, sons, brothers and lovers who are the perpetrators of sexual harassment against black women? White women in the workforce have higher status and most often are in positions of superior power to black women who have historically been in the workforce in greater numbers and over longer time periods.

Sexual Politics

Contemporary white feminists often attempt to impose upon black women a definition for black male/female relationships based upon their perspectives which identify all men as the enemy. Such women point to examples of black male abuse of black women and call to black women for disassociation with black males as if such men were in the same positions of power as white males.

Clearly, sexism and abuse of black women by black men can be observed and may be documented to exist as a serious problem within the black community. However, the black community vis-à-vis black women, must define their own problems and the means through which those problems might best be resolved with minimal injury to all.

Historically, black women have functioned in different relationships to black men than have white women with white men. More importantly, when we view sexual politics as expressed through rape and other violent crimes, a point of orientation must be the extent to which black on black crime results most ostensibly from white on black crime.

Some black feminists have observed that rape is an emotional issue which emerges as a concern for white women primarily as an emotional attention-getting issue. They point out that the white woman's primary victimization by white men is in less violent forms, such as economic and political sexual politics. In particular, when calling attention to abuses of black women by black men, white feminists point to the black man as the potential rapist of white women. A key issue for black women must also be the extent to which the white female/male focus upon the black male as rapist is a focus upon a presumed black female promiscuity. As Angela Davis reports, "the mythical rapist implies the mythical whore." She adds:

> ...It cannot be denied that Brownmiller's book, *Against Our Will: Men, Women and Rape*, is a pioneering scholarly contribution to the contemporary litera-ture on rape. Yet many of her arguments are unfortunately pervaded with racist ideas. Characteristic of that perspective is her reinterpretation of the 1955 lynching of fourteen-year-old Emmett Till. After this young boy had whistled at a white woman in Mississippi, his maimed body was found at the bottom of the Tallahatchie River. "Till's action," said Brownmiller, "was more than a kid's brash prank."
>
> While Brownmiller deplores the sadistic punishment inflicted on Emmett Till, the Black youth emerges, nonetheless, as a guilty sexist—almost as guilty as his white racist murderers. After all, she argues, both Till and his mur-derers were exclusively concerned about their rights of possession over women.[5]

Davis continues by citing the work of Jean MacKeller:

> Blacks raised in the hard life of the ghetto learn that they can get what they want only by seizing it. Violence is the rule in the game for survival. Women are fair prey: to obtain a woman one subdues her.
>
> ... MacKeller has been so completely mesmerized by racist propaganda that she makes the unabashed claim that 90 percent of all reported rapes in the United States are committed by Black men. Inasmuch as the FBI's corre-sponding figure is 47 percent; it is difficult to believe that MacKeller's state-ment is not an intentional provocation.[6]

If these discussions which link rape (for which the black woman is most often the victim) as a primary preoccupation by black men and with a so-called promiscuity of black women (a link which emerged as a justification for white male rape of slave women), even more devastating are the works by black male writers of the 1960s, such as Claude Brown's *Manchild* or Calvin Hernton, who support myths established by white males. As Davis critiques:

> "the Negro woman during slavery began to develop a deprecatory concept of herself, not only as a female but as a human being as well." According to Hernton's analysis, "after experiencing the ceaseless sexual immorality of the white south," ... the Negro woman became "promiscuous and loose," and could be "had for the taking. Indeed, she came to look upon herself as the South viewed and treated her, for she had no other morality by which to shape her womanhood."
>
> Hernton's analysis never penetrates the ideological veil which has resulted in the minimizing of the sexual outrages constantly committed against black women. He falls into the trap of blaming the victim for the savage punishment she has historically been forced to endure.[7]

When black women have worked throughout history to manifest what Davis calls "a collective consciousness of their sexual victimization," they have labored alone in their appeal before receiving support by white women. One must move into historically recent times, for example, before we find Jessie Daniel Ames and the Association for Southern Women for the Prevention of Lynching. They worked against lynchings purported to be in defense of white women victims of black male rape. Again, as Davis reports:

> One of the major weaknesses of Susan Brownmiller's study on rape is its absolute disregard of Black women's pioneering efforts in the anti-lynching movement. While Brownmiller rightfully praises Jessie Daniel Ames and the Association of Southern Women, she makes not so much as a passing mention of Ida B. Wells, Mary Church Terrell or Mary Talbert and the Anti-Lynching Crusaders.[8]

If one is lacking a clear understanding of the relative value placed upon black women versus white women as violence victims, one need only consider these facts reported by Gloria Joseph:

> Rape is America's fastest-growing violent crime. Black women are eighteen times more likely to be rape victims than are White women... No White male in the history of this country was ever given the death penalty for raping Black women.[9]

Black men who rape black women are given lighter sentences (if sentenced at all) compared to sentences for the rape of white women. The victim of the black male rapist is overwhelmingly the black female. The rate of black female rape by white males is almost three times higher than the rate of white female rape by black males. That the dominant society (white male/ female) has internalized the value association of white as good and black as bad appears to be supported by the data reporting crime and punishment by race.

The homicide rate for black women is superseded only by the homicide rate for black men. Without a doubt, varying degrees of violence are a part of the life of large numbers of black women. While much publicity is given to the disproportionate number of black males in the nation's prisons, limited attention is given to the fact that 48 percent of the women's prison population is black. Little research has been conducted to determine why this black female prison population is so high. It is reasonable to speculate that black women (like black men) often find themselves swept up in life situations that are so desperate that violence appears to be the easiest if not the only avenue for a statement of self-hood, or for the resolution of a threat crisis.

To combat these devastating and self-destructive situations within the African American community, the historic alliance between black men and black women, politically and socially as defenders, developers and lovers of each other must be strengthened, and in many instances completely reestablished. The gender divisions which the contemporary white feminist movement could promote among black women would be counter-productive to this vital unifying effort. To be respected by others and in order to be in a workable coalition posture, an oppressed people must first and foremost seek to address their own personal/internal issues.

Economic Inequality by Race and Sex

The stratification patterns of economic inequality are well known. In 1980 the median earnings for full-time white women workers was $11,703 compared to $19,720 for white men, or an income gap of approximately 50 percent. The income gap between black women and black men has narrowed over the years; however, the true indicator of economic viability is obtained only when median income by race is compared to that of white men. As the data indicate, the income gaps between black and white women must be viewed in terms of part-time and full-time working women. The highest national rate of unemployment is among young black women. Single parent white women are more likely to be employed than black women.

NOTES

1. Blalock, Hubert M. *Race and Ethnic Relations.* Englewood Cliffs, N.J.: Prentice Hall, 1982, pp. 109–112.

2. Lerner, Gerda. *Black Women in White America*. New York: Vintage Books, 1974, preface.

3. Discussion supported by a number of works including: *The Slave Community* by John Blassingame; *Black Women in White America* by Gerda Lerner; *The Black Community* by James Blackwell; *Slavery and Race Relations in the Americas* by H. Hoetnick.

4. Gidings, Paula. *When and Where I Enter*. New York: William and Morrow, 1984, p. 43.

5. Davis, Angela. *Women, Race and Class*. New York: Random House, 1981, chapters 1, 2.

6. *Ibid.*, chapter 11.

7. *Ibid.*

8. *Ibid.*

9. Joseph, Gloria I., and Jill Lewis. *Common Differences*. New York: Anchor Press/Double Day, 1981, pp. 27, 38–39, 278–279.

13. "Feminist" or "Womanist"? A Black Woman Defining Self

Shawn R. Donaldson, Ph.D.
Associate Professor of Sociology
Richard Stockton College of New Jersey

In the process of self definition we must first recognize the power of language to symbolically represent, distort and even create social reality, for terminology "predisposes us to make a particular interpretation of [social] reality" (Robertson, 1987, p. 79). In this vein, I have always been uncomfortable with the label feminist, particularly without the qualifier "black," because of the negative connotations associated with the term both past and present. The major point here is the brass contrast between feminism as an ideology that should envelope, at the very least, the liberation of all women and the historical practice that has served to forge a race and class specific agenda to the exclusion of those unlike the leadership of the nineteenth and twentieth century women's movements (Hooks 1981). In other words, my comprehension is overshadowed by the images of white middle/upper class women who while embracing feminism simultaneously denied the implications of their race and class privilege. In the words of my grandmother, "Old wounds are hard to heal especially when salt is rubbed in them."

My aversion for the term in no way fails to recognize the contributions of my foremothers in spite of social marginality, their contribution to the movement or what they or my sisters brought or will bring to light in this regard. For example, at the earlier meetings of the nineteenth century suffragists' movement, black women were not only present but in the forefront, much to the consternation of their white counterparts. Even though women such as Sojourner Truth did not qualify as a woman in the nineteenth century, "cult of true womanhood" (Hooks, 1981, p. 48)—gentility, decency and of course, white skin—she defied the social etiquette of "proper women" of her time by addressing a public gathering of both men and women and furthermore bared her breasts while exclaiming "Ain't I a Woman" in response to a white male heckler who questioned her femaleness (Davis 1981; Hooks 1981). Rather than accepting this demonstrative action as an affirmation of Sojourner's femaleness, they viewed her audacious behavior as further proof of her failure to meet the criteria of "womanhood." Stereotypically, women of African descent were perceived as "immoral, licentious and insolvent" (Hooks 1981, p. 133). Yet today, Sojourner Truth has been "grandmother claused" into the mainstream literature as a champion for women's rights as if her presence at those earlier meetings were met with an overwhelming receptivity.

Historically, we have been included (or as Hooks (1981) so appropriately states, asked to join "'their' movement") when it has been politically correct, convenient and expedient. Even today, we are "told" by some white feminists to choose between our blackness and our femaleness as if it were physically and philosophically possible. In the same breath we are "advised" to choose between alliances with men of color and white females as if interracial sisterhood has been based on mutual trust and respect. As our foremothers, we have delivered the same message about the intersection of race, gender and class oppression. And, as our foremothers, we have observed "a whole lotta motion but no movement" within the core feminist tradition.

The social marginality experienced by women of African descent within the feminist/women's movement is simply symptomatic of a greater societal ill: racism, most specifically white supremacy. White women are direct benefactors of such a system and many if not most have assisted either consciously or subconsciously—as aware/blatant, aware/covert, unaware/unintentional or unaware/self-righteous racists (Yamato 1988)—in the continued subjugation of people of color. I, too, feel a part of the struggle exemplified by Sojourner Truth, Mary Church Terrell and my grandmother, Bernice Bowens. I applaud their strengths and stand on their shoulders as I commit these thoughts to paper. I also resent the disrespect and degradation they endured in society and within yet outside of the formal and informal women's movements. I must also endure the same indignities by virtue of my race and sex. So, when we discuss their accomplishments and our contributions within the context of feminism is it for lack of a more precise, culturally grounded, more African-centered term?

In her introduction of the term "womanist" into the literature, Alice Walker offers an alternative self identification that better speaks to our concerns:

> 1. From *womanish* (opposite of *girlish*, i.e., frivolous, irresponsible, not serious). A black feminist or feminist of color. From the black folk expression of mothers to female children, "You acting womanish," i.e., like a woman. Usually referring to outrageous, audacious, courageous, or *willful* behavior. Wanting to know more and in greater depth than is considered "good" for one.

Interested in grown-up doing. Acting grown-up. Being grownup. Interchangeable with another black folk expression: "You trying to be grown." Responsible. In charge. *Serious.*

2. *Also*: A woman who loves other women, sexually and/or nonsexually. Appreciates and prefers women's culture, women's emotional flexibility (values tears as natural counter-balance of laughter), and women's strength. Committed to survival and wholeness of entire people, male *and* female. Not a separatist, except periodically, for health. Traditionally universalist, as in: "Mama, why are we brown, pink, and yellow, and our cousins are white, beige, and black?" Ans: "Well, you know the colored race is just like a flower garden, with every color flower represented." Traditionally capable, as in: "Mama, I'm walking to Canada and I'm taking you and a bunch of other slaves with me." Reply: "It wouldn't be the first time."

3. Loves music. Loves dance. Loves the moon. *Loves* the Spirit. Loves love and food and roundness. Loves struggle. *Loves* the Folk. Loves herself. *Regardless.*

4. Womanist is to feminist as purple is to lavender [Alice Walker 1983, p. xi].

The fact that one may add the descriptive noun of black to feminist certainly adds credibility to the latter label and aligns the label with "pure feminism," but to quote Brown (1989, p. 10),

> Womanist can certainly mean black feminist as Walker indicates in that womanist refers to black women's struggle against gender oppression. But womanist must mean more than this. When studied against the background of her relationship with white women, a womanist is epitomized by struggle and politics of Sojourner Truth. As suggested by Walker's remark, "womanist is to feminist as purple is to lavender," there is a "shade" of difference between the meaning of feminist and womanist. Being black adds crucial historical dimensions to the fight for women's equality.

Walker's analogy between feminist/womanist and gradations of a color spectrum recognizes the primacy of womanist tradition to feminist activism and thought. Likewise, in her description of "true feminism," Steady concludes "with much justification that the black woman is to a large extent the original feminist" (1981, p. 36). Primarily, Walker's definition of womanist is written from a position of strength with a spiritual warmth that embraces a humanist stance as well as a people. Above all, womanist speaks to black women's struggle to implement survival imperatives when facing racism, sexism, classism and other types of oppression.

According to Brown (1988), womanist theology articulates the uniqueness of black women's experience, an experience overlooked by most black theologians (primarily male) and feminist theologians (primarily white). Rarely does either group address the elements of religion life that support the oppression of black women. For example,

Because of the problems associated with the maleness of Jesus, some feminist theologies either discard him as unimportant to understanding God, or de-emphasize his centrality as the Christ. Black theologies tend to ignore the oppressive quality which often results from the fact of Jesus' maleness. Womanist theology however cannot discard Jesus, de-emphasize his centrality or ignore the problematic nature of his maleness [Brown, 1988, p. 15].

As a result, a womanist Christology must question the interpretations of biblical passages that substantiate and perpetuate the subordinate position of black women in the church, home and society. As for the implications of Jesus' gender, Brown insists that the focus must be on Christ's humanitarian work and liberating power rather than his physical appearance.

In addition to Brown's work in theology, Bess also applies a womanist perspective to her scholarship. In her eloquent literary critique of Naylor's *The Women of Brewster Place* and Jones' *Corregidora*, Bess (1992) analyzes the barriers both symbolic and ideological that the society erects to keep the "untouchables" out. She writes in her conclusion,

Because womanist thought is about the coming together of a people for the collective good, and because it is about people loving and embracing each other regardless of sex or sexual orientation, class or education. It allows us, if we embrace it, to collapse "wallisms"; heterosexism, homophobia, classism, sexism and racism. In collapsing those walls we are consequently, able to raise new images of people loving, helping, sharing, needing, caring for each other. Ultimately this embrace allows us to blend our voices, share our pains and joys, join our energies and efforts to heal.

As shown in the works of Brown and Bess, the potential for application of a womanist perspective in activist scholarship across disciplines and beyond a passing reference to the concept is immense and invigorating.

However, in the process of investigating the literature of African American women in a number of disciplines who identify themselves as womanist or feminist, I recognize the potential for decisiveness arising out of the very question of terminology. Given that the expressed agendas of all these women, regardless of how they identified themselves, seem to agree with Brown's interpretation of womanist that is "the struggle to survive and be free from racism and sexism as it is manifested within the various social contexts of which black women are an integral part" (Brown, 1989, p. 12), I suggest that regardless of our preference for one term over the other we must avoid the temptation to denounce other sisters, their work and their contributions to our common cause on their seeming affiliation with the adversarial camp.

Instead of attempting to advance a humanist movement under a tainted label, I still advocate switching to womanist in the spirit of the Kwanzaa principle Kujichagalia—self determination and self definition. To quote Akinwole (Robinson, 1995, p. 22): "... part of the redefinition or just self definition of our movement will help Black women to identify with something we've created and named." In essence, I prefer the shift in terminology because it signals a strategic move from the periphery to the center. Audre Lorde once said, "You can't use the master's tool to dismantle the master's house." What I suggest is that "You also can't use Miss Ann's tool to dismantle Miss Ann's house." In closing, I must concur with Alice Walker's rationale for embracing the term:

> I choose it because I prefer the sound, the feel, the fit of it. Because I cherish the spirit of women (like Sojourner) the words call to mind and because I share the old ethnic-American habit of offering society new word when the old word it is using fails to describe behavior and change that only a new word can help it more fully see [Kramarae and Treichler 1985, p. 495].

WORKS CITED

Bess, Georgene. "Collapsing Walls, Raising New Images and Blending Voices to Heal: A Womanist Analysis of Gloria Naylor's *Women of Brewster Place* and Gail Jones' *Corregidora*." (Unpublished manuscript). (1992).

Brown, Kelly D. "God Is as Christ Does: Toward a Womanist Theology." *The Journal of Religious Thought* 46, 1 (1989): 7–16.

Davis, Angela. *Women, Race and Class*. New York: Random, 1981.

Hooks, Bell. *Ain't I a Woman: Black Women and Feminism*. Boston: South End, 1981.

Kramarae, Cheris, and Treichler, Paula A., eds. *A Feminist Dictionary*. Boston: Pandora, 1985.

Robertson, Ian. *Sociology*, 3rd ed. New York: Worth, 1987.

Robinson, Lori S. "A Feminist Vision." *Emerge* (March 1995): 20–23.

Steady, Filomena. "The Black Woman Cross-culturally: An Overview." In Filomena Steady, ed., *The Black Woman Cross-Culturally*. Cambridge: Schenkman, 1981; pp. 7–41.

Yamato, Gloria. "Something About the Subject Makes It Hard to Name." Rpt in Margaret L. Andersen and Patricia H. Collins, comps. (1995). *Race Class and Gender: An Anthology*, 2nd ed., pp. 71–75. Belmont, California: Wadsworth.

Walker, Alice. *In Search of Our Mothers' Gardens, Womanist Prose*. New York: Harcourt Brace Jovanovich, 1983.

14. On the Myth of Male Supremacy: Adam and Eve and the Imperative of a New Afrikan-Centered Epistemology of Gender

Ahati N.N. Toure

The strength of the notion of male supremacy, like the notion of white supremacy, rests merely and solely in the fact that people believe it to be true. Aside from the fact that neither notion is factually compelling and can be facilely dismissed on any number of grounds, the tenaciousness with which far too many men and women feel compelled to cling to them is rather remarkable. In European societies, and in various non–European societies profoundly influenced by European culture, the conceptual validity of sexism is deeply and fundamentally rooted in the divine sanction of the Judaeo-Christian religious tradition. It is, indeed, a strange state of affairs, especially when one considers that, with scant critical examination, the myth of male supremacy as illustrated in the biblical myth of Genesis is, at best, a clumsy and thinly-veiled attempt not only to justify and maintain male hegemony within the social order, but reveals itself to be a rather bitter, and perhaps unwitting, expression of male envy of the female.

The reason, however, that sexism has become so entrenched and nearly ineradicable in social belief (and we are particularly concerned with United States Afrikan culture) is that no one has created an alternative, egalitarian and Afrikan-focused epistemology of gender—that is to say, a global and fundamental understanding of the nature and purpose of human existence that also explains the significance of gender specification, differentiation and inter-relation within the cosmic and social orders. All that exists at present is the inadequacy of an epistemology of gender inherited from the Bible, the Adam and Eve story, and the criticisms and weaknesses of that epistemology.[1] The challenge and the imperative for the Afrocentric development and revitalization of United States Afrikan culture is to create an explanatory myth that redefines values and ontology in such a way as to establish a new cosmic (or spiritual) and social understanding that is more humanistic, egalitarian and productive for Afrikan community. Until we recreate such an epistemology for ourselves, all that will exist is the epistemological hegemony and corruption of the Adam and Eve myth.

The story is almost universally known. A male creator god, toward the conclusion of his creation, decides to make a being in *his* own image and likeness. The resulting creature, manufactured from the earth and into which the god personally breathes life, is a male. The male is then made master of all the male god has created. Before him are paraded all the animals of the god's creation, whom the male names, thus indicating his authority over the lesser creation. As an afterthought, the male creator god realizes that the male creature is alone and that none of the animals his creature has named is a fit partner for him. "It is not good that man should be alone," the creator god says. The god subsequently anesthetizes his male creature, during which time he performs an operation, removing a rib, out of which he fashions a female. He awakens the male, presents the female to him, and the male names her. The god then tells them to be fruitful and multiply and to jointly exercise dominion over all creation.

Later, a serpent—which not before the first century B.C.E. becomes identified as Satan[2]—enters the picture and persuades the woman to eat the one thing forbidden them in all creation: the fruit of the tree of the knowledge of good and evil. The woman, disobeying the god's commandment, swayed by the serpent's beguiling words, eats the fruit and gives it to her husband, who also eats and who had been all the while standing alongside listening to the conversation.[3] As a consequence, they become estranged from their creator, who in anger throws them out of the paradise in which he had originally placed them, punishing the man with hard labor, the woman with painful childbirth and enslavement to her husband,[4] and both of them with mortality.[5]

Of course, for Biblical apologists what preceded represents a gruesome distortion. To them the story of the creation of humanity—at least before the expulsion from paradise—bespeaks of the sublime egalitarianism of the genders. Writes Nahum M. Sarna: "Both sexes are created on the sixth day by the hand of the one God; both are made 'in His image' on a level of absolute equality before Him. Thus the concept of humanity needs both male and female for its proper articulation."[6] Consistent with this thesis, some Biblical scholars point to the accounts of human creation in Genesis 1 and 2 as authored by two differing traditions—one egalitarian, the other patriarchal.

Genesis 1:27 reads: "And God created man in His image, in the image of God He created him; male and female He created them."[7] In these words biblical apologists see the intimation of a simultaneous, as opposed to ordinal, creation. Even if that were the case, however, the "egalitarian" interpretation is, at best, vague, fragmentary and fleeting, drowned in a flood of unabashed patriarchy throughout the entire Judaeo-Christian text. The central figures in this story are the male creator god and the male creature he has made; the woman exists only in relationship to the purposes of the male egos. She is an object and not a subject of the tale.

There are a number of examples to illustrate this. In the first instance, although male and female are created in the same day, the male is created first and the male is created alone. The female is created for the male's benefit and not for her own or even the god's benefit. The male even names her—she does not name herself—as he had earlier named the animals, implicitly demonstrating his god-given authority over her. Not only does the man name the woman before the expulsion from paradise, but he names her after the expulsion as well,[8] when the male god curses the woman for disobedience, saying "I will make most severe your pangs in childbearing; in pain shall you bear children. Yet your urge shall be for your husband, and he shall rule over you."[9] Hence, male supremacy does not arise as a consequence of estrangement from god, but as a consequence of the natural order the male creator god instituted from the very beginning.

The fact that ancient Hebrew society was misogynistic reveals that the interpretation of male supremacy as arising from a "fall from grace" cannot be upheld. For if egalitarianism were the ideal the male creator god had intended, egalitarianism, like obedience to god, would have been a good advocated by the religious and social order. Nothing about the Genesis story—either before or after the expulsion—contradicts this impression. The fundamentalists La Sor, Hubbard and Bush admit as much, albeit they do so rather lamely, when they observe that the notions that informed the male creator god's ordination of female subjugation

> show a certain amount of cultural conditioning; they reflect the social milieu and institutions of ancient Israel through which vehicle, under divine inspiration, they were formulated and set down. This is reflected especially with regard to the status of the woman, who was little more in the ancient world than a chattel of her husband.[10]

The notion of human superiority and inferiority, which is central to the gender myth, brings us to the issue of the qualitative nature of being. It is on this question that woman is cast—by virtue of the order in which and the purpose for which she was created—in the subordinate and inferior role. In fact, in the Genesis myth, which is fundamentally an epistemology of gender, not only is the female made (ontologically) to serve the needs and interests of a male, but the debate legitimately extends to whether she is even as human (ontologically) as the male, contrary to Sarna's rather charitable interpretation. The apostle Paul, perhaps the chief of misogynists,[11] makes this point quite clearly in one of his epistles when he writes that man "is the image and glory of God; *but woman is the glory of man* [emphasis mine]."[12] Indeed, Paul bases male supremacy on the nature of the order of creation, declaring that "man *did not come from* woman, but *woman from man*; neither was man created for woman, but woman for man [emphasis mine]."[13] It is, as well, on the basis of the creation that he declares: "A woman should learn in quietness and full submission. I do not permit a woman to teach or to have authority over a man; she must be silent. *For Adam was formed first, then Eve* [emphasis mine]."[14] Clearly, it is because the female is inferior as a matter of ontology, as a consequence of the creative order, that women are instructed to "submit to their husbands *in everything* [emphasis mine]."[15]

Nor is Paul's interpretation that women are less human than men because they were not created in the image of God an utterly implausible or extremist position. The language of the so-called egalitarian tradition is both curious and striking. It reads: "in the image of God He created *him*; male and female He created *them* [emphasis mine]."[16] The message of both Paul and the Genesis myth is unambiguous. Woman is inferior to man. She is less human or not quite as human as man. She is one step removed from the image of the divine (male god). She is, in essence, merely a refraction of the divine image, connected to it only because of and through the man. Such an observation is inescapable. And it can never be overemphasized that the divine is not female. In other words (and this is what the tradition is really saying; it cannot be explained away), only the male is created in the image of god!

The apostle Peter is essentially in agreement. No less sexist, but perhaps less strident than Paul, Peter in more avuncular fashion urges that wives adorn themselves in "the unfading beauty of a gentle and quiet spirit"—a demeanor most pleasing to the male god—and emulate the wifely submissiveness of the women of old, "like Sarah, who obeyed Abraham and called him master."[17] Husbands, on the other hand, are advised to live with their wives patiently, knowing she is the weaker sex because she is a woman.[18]

Paul's male supremacist argument does, however, bring up a point that bears closer scrutiny precisely because it makes no logical or experiential sense and because it exposes the hidden agenda of the creation tale—the justification of a male supremacist social order motivated by envy of the female. It is his Biblically-based assertion that man does not come from woman, a claim that is absurd on its face because it is a denial of irrefutable fact. No man in history—not even Jesus—can or could ever claim that he did not come from a woman.[19] Adam is the only man in "history" for whom the claim is made.[20] But if Adam had no mother, why is he the exception to all other men? Or put another way, why is the woman now giving birth to both men and women?

Why did Adam cease to give birth to anyone after Eve? Why is it that not a single man in history has given birth to anyone?

One of the most glaring contradictions in patriarchal Judaeo-Christian mythology is precisely this treatment of the life-giving function. It was man who gave birth to woman. The life-giving function was given to man, but notably and curiously, through an unnatural operation of the male god. Man did not give birth to woman by any natural process. It was the intervention of a male creator god—an extraordinary and unusual act—that gave birth to woman. Then, even more strangely, when man and woman are expelled from paradise, the life-giving function is transferred to the woman, albeit in the form of a punishment. Nowhere is it explained how the woman receives the power to give life that originates with the man, nor why the life-giving function is a curse to the woman when it was not to the man. Nor are we told why the man does not retain the power to give life to humankind.

It is obvious the writers could not plausibly conceive of man giving life. That is why it took an extraordinarily unusual and unduplicable act of god for man to give life to woman. No one then or now can understand how a man can give birth naturally, which is why an operation was devised as an inept and awkward explanation. This also explains why the woman's life-giving ability is first introduced as a punishment by the male creator god. Because of man's envy of the woman's ability to give life, the writers of Genesis created the myth of a male god who would curse the woman's life-giving function. The mythology of male supremacy, then, arises from envy of the life-giving power of the woman's body, a manifestation of his own feeling of ontological inferiority. To convince women of their inferiority, the man had to create the notion that the divine-like power of the woman's ontology was accursed, and to facilitate that the nature of the genesis of the human experience, or an epistemology of gender, had to be falsified and usurped.

It is clear that the life-giving power of the woman's womb makes her more like the divine because it is the power to give life that is the power of divine creation. Hence, it is really woman who is more logically created in the image of the creator god, making the creator god female rather than male. The Judaeo-Christian construction appears merely a reversal of what is the more logical and natural construction on any myth concerning human origins.[21] And in this vein, it appears that the sustained attack on woman in the Genesis story represents a projection of man's own ontological insecurity, his profound sense of inadequacy and inferiority in the face of superior woman in a female-centric universe. The Genesis account, from this perspective, presents itself as a fraudulent account of human origins, as an epistemological usurpation of the natural or divine order by means of a falsified religious text. Upon close examination, the story reads much too clumsily even to pass as persuasive fiction. What the authors constructed in Genesis was, apparently, a part of a socio-cultural putsch, a repudiation of either a female-dominated or egalitarian, but female-centric, social order.[22]

Further, the myth flies patently and headlong in the face of human experience. Among humans, it is woman who comes first, not man. This cannot be overstated. Woman is the source of life and its sustenance. With sober reflection, the magnitude of the epistemological subversion that the Genesis myth has engendered can with difficulty be properly appreciated. The Adam and Eve story is a stultifying falsification, if only because over several millennia male supremacists, by virtue of the Bible's authority as "the Word of God," have successfully declaimed the primacy of man when experience demonstrates daily, inexorably, the indisputable primacy of woman. This is not to suggest a womanist supremacy; it is simply to acknowledge the reality of the human experience. It is a simple recognition of the truth.[23]

Perhaps the most powerful argument in favor of this conclusion comes—remarkably and ironically enough—not from skeptics but from the fundamentalists La Sor, Hubbard and Bush, who, in a paroxysm of double-talk, academic foot-in-mouth and the classic fallacy of circular reasoning, underscore the fact that the Genesis tale had an epistemological intent (although we are dismissing their description of that intent) and establish beyond doubt the fictionality of its account. In their *Old Testament Survey: The Message, Form and Background of the Old Testament* the authors state (with what appears to be some slight embarrassment) that the creation story cannot be taken literally because it is fiction. The Genesis author, they admit, "is writing as an artist, a story teller, who uses literary device and artifice."[24] In fact, they continue,

> Recognizing the literary technique and form and noting the literary background of [Genesis] chs. 1-11 does not constitute a challenge to the reality, the "eventness," of the facts portrayed. One need not regard this account as myth; however it is not "history" in the modern sense of eyewitness, objective reporting. Rather, it conveys theological truths about events, portrayed in largely symbolic, pictorial literary genre. This is not to say that Gen. 1-11 conveys historical falsehood. That conclusion would follow only if it purported to contain objective descriptions. The clear evidence already reviewed shows that such was not the intent. On the other hand, the view that the truths taught in these chapters have no objective basis is mistaken. They affirm fundamental truths: creation of all things by God; special divine intervention in the production of the first man and woman; unity of the human race; pristine goodness of the created world, including humanity; entrance of sin through disobedience of the first pair; depravity and rampant sin after the Fall. All these truths are facts, and their certainty implies the reality of the facts.[25]

The damage, of course, has been done. And perhaps realizing this, the authors attempt to rescue their explanation from the perilously intractable contradictions of their faith and their scholarship, noting in a final and suicidal effort: "Put another way, the biblical author uses literary traditions to describe unique events *that have no time-conditioned, human-conditioned, experience-based historical analogy* and hence can be described only by symbol [emphasis mine]."[26]

What emerges, then, (and this is why these admissions are so remarkable), is that the Adam and Eve account never happened; it is fiction, imaginary. Absent any historical validity, it can, for the Christian, only be embraced as an article of faith despite the fact it purports to speak of "truths" or "events" that cannot be based in any time or place and that involved no real people. Understood realistically, its intent is evidently epistemological and ideological: to refute prevailing Near Eastern mythological conceptions of the female-centric nature of the cosmos and to justify the validity of male supremacy as a normative value in the Hebrew social order.

Barbara G. Walker makes precisely this point when she notes that Adam's birth-giving to Eve merely constituted a "syncretic product of numerous local notions of the male mother." To construct the creation myth, the ancient Hebrews drew from sources that included the Hittites and the Sumerians (Near Eastern Afrikans).

> The idea for Adam's birth-giving rib came from Sumerian childbirth-goddess, Nin-ti, 'Lady of the Rib.' Since *ti* means both 'rib' and 'life,' she was also Lady of Life. She made infants' bones *in utero* from their mother's ribs, which is why biblical writers thought ribs possessed the magic of maternity.[27]

She further observes that the concept of the "male mother" became a psychological imperative in the male supremacist quest to formulate a new understanding of the qualitative nature of gender because "it was hard for men to see themselves as perfect, when they conspicuously lacked the ability to bring forth and nurture new members of their race. This endless quest for superiority nearly always required some travesty of motherhood."[28] Hence, in the same way that European ("white") supremacists fraudulently appropriated Afrikan history and cultural contributions as their own, the male supremacist authors of the Genesis myth appropriated feminine models to legitimize their quest for hegemony. The correspondence is sobering. But it also underscores the fact that there were no uniquely masculine models of divinity to appropriate![29]

Again, the fundamentalists La Sor, Hubbard and Bush reluctantly admit to the tremendous degree to which the ancient Hebrews were influenced by and borrowed from other cultures when they claim that shared themes and elements between Hebrew and other Near Eastern mythologies is a reflection of "a diffuse influence or common cultural atmosphere." While, for their part, this fact does not disprove divine inspiration or originality of the Hebrew version (the notion that Hebrew myth is derivative), it does demonstrate that the Genesis "narrative moves in the same circle of ideas and that the inspired authors of the primeval prologue knew and drew on material and manner of speaking about origins that was part of their cultural and literary tradition."[30]

Indeed, Walker's case is made more compelling by such admissions, especially because the Genesis account demonstrably lacks the originality of alleged divine inspiration and constitutes, instead, a mere revision of contemporary mythology.

> The biblical idea was a reversal of older myths in which the Goddess brought forth a primal male ancestor, then made him her mate—the ubiquitous, archetypal divine-incest relationship traceable in every mythology. The reversal was not even original with biblical authors. It was evolved by Aryan patriarchs who called Brahma the primal male ancestor. They claimed their god brought forth the Mother of All Living from his own body, then mated with her, so she gave birth to the rest of the universe. In the Hebraic version, a wombless God made his offspring with his hands, and the actual birth-giving was left to Adam. The Bible as revised by patriarchal scribes said nothing about divine birth-giving, since the scribes were determined to separate the concepts of "deity" and "mother" insofar as possible.[31]

That the Genesis account of the beginnings of the human social order is fictional is also well established on the ground of history and anthropology.

> The idea of the primacy of patriarchy, with its male head and a subordinate position for women was held to be the very foundation of human society. This theory is no longer tenable, for we now know that the patriarchal family was not the primal human group. The first type of family was matriarchal, since the role of the father in procreation was unknown. ... The evidence at hand points to the conclusion that the primordial human group consisted not of a father and their descendants, but instead, of a mother and her descendants in the female line, since no other line of descent was then known.[32]

Naturally, then, the supreme and universal deities in the older matriarchal societies were female, while in succeeding patriarchal societies, a supreme male god was created.[33] The former situation, however, evolved from an understanding that women were both socially and cosmologically a powerful force in the world.

> Prehistoric woman was ... assertive and forthright on her own, sometimes wielding the power of a god.... Some [prehistoric cave art] works show her as Primal Mother Creator, with fertilizing and nurturing powers which extended from the firmaments down into the earth below. Her powers of fertility in the universe were not confined to human beings but could be magnified to affect vegetation, animal husbandry, and the atmosphere. Because of her contact with the atmosphere, she too was Rainmaker. In times of severe crisis such as extremes of drought, it was the female, a virgin, who was sacrificed, because her fertilizing capacity was thought to be potent

enough to bring down showers to slake the thirst of humanity. Woman was the "Giver of Life." She was also the "Mother Killer," associated with the symbol of the vulture, thus equipped to scavenge whatever was necessary for the race to survive.[34]

What is particularly intriguing about this are the powerful cosmological and sociological connections to woman. It is the woman's capacity to give and to sustain life in human experience that is understood as an analogy of the nature of the operative power or force in the universe, and this leads to the conception of the divine in terms of the physical, earthly capacity of the female's power. Hence, humankind's earliest and original understanding of the cosmos—and we cannot forget that these are ancestral understandings— was female-centric. The female deity was "in the earliest times ... an all-encompassing influence and was universally acknowledged as the greatest and ultimate seat of power. She was both the giver and sustainer of life."[35] In other words, the divine was understood to be in the image of woman, not man! This conception of woman as linked to cosmological forces had, obviously then, corresponding implications for the status of women within the social order.

In North Afrika, as in Central/East Afrika, where we witness the beginnings of our ancestral conceptions of the divine, we find the goddess Neith, "one of the earliest of North African goddesses," who can be "traced back to at least 4000 B.C. She is one of the 'oldest of all the gods, who was already when nothing else existed.' Like Ptah, she was self-begotten and self-produced."[36] In the same way Isis (Aset), the great goddess of ancient Kemet, declared of herself:

> I am Nature, the universal Mother, mistress of all the elements, primordial child of time, sovereign of all things spiritual, queen of the dead, queen also of the immortals, the single manifestation of all gods and goddesses that are. My god governs the shining heights of Heaven, the wholesome sea-breezes, the lamentable silences of the world below.[37]

Similarly, Rosalind Jeffries observes that the oldest Akan conception of the divine was female, a Supreme Mother.

> Her name was Atoapoma and she was said by them to be self-begotten, self-produced and self-born, eternal and infinite. She created the firmament with its stars and sun and she did so without the help of a male partner. ... She was venerated not only as the "Giver of Life" but also "the Giver of Death." She was Odiawuono, literally "the Mother Killer," mother of the living, mother of the dead, the sky and earth. Her underworld reference was envisioned as the barren soil in which the dead lay buried.[38]

Consequently, what the evidence demonstrates is that the Genesis myth was created for a specific purpose and that it entailed a reinterpretation of existing myth and the appropriation of existing themes and elements to serve a new social purpose. In the United States Afrikan case, our quest is a repudiation of existing male supremacist Judaeo-Christian myth and an appropriation from Afrikan myth of a set of presuppositions and paradigms that can establish the ground for understanding the distinctions of gender and their interrelation in the social order. The emphasis is primarily ethical, but it is important to look also at the cosmological issues that are extant within myth and their implications for Afrocentric spiritual and social understanding. There must take place, then, not only a redefinition of the nature and purpose and interrelation of men and women in the social order that we are creating, but a redefinition of the divine, as well. It is evident that the invention of the Judaeo-Christian god in the Genesis myth represented precisely that: a redefinition of the divine in the male image; it was in a very real sense an idolatry (by Judaeo-Christian standards), for the original human conceptions (which were simultaneously Afrikan) were female, and the nature of the first human social order was female-centric. It is not altogether clear as to whether these were female supremacist orders. What is clear is that both women and men recognized the centrality of women in the social and cosmological orders due in part to ignorance of the male role in human reproduction, but equally in recognition of the primary and vital role that women played in the sustenance of human life and its significance for continued human existence and society.

For sexism to be eradicated in United States Afrikan culture, it must be attacked on the level of epistemology—just as the prevailing Near Eastern female-centric notions were eradicated within ancient Hebrew society through the invention of a male supremacist epistemology in Genesis. A new, Afrikan-centered model of understanding the divine and the nature and purpose of human existence must be forged. It is, of course, not important that it be explained purely on the level of scientific materialism (which, in any event, is a Eurocentric paradigm). The Afrikan mentality requires that it be forged, as well, on the level of "scientific spiritualism," on our recognition that there is a metaphysical dimension to human experience—a dynamic interactiveness—that invests the material dimension with meaning and vitality. This new epistemology will entail, then, a reconceptualization of the nature of gender interrelations and differences that serve as lessons for the roles of men and women in United States Afrikan society and family. It will even call forth the necessity of the creation of new language—both gender specific that is denuded of the derogatory meanings associated with the female, and gender neutral that allows for a true equality of gender.

In any event, we are not seeking to obliterate differences and distinctiveness, but to create a cultural atmosphere that is accepting of them and that celebrates them. The social imperative for Afrikan men and women is the attainment of a new ontology of Maat, a state of spiritual, intellectual and emotional being in which Afrikan women and men can engender mutual respect, love, support, balance, interconnectedness and Afrikan community. One must never forget that myth serves social need, that it is a human creation subordinated to a specified social purpose (or that, in its passive aspect, it is an understanding that reflects material conditions and imperatives). For the United States Afrikan people, it is only with the emplacement of a new epistemology of gender that we can arrive at a paradigm upon which we can interpret and define Afrocentric human society. Our social purpose is to so strengthen the bonds of our nation through a new vision of community that we can ensure liberation for all of us.

NOTES

1. Evolutionary science offers another epistemology as to human existence—namely, that humans were evolved and not created—but it does not offer an epistemology of human purpose, as does the Genesis myth. Nor does it offer an explanation of the purpose and interrelations of genders within the cosmological and social orders. It is incomplete. What it does not explain is simply filled in by the explanatory power of the Adam and Eve myth, which is why the language of science references to the emergence of "Man" and "Mankind" in discussions of the evolutionary process. There can be no mankind without womankind; therefore, to talk of Man without Woman is to be both ahistorical and supremely arrogant. The human experience begins with the female. The fact that this is never mentioned demonstrates the continued epistemological preeminence of the Genesis myth in European and European-influenced cultures as it relates to the contemporary understanding of gender and human ontology.

2. Nahum M. Sarna, ed., *The JPS Torah Commentary: Genesis,* Philadelphia: The Jewish Publication Society, 1989, p. 24.

3. *Ibid.,* p. 25. Paul argues in 1 Timothy 2 that Eve was deceived. But if Adam was there listening to the conversation, why did he eat? Was he not also deceived? Paul's charge against Eve—in the context of his condemnation of a woman teaching a man—goes really to the question of a woman's intelligence. He is very simply saying that a woman is not intelligent enough to teach a man anything because she is weak-minded, gullible.

4. Enslavement is not by any means too strong a characterization, as the fundamentalists William Sanford La Sor, David Allan Hubbard and Frederick William Bush admit in *Old Testament Survey: The Message, Form and Background of the Old Testament* (Grand Rapids, Mich.: William B. Eerdmans, 1982), p. 84.

5. Genesis 2:4–3:24.

6. Sarna, *The JPS Torah,* p. 13.

7. *Ibid.,* pp. 11–13.

8. Genesis 3:20.

9. Genesis 3:16 (*JPS Torah*). Interestingly, John G. Jackson in *Introduction to African Civilizations* (New York: Carol Publishing Group, 1990), p. 55, notes that males established patriarchy, among other reasons, to control female sexuality. The language here speaks directly to that interest.

10. La Sor et al., *Old Testament,* p. 84. One wonders if they are arguing that misogyny was ignored or acquiesced to by their god. If so, misogyny was not, apparently, a sin to their god but an acceptable form of belief and practice. How can that be if woman is made in the image of their god?

11. Paul in 1 Timothy 1:15 (King James Version) called himself the chief of sinners because he persecuted the church. Aside from the pun, Paul is singularly harsh and abusive in his statements about women.

12. 1 Corinthians 11:7 (New International Version).

14. On the Myth of Male Supremacy 191

13. 1 Corinthians 11:8–9 (NIV).
14. 1 Timothy 2:11–13 (NIV).
15. Ephesians 5:24 (NIV).
16. Hence, although both were formed on the same day, they are not equals, which is the same thing as saying they were not formed simultaneously. Had they been, we would reasonably have expected to read language of this nature: "in the image of God He created *them*; male and female He created *them*." In the *First Book of Adam and Eve* in *The Lost Books of the Bible and the Forgotten Books of Eden* (World Bible Publishers, Inc., nd.), p. 7, we have this interpretation, Eve speaking: "and Thou didst make me after the likeness of his [Adam's] countenance, by Thy mercy and power. O Lord, I and he are one, and Thou, O God, art our Creator. Thou are He who made us both in one day."
17. 1 Peter 3:4–6 (NIV).
18. 1 Peter 3:7 (New American Standard Version).
19. Perhaps ironically, the Christian gospels claim that Jesus had no human father. The idea of not having a mother was inconceivable. In this sense, I suppose it is inappropriate for Jesus to be seen as the "second Adam."
20. The Adam and Eve story, in any event, is admittedly a fictional tale, and as such, has no historical validity, making Paul's contention even more absurd. See La Sor et al., *Old Testament*, pp. 72, 74. On page 72 they write: "Surely, when an author of a story names the principal characters Mankind and Life, something is conveyed about the degree of literalness intended!"
21. Perhaps androgyny fits even better as an explanation. Although it seems a later formulation, it appears *the most logical*. An androgynous god, as in the Kemite god Amon, is both female and male, although it is unclear if the masculine character predominates. Inasmuch, however, as the human species is male and female, it would seem that a creator god would be expected to reflect that dualism. See Cheikh Anta Diop, *The African Origin of Civilization: Myth or Reality* (Westport, Conn.: Lawrence Hill, 1974), pp. 112, 137.
   Rosalind Jeffries notes in "The Image of Women in African Cave Art" in Ivan Van Sertima, ed., *Black Women in Antiquity* (New Brunswick, N.J.: Transaction Books, 1989), p. 103, that in Akan belief, the supreme god Nyame "is thought to be strong enough to encompass both genders, male and female, or else conceived of as beyond the abstract idea of sexual identity." She also notes this conception contains a male dominance and is more recent than an originally female conception.
   Interesting, as well, is the Dogon conception of human ontology. Diop observes in *African Origin*, p. 137, that circumcision of male and female is intended to remove the ontological gender ambiguity of infants, since, like the divine, they are believed to be born into a certain degree of androgyny.
22. This kind of thinking and behavior is very Aryan (European) in character, and suggests the Aryan origin of this aspect of ancient Hebrew culture. For Afrikans, among other majority world peoples, it is a familiar modality and rationality, clearly reflected in the construction and practice of white supremacy; the xenophobic psycho-cultural dynamics of superiority/inferiority strongly suggest the possibility of European thought and behavior. It is because of this that one may speculate that perhaps what the authors were rejecting was the influence of a foreign—most likely Afrikan—matriarchal culture. The establishment of patriarchy may have been allied with a rejection of Afrikan cultural norms and influence. After all, the Hebrews claim to have been enslaved in Kemet, a claim that is doubtful, but that underscores a certain level of hostility toward the country and culture. Certainly the cultural insularity and chauvinism that is manifest in Old Testament religion is worth noting, particularly in light of the cultural indebtedness of Hebrew culture to other Near Eastern and continental Afrikan cultures. This fact provides a context in which to seek a connection for what is evidently an epistemological refutation of all non Hebrew (possibly Aryan) cultural influences and the ideological justification for a new, and patriarchal, social order.
   Interestingly, Jackson in *Introduction*, p. 94, quotes the ancient Greek historian Diodorus Siculus regarding common Kemite social practice. According to Diodorus, " 'Among private citizens ... the husband by terms of the marriage agreement, appertains to the wife, and it is stipulated between them that the man shall obey the woman in all things.' " It is worth noting, however, that Diodorus was a European man. His statement could well have been an extreme interpretation of the Afrikan situation, representing the hard-line misogyny of his own society

and, consequently, overstating the degree of egalitarianism in the Afrikan one. Ifi Amadiume, for example, observes in *Afrikan Matriarchal Foundations: The Igbo Case* (London: Karnak House, 1987), p. 84, that despite the existence of matriarchal systems "men sought incessantly to control women and their services, and succeeded more often than not."

23. Even the patriarchal writers of the Genesis myth call woman "The Mother of All Living" and "The Giver of Life." To have been consistent, they should have called her "The Mother of All Living Except One" and "The Giver of Life To All But One." If woman is, indeed, "The Mother of All Living" and "The Giver of Life," then she is obviously and unarguably first.

24. La Sor et al., *Old Testament*, p. 72.

25. *Ibid.*, p. 74.

26. *Ibid.*

27. Barbara G. Walker, *The Woman's Encyclopedia of Myths and Secrets*, New York: HarperCollins, 1983, pp. 107-108.

28. *Ibid.*, p. 109.

29. Daniel P. Reid makes this statement in his *The Tao of Health, Sex and Longevity* (New York: Fireside, 1989), p. 282: "Taoists advocate living in complete harmony with the great patterns of nature, and they venerate womanhood precisely because women are by nature far closer to the primordial powers of the cosmos than men."

30. La Sor et al., *Old Testament*, p. 74.

31. Walker, *Woman's Encyclopedia*, p. 298.

32. Jackson, *Introduction*, p. 51.

33. *Ibid.*, p. 56.

34. Jeffries, Image, p. 98.

35. Runoko Rashidi, "African Goddesses: Mothers of Civilization," in Ivan Van Sertima, ed., *Black Women in Antiquity*, New Brunswick, N.J.: Transaction Books, 1989, p. 72.

36. *Ibid.*, p. 73.

37. Eloise McKinney-Johnson, "Egypt's Isis: The Original Black Madonna," in Ivan Van Sertima, ed., *Black Women in Antiquity*, New Brunswick, N.J.: Transaction Books, 1989, p. 66.

38. Jeffries, "Image," p. 103.

Part Four:
Cultural Aesthetics

15. Culture, Language, and Symbols in Africana Studies: An Etymological Study

James L. Conyers, Jr., Ph.D.
Associate Professor of Black Studies
Chair, Department of Black Studies
The University of Nebraska at Omaha

Introduction: Rationale and Context

There is an Akan proverb that reads, "Wisdom Is Not Like Money to Be Tied Up and Hidden."[1] Often times African Americans do not connect their individualism to their ancestral communalism. This is a given, considering the exodus of Africans to America was the result of involuntary migration. Na'im Akbar and Wade Nobles explain this phenomena of inter-connectedness as the "KA." Nobles explains this metaphysical conceptualization of spirituality by writing, "Conceptually or more accurately the intuitive vision of the Ancients saw no firm and final dividing line between gods and men. To the ancients, all elements of the universe were consubstantial. That is to say the nature of all things were of the same spirit or KA."[2] The objective set forth in this essay is to examine culture, language, and symbols in Africana studies. The paradigmatic emphasis is to conduct an etymological study of the enterprise of Africana Studies. Africana Studies regulates an academic discipline; as such, a common state of mind and language are the essential grounds for the development and transcendence of a discipline. There have been arguments presented by scholars of African and European descent questioning the issue of commonality in African American culture from continental Africa. Admittedly, these scholars thought about African culture being the result of survival techniques and strategies of slavery. Lorenzo Dow Turner, in his study on African oral retention in the Gullah community, advances the notion of linguistic survival in African American patterns of speech. Margaret Wade-Lewis defines the term Gullah as, "...an American

English-based creole spoken along the coast of Georgia, South Carolina, and in the Sea Islands."[3] To explore his thesis, I conducted an interview with Mrs. Agnes Dingle, who was raised in the Gullah community. She confirmed the ideas and theories of Turner on the survival and retention of West African culture in this community.[4] From my examination of linguistics, I have found they offer an alternative and culturally aesthetic method of studying language with emphasis on African phenomena from an Afrocentric perspective.

Keto expounds on the use of language from an African-centered perspective as pluriversal for the advancement of African people worldwide. His analysis is the following:

> Language is so important, when we communicate about Africa, Africans and the descendants of Africans in the Americas, Europe and Asia that adopting the criterion of European language use as an organizing principal of understanding the African reality has profound implications. We can arrange the study of Africa, the Caribbean or the Americas into Anglophone, Francophone, Lusophone or Hispanic areas.... However, when we study, integrate and analyze this same literature with literature in Arabic, Yoruba, Akan, Wolof, Kiswahili, Amharic, Chibemba, Hausa, Zezuru, Isizulu and Sesotho, we are closer to employing a truly Africa-centered perspective of the literature because what binds the literatures together is the African's experience and not simply the medium of expressing that experience.[5]

Asante addresses language liberation by writing:

> All language is epistemic. Our language provides our understanding of our reality. A revolutionary language must not befuddle; it cannot be allowed to confuse. Critics must actively pursue the clarification of public language when we believe it is designed to whiten issues. We know through science and rhetoric, they are parallel systems of epistemology. Rhetoric is art and art is as much a way of knowing as science. When the oppressor seeks to use language for the manipulation of our reality; Nommo, for ourselves, and of ourselves, must continue the correct path of critical analysis.[6]

The issue of language and choice of terms identifies the ideological location and repertoire—this refers to the cosmology, epistemology and ontology of the subject. Data and analysis will decide where the researcher can advance, neutralize and interpret phenomena. Method and theory are critical tools of analysis for procedure, examination, critique and review of the commonalities in the African Diaspora experience, in the form of culture, language, and symbols.

Indeed, the use of terms transforms one's thinking. In presenting this chapter from an Afrocentric perspective, I've attempted to conduct a qualitative study to substantiate the merit of my proposition. Thus, use of indigenous African terms assist method and theory in developing African centrality in this study. Equally important, African languages allow me the opportunity to study African American culture and history from an Afrocentric cosmology. The rationale and context of this study is two-fold: (1) to illustrate the impact and effect of culture, language, and symbols in Africana Studies; and (2) provide an Afrocentric perspective of linguistic pedagogical studies. Indigenous African languages valorize Africana scholars studies to express ideas from a cultural and intellectual mode of communication. For example, Marimba Ani has written about the inter-relationship of culture and language in this way:

> The argument of Europeans is all too easy for us to accept. We look around us and, while in the Caribbean and in the black communities of South America, African retention are often quite visible, black existence in North America is problematical. "How are we African?" We blacks ask. We do not know where to look for likeness? Not knowing ourselves, we have not known how to recognize manifestations of our heritage. If we look deep enough, we will find that our deepest beliefs are shared beliefs, and that deep within we are one people.[7]

Asante adds:

> ...Okomofo Anokye, who lived in Ghana during the seventeenth century. Anokye helped to construct a set of concepts that applied to the spiritual kinship. Thus, *okra, sunsum, ntoro,* and *mogya* represent the major components of the individual. The *okra* is a person's destiny or mission; *sunsum* is character, genius, morality. *Ntoro,* from one's father, is personality; and *mogya* is blood which one inherits from his or her mother.[8]

Janet Cheatham Bell goes on to write:

> I had always known, that multifarious images abound in the languages we use. These images are both fecund and powerful whether the quotation is from the oral tradition of an indigenous African language, or written/spoken in one of the several European languages that people of African descent have made their own.[9]

This chapter attempts to describe and evaluate culture, language, and symbols in Africana studies: develop critical thinking and query the use of indigenous African languages in the disciplinary matrix of Africana Studies. Ani advocates the necessity of a linguistic transformation and transcendence, from an Afrocentric perspective, writing:

> Retention in other areas are fascinating and point to the strength and resilience of African culture; but many of these retention have already been well examined and they do not help to explain how all of us are African. The attempt to understand our experience in North America, however, has something critical to teach us about ourselves throughout the diaspora.[10]

Wade-Lewis provides insightful analysis on this issue, stating: Africanism is not only important because it provides proof.

African Diasporic vernacular and ebonics are secondary analysis qualifying the language issue. Whereas the use of indigenous African languages in Africana Studies is not to underscore the use of English, but rather, a procedure of studying African phenomena from an African-centered perspective. An Afrocentric cosmology regulates a synthesis to use language as a cultural tool of expression. Karenga notes, "Blassingame observes that most distinctive survivals or retention are dances, folktales, music, magic, and language patterns."[11] Folktales, proverbs, names and other uses of oral communication illustrate, in general, the interconnectedness between African Americans and continental Africans.

Significance of Culture

Queries raised to discuss the relevance and significance of culture, language, and symbols are the following: (1) What is the necessity of using indigenous African terms in Africana studies? and (2) Does an etymological study of Africana studies present a counter-cultural perspective of American higher education?

First, I propose the use of indigenous African languages will allow Africana Studies scholars the opportunity to develop a linguistic epistemology from an African-centered worldview. Such a theoretical and practical application of pedagogy provides the synthesis for an Afrocentric prism of examining African phenomena. Jacob Carruthers points out that in order to restore a Pan-Africanist worldview, Africans must return to indigenous languages, such as Mdw Ntr, in order to understand the essential function of their ancestors.[12] Within popular culture, African Americans use Mdw Ntr to express greetings, interchangeably with the English language.

Secondly, the transition of Africana scholars using terminology could be a pedagogical advancement, in the way of conducting an operational scheme infusing the axiology of culture, language, and symbols in a disciplinary matrix.

As a result of European colonization of Africa, black Americans sojourn to locate cultural representations of authenticity, pertaining to language and motifs. Of course, there will be resistance and reservations drawn about the use of indigenous African languages in Africana Studies. Simply put, Africana Studies scholars must be rigorous in their scholarship to provide an ontology for studying the roots of African American history, culture, and ethos. Wole Soyinka provides critical analysis, writing, "I cannot accept the definition of collective good as articulated by a privileged minority in society, especially when that minority is in power."[13] Karenga expounds on this issue by stating:

Liberation as a human possibility must express itself as both an intellectual and social situation and practice. But cultural or intellectual liberation precedes and makes possible social liberation. In a word, until we break the monopoly the oppressor has on our minds, liberation is not only impossible, it's unthinkable. For one is not likely to achieve what one cannot even conceive.[14]

Variables such as culture, language, and symbols, queries emotion and logic of an Eurocentric hegemonic perspective. Asante addresses this point by writing:

This raises the question of objectivity in research. Richards has pointed to the problems inherent in the concept that suggests that the scholar maintains a mental distance from the object of study. She shows that this is difficult to maintain and is at best an illusion. Why would a scholar want such a mental distance in the first place? Perhaps a more appropriate concept is decentration which is the process to reduce mental distance between subject and object of study. Although the Afrocentric method considers the separation of subject and object to be a transitory separation, the idea of a practical separation to allow engagement between scholar and subject is acceptable."[15]

Simply put, indigenous African languages taught in Africana Studies would support the proposition of the cultural continua. Culture, language, and symbols are relative to the ontology that describes and evaluates the ethos of African Americans. Africana Studies as a holistic academic enterprise seeks to serve as an alternative epistemology to transcend the essential function and nature of science.

Written and oral communication illustrates the humanity and centering of a group's systematized method to convey or express ideas and feelings. Symbols are aesthetics used to affirm and represent the historical and cultural experiences of that particular group. Consequently, the black experience in America illustrates xenocentrism. Labeled as a subculture or counter-culture, African Americans have been removed from their culture, history, and linguistics. Therefore, I contend, culture is the ontology to begin with concept of formation in space, place, and time. Ontology identifies culture, language, and symbols for oral communication and the development of a script as Africana Studies scholars seek to examine the Eurocentric hegemonic perspective in world history. This critical examination must explore the emotion, logic, and reasoning concerning the systematic creation and consequence of subordinate groups' status. Colonization, being one of the key variables in the creation of subordinate group status, refers to the termination of a people's culture, language, motifs and ethos. Indeed, African Americans have been able to retain certain aspects of oral and written communication in folklore, history, and mythology. Indigenous African languages have transcended into African Americans' dialogue of oral expression, in the way of accent and pronunciation. For example, Amuzie Chimezie says, "African marital practices, child rearing, religions, languages, family structures, music, cosmology beliefs, folklore, etc."[16] Richards adds critical analysis, stating:

> "Once we understand the nature of the traditional African world view, we will see that it explains the African American ethos and response to Western European culture and the experiences forced on us by the culture in its New European setting. We must begin, therefore, with an explanation of the traditional African world view, for this knowledge will enable us to recognize its expressions and manifestations in African American life and culture."[17]

From the collection of linguistic data, the formation of a resource directory of African American terminology could be published. I think this would be functional for two reasons: (1) using these terms will initiate a mental, physical, and spiritual transformation of the enterprise of Africana Studies; and (2) requirement for rigor and intellectualism in developing an epistemology to examine Pan-Africanist phenomena from an Afrocentric perspective. I propose that culture, language, and symbols are the research tools that provide a contextual analysis for the essential function of Africana Studies. Paradoxically, scholars who hold positions in Africana Studies may be confronted with an "intellectual rites of passage," challenging their competence of Afrocentric scholarship and knowledge of indigenous African languages. Indeed, it is essential that scholars from this academic enterprise be visionaries to transcend the conceptual view of Africans throughout the diaspora, from an Afrocentric perspective.

Africanisms in African American Oral Communication

The inter-connectedness of language and oral communications between continental and diasporan Africans can also be detected in folklore. Blassingame and Berry present these linkages, citing:

> Whatever, the situation in the twentieth century, about sixty-five percent of the folktales of slaves in the nineteenth century American South came from Africa. The 200 slave tales recorded by Abigail Christensen in South Carolina, Joel Chandler Harris and Charles C. Jones, Jr., in Georgia, Alcee Fortier in Louisiana, and the Hampton Institute's black folklorist throughout the South between 1872 and 1900 were generally identical in structure, detail, function, motif, attitudes, and thought patterns to African ones. Rarely did the slaves tales show any trace of the sentimentality and romanticism characteristic of European folklore. The African origin of nineteenth century black folktales has long been recognized by the collectors of African folklore. In 1892, A. Gerber compared Afro-American and African folklore and asserted that "not only the plots of most the stories, but even the principal actors, are of African origin." African scholars found striking parallels between the Uncle Remus stories collected by Harris and West African folktales. According to Alta Jablow, the traditional West African animal stories "served as the prototype of the well known Uncle Remus stories." And in 1966, Hugh Anthony Johnston, after studying more than 1,000 traditional Hausa and

Fulani folktales in Nigeria, asserted: Brer Rabbit is undoubtedly the direct descendant of the hare of African folktales. Not only are his characteristics exactly the same as those of the Hausa Zomo but the plots in the last thirteen of the Uncle Remus stories are parallels of those in Hausa stories.[18]

Lawrence Levine points out that there is often a misunderstanding concerning Africans sharing their folktales and traditions with Europeans. He continues by inferring that African Americans retained their oral and written forms of communication as a means of survival for two reasons: (1) the necessity of rhetoric; and (2) because of caution.[19] Levine's thesis addresses culture and nationalism as key variables concerning the collective consciousness of African American's survival of the "Great Maafa" (i.e., Holocaust).

In addition, Blassingame and Berry provide a schematic framework for comparative analysis between African American and African proverbs.

Figure 9
Slave Proverbs and Their African Parallels[20]

Slave Proverb	African Parallel	Meaning
If you play with a puppy, he will lick your face.	If you play with a dog, you must expect it to lick your mouth. (Ashanti)	Familiarity with inferiors may cause them to lose respect for you.
Distant stovewood is good stovewood.	Distant firewood is good firewood. (Ewe)	Things look better from a distance.
"Almost kill bird" don't make soup.	"I nearly killed the bird." No one can eat "nearly" in a stew. (Yoruba) "Almost" is not eaten. (Zulu)	Literal
One rain won't make a crop.	One tree does not make a forest. (Ewe, Kpelle, Ashanti)	One part does not equal the whole.
The pitcher goes to the well every day; one day it will leave its handle.	If there is a continual going to the well, one day there will be a smashing of the pitcher. (Hausa)	One's evil deeds will one day be discovered.
A seldom visitor makes a good friend.	If you visit your fellow (friend) too often, he will not respect you. But if you make yourself scarce, he will pine for your company. (Jabo)	Literal
A scornful dog will eat dirty pudding.	When a dog is hungry, it eats mud. (Zulu)	Adversity causes one to do things he would not do in good times.
He holds with the hare (or fox) and runs with the hounds.	They forbid ram and eat sheep. (Ibo)	A deceitful person
The best swimmer is often drowned.	The expert swimmer is carried away by the water. (Zulu, Tonga)	There is no absolute certainty of anything.

The purpose for this comparative analysis is three-fold: (1) to give the African parallel; (2) to give the meaning of the proverb; and (3) to illustrate the retention of Afrikanisms in proverbs. Oftentimes Africana Studies scholars use proverbs to give examples and make relative the analysis drawn from examining African phenomena. Using proverbs is a pedagogical method that infuses satire, irony, and semiotics collectively. Levine discusses the function of African American proverbs by writing:

> In their songs, as in their tales, aphorisms, proverbs, anecdotes, and jokes, Afro-American slaves, following the practices of the African culture they had been forced to leave behind them, assigned a central role to the spoken arts, encouraged and rewarded verbal improvisation, maintained the participatory nature of their expressive culture, and used the spoken arts to voice criticism also to uphold traditional values and group cohesion.[21]

Blassingame and Berry add:

> Among the Ashanti, when a master called his slave's name, the bondsman always answered with a proverb. As a relation of the philosophy of a people and as a way of using the past to cope with a new situation, the West African proverb differed little from those found among Europeans. But West African proverbs, in general, had greater flexibility of imaginary and application, symmetrical balance, poetic structure, and rhythmic quality than Europeans. Africans used proverbs to teach modes of conduct, religious beliefs, hospitality, respect for elders, caution, bravery, humility, and cooperation by drawing on the lessons learned from history, mythology, and the observation of flora, fauna, and human behavior.[22]

African Americans continue to use proverbs as informal cliches (i.e., vernacular) to convey ideas and thoughts. Drums, beats, horns, and syncopation are attributes of traditional African culture that can be found in black popular cultural music such as rap-jazz, hip-hop dancing, fusion, and rhythm 'n' blues. These illustrate genres of music retention of indigenous African culture, language, and symbols; an Afrocentric cosmology provides a prism to view this aspect of Africana Studies holistically.

Interestingly, when examining the concept of spirituality in music, there are retentions of African culture illustrated in work-songs, blues, and gospel. It's clear to understand that during the Civil Rights movement, protesters often sung work-songs and gospel music for spiritual sobriety to persevere adversity.

How a group defines itself is important, as it is relative to culture, language, and symbols. For example, John Henrik Clarke uses the term "Africana Studies" in reference to Black Studies. He qualifies this point by stating that people must always be connected with land, history and culture.[23] Therefore, Clarke has consciously chosen this term to exercise language which operationalizes the existence of African Americans as a world people and not a minority. Naming of African American religious, fraternal, educational, and political institutions during the seventeenth and eighteenth centuries often identified Africa in their name or the organizations' ideological worldview. The intellectual history of African Americans maps out the cultural continua; simply put, blacks understood their cultural, social, and kinship roots to Africa. Black expressions such as nicknames and names retained from their ancestral homeland provided symbolism and social responsibility. To provide additional analysis on this issue, Blassingame and Berry cite:

> Until the end of the eighteenth century, the slaves retained their African names. Most of what scholars know about this phenomenon comes from ads placed in colonial newspapers by masters trying to recapture fugitive slaves. In attempting to anglicize the names, the masters distorted many of them as they had done in Africa; the slaves continued to name their children according to the day of the week on which they were born. Although day names appeared in South Carolina runaway ads alone. African names, showing a connection to the ancestral home, continued to be marks of status in free black community throughout the nineteenth century. Significantly, many of them appeared in Carter G. Woodson's list of free blacks included in the census of 1830. Between 5 and 10 percent of the given names of free blacks were African derivatives, with Juba, Cuffy, Abba, Cudjo, Tinah, Quashee, Chloe, Selah, Mingo, Sawney, Ferriba, Garoh, Wan, and Bena being the most popular. Occasionally, the free blacks had such African-derived surnames as the following: Quashy Baham, Wilson Africa, Edward Affricaine, Kedar Africa, Elikaim Bardor, Byer Africa, Gadock Coffe, Pryor Biba, Alford Bim, Cuff Cawon, Ally Africa. African appellations disappeared from the lists of slaves in the nineteenth century because masters frequently chose their slaves names.[24]

In contemporary times, African Americans are giving their children African and Arabic names. This exists for four general reasons: (1) to identify with their cultural past; (2) to promote self-esteem and social responsibility; (3) to enhance a concept of nationhood; and (4) a form of "popular culture Afrocentricism."

> *It is an historical fact that whenever the oppressor is called upon to define an indigenous product of the oppressed that product loses its functional value.*[25] —James G. Spady

Analysis of Language

Afrikanisms or the retention of culture in oral communication illustrate the relevance of culture, language, and symbols. Language provides the ontology of a lexicon in oral communication. Contemporary scholars such as Ani, Madhubuti, Karenga, Julius Thompson, and Carruthers have provided an alternative epistemology for language, emphasizing the use of Kis-Swahili and Mdw Ntr. Their scholarship is grounded from an African-centered perspective; in fact, they propose that this ideological repertoire is the common school of thought among scholars in the discipline of Africana Studies. Madhubuti notes the importance of language, writing, "No one, not even the elders, could speak the language of their foreparents. With the killing of the language, the transfiguration of the Africans was complete and lasting."[26]

The Eurocentric hegemonic perspective presents the idea that one particular view is universal. As an alternative to this perspective, Africana Studies endorses a cultural pluralist perspective to examine culture, language, and symbols. Ironically, Euro-Americans have impowered themselves as authentic Americans. Carruthers attributes the language connection among Africans, stating: "When one analyzes the iconographic data (i.e., the statues, wall engravings and murals) one finds that the race of the Egyptians is not substantially different from the Nhsi. The linguistic data settles the argument."[27] Ani and Karenga use Kis-Swahili and Mdw Ntr concepts ambidextrously in their scholarship.

For example, Karenga established the holiday Kwanzaa. Kwanzaa uses Kis-Swahili as its base language. He explains his rationale for using Kis-Swahili in this way:

> We chose Swahili as the most appropriate cultural language in 1965 for Afro-Americans for three basic reasons. First, it is "non-tribal" and thus, shows no ethnic or so-called "tribal" preference. Choice of any other language in Africa would in fact show this. Secondly, we chose it because being "non-tribal", it is Pan-African in character, and so are we, Afro-Americans claim all the people and the whole continent of Africa than one people or place on the continent. In fact, we argued then that we, Afro-Americans, were the first Pan-Africanists. Finally, we chose Swahili as a matter of self determination according to our own needs and understanding and reject racists' attempts to identify it with slavery or any other negative in order to discredit it. First, not only is that false, but if we're to reject speaking all languages associated with slavery, by the same logic, we'd have to begin by rejecting English and all other European languages.[28]

Karenga has captured the essence of locating African Americans in their own historical experiences—providing an Afrocentric analysis of etymology. Kwanzaa is the celebration of the first fruits of the harvest, which is referred to as the Nguzo Saba. The Nguzo Saba is based on the seven principles of moral and ethical conduct:

1. UMOJA (Unity)
   To strive and maintain unity in the family, community, nation, and race.

2. KUJICHAGULIA (Self-determination)
   To define ourselves, name ourselves, create for ourselves and speak for ourselves instead of being defined, named, created for and spoken for by others.

3. UJIMA (Collective Work and Responsibility)
   To build and maintain our community together and make our sister's and brother's problems our problems and to solve them together.

4. UJAMAA (Cooperative Economics)
   To build and maintain our own stores, shops and other businesses and to profit them together.

5. NIA (Purpose)
   To make our collective vocation the building and developing of our community in order to restore our people to their traditional greatness.

6. KUUMBA (Creativity)
   To do always as much as we can, in the way we can, in order to leave our community more beautiful and beneficial than we inherited it.

7. IMANI (Faith)
   To believe with all our heart in our people, our parents, our teachers, our leaders and the righteousness and victory of our struggle.[29]

Ani has made a significant contribution to the intellectual (tradition) history of Africana Studies, with emphasis on language. *Yurugu* is a critical examination of the misorientation of European culture, philosophy, ethos, and history. Ani's use of Kis-Swahili provides an Afrocentric etymological critique of the Eurocentric hegemonic perspective.

The Hausa have a proverb which says, "Strategy is better than strength."[30]

Conclusion

The enslavement and colonization of Africans, by Europeans, created a holocaust. This holocaust has had lasting effects that can be seen in contemporary times. This can be illustrated in five ways: (1) low percentage of representation in the political arena; (2) dislocation and peripheral analysis about culture; (3) economic inequality and caste stratification in African American communities; (4) consistent practice of institutional and individual racism; and (5) development of scholarship and ideologies that reinforce the inability of blacks to be successful. Ethos and psychology are the essential grounds that explain the axiology of culture, language, and symbols from an Afrocentric perspective. An epistemological system that uses motifs, icons and cultural concepts provide an ontology which defines the nature of spirituality and the "KA."

The intellectual tradition of Africana studies has always challenged scholars to transform and transcend, working toward the higher ground: The use of indigenous African languages perhaps can provide cultural transmission in developing (Maat) balance in attempting to understand the essential function of culture, language, and symbols in Africana Studies.

BIBLIOGRAPHY

Akbar, Na'im. *Chains and Images of Psychological Slavery.* Jersey City, N.J.: New Mind Productions, 1986.
Alkalimat, Abdul. *Introduction to Afro-American Studies: A Peoples College Primer.* Chicago: Twenty First Century Books and Publications, 1986.
Anderson, Talmadge, ed. *Black Studies: Theory, Method, and Cultural Perspectives.* Pullman: Washington State University Press, 1990.
Asante, Molefi. *The Afrocentric Idea.* Philadelphia: Temple University Press, 1987.
_____. *Afrocentricity.* Trenton, N.J.: Africa World Press, 1988.
_____, and Asante, Kariamu Welsh, eds. *African Culture,* Westport, Conn.: Greenwood Press, 1985.
Bell, Janet Cheatham. *Famous Black Quotations.* Chicago: Sabayt Publications, 1986.
Blassingame, John W., and Berry, Mary Frances. *Long Memory.* New York: Oxford University Press, 1982.
_____. *The Slave Community.* New York: Oxford University Press, 1979.
Carruthers, Jacob. *Essays in Ancient Egyptian Studies.* Los Angeles: University of Sankore Press, 1989.
Chimezie, Amuzie. *Black Culture.* Shaker Heights, Ohio: Keeble Press, 1984.
Holoway, Joseph E. *Africanism in American Culture.* Bloomington: Indiana University Press, 1990.
Jahn, Janheinz. *Muntu: African Culture and the Western World.* New York: Grove/Weidenfield, 1989.
Karenga, Maulana. *Introduction to Black Studies,* Los Angeles: Kawaida Publications, 1984.
_____. *Kawaida Theory.* Inglewood, Calif.: Kawaida Publications, 1980.
_____. *Kwanzaa: Origins, Concepts, and Practice.* Los Angeles: Kawaida Publications, 1977.
Levine, Lawrence. *Black Culture and Black Consciousness.* New York: Oxford University Press, 1977.
Madhubuti, Haki R. *Earthquakes and Sunrise Missions.* Chicago: Third World Press, 1984.
Nobles, Wade. *African Psychology.* Oakland, Calif.: Black Family Institute, 1986.
Woodson, Carter G. *The Mis-Education of the Negro.* Washington, D.C.: Associated Publishers, 1933.

NOTES

1. Janet Cheatham Bell, *Famous Black Quotations*, Chicago: Sabayt Publications, 1986, p. 53.
2. Wade Nobles, *African Psychology*, Oakland, Calif.: A Black Family Institute Publication, 1986, p. 45.

3. Margaret Wade-Lewis, *Lorenzo Dow Turner: First African American Linguist*, Philadelphia: Temple University, Institute of African and African American Affairs, Department of African American Studies, Spring 1988.

4. Interview of Agnes Dingle-Conyers, September 5, 1994, by James L. Conyers, Jr.

5. Keto, *op. cit.* p. 9.

6. Molefi Kete Asante, *Afrocentricity: The Theory of Social Change*, Trenton, N.J.: Africa World Press, 1988, p. 32.

7. Dona Marimba Richards, "The Implications of African Spirituality," in Molefi Kete Asante and Kariamu Welsh-Asante, eds., *African Culture: The Rhythms of Unity*, Westport, Conn.: Greenwood Press, 1985, pp. 207–208.

8. Molefi Kete Asante, *Kemet, Afrocentricity, and Knowledge*, Trenton, N.J.: Africa World Press, 1991, p. 227.

9. Janet Cheatham Bell, *Famous Black Quotations*, Chicago: Sabayt Publications, p. xi.

10. Dona Marimba Richards, "The Implications of African Spirituality," in Molefi Kete Asante and Kariamu Welsh-Asante, eds., *African Culture: The Rhythm of Unity*, Westport, Conn.: Greenwood Press, 1985, p. 208.

11. Maulana Karenga, *Introduction to Black Studies*, Los Angeles: Kawaida Publications, 1983, p. 89.

12. Jacob Carruthers, *Essays in Ancient Egyptian Studies*, Los Angeles: University of Sankore Press, 1989, p. 21.

13. Janet Cheatham Bell, *Famous Black Quotations*, Chicago: Sabayt Publications, p. 8.

14. Jacob Carruthers, *Essays in Ancient Egyptian Studies*, Los Angeles: University of Sankore Press, 1989, p. viii.

15. Molefi Kete Asante, "Afrocentricity and Human Knowledge," *Working Paper*, Temple University, 1989, p. 139.

16. Amuzie Chimezie, *Black Culture*, Shaker Heights, Ohio: Keeble Press, 1984, p. 3.

17. Dona Richards (aka Marimba Ani), Molefi Kete Asante and Kariamu Welsh Asante, *African Culture*, p. 210.

18. John Blassingame and Mary Frances Berry, *Long Memory*, New York: Oxford University Press, 1984, p. 17.

19. Lawrence Levine, *Black Culture and Black Consciousness*, New York: Oxford University Press, 1977, p. 101.

20. John Blassingame and Mary Frances Berry, *Long Memory*, New York: Oxford University Press, 1982, p. 21.

21. Lawrence Levine, *Black Culture and Black Consciousness*, New York: Oxford University Press, 1977, p. 6.

22. John Blassingame and Mary Frances Berry, *Long Memory*, New York: Oxford University Press, 1982, p. 19.

23. James Turner, ed., *The Next Decade*, Ithaca, N.Y.: Africana Studies and Research Center, 1984, p. 31.

24. John Blassingame and Mary Frances Berry, *Long Memory*, New York: Oxford University Press, 1982, pp. 18 and 19.

25. Janet Cheatham Bell, ed., *Famous Black Quotations*, Chicago: Sabayt Publications, 1986, p. 9.

26. Haki Madhubuti, *Earthquakes and Sunrise Missions*, Chicago: Third World Press, 1984, p. 123.

27. Jacob Carruthers, *Essays in Ancient Egyptian Studies*, Los Angeles: University of Sankore Press, 1989, p. 21.

28. Maulana Karenga, *Kwanzaa: Origins and Concepts*, Los Angeles: Kawaida Publications, 1980, pp. 53–54.

29. Maulana Karenga, *Kwanzaa: Origins and Concepts*, Los Angeles: Kawaida Publications, 1980, p. 9.

30. Janet Cheatham Bell, *Famous Black Quotations*, Chicago: Sabayt Publications, 1986, p. 15.

16. The Black Poet in Mississippi, 1900–1980

Julius E. Thompson, Ph.D.
Director of Black Studies
University of Missouri at Columbia

The history of the black poet in Mississippi extends from the first slave songs to rise from the fields and riverbanks during the slavery era of the Mississippi to the most recently published poems by the state's black poets in book, magazine and tape media. This history takes us back 300 years.

The focus of this chapter however, will be to place in historical perspective the role and accomplishment of black poets in Mississippi, from the late nineteenth century to the present. It seeks to identify the poets of each period; to note their chief publications in all forms: books, work in anthologies, and to evaluate the historical importance of their work and lives, as their achievements relate to the wider experiences of the Afro-American people in Mississippi, and the United States.

This chapter seeks also to determine the historical vision, direction and meaning of the works which have been produced by Afro-American poets in Mississippi, from the Emancipation generation to the post–Civil Rights movement era, in an effort to relate these themes to the contemporary poets who are active in the state today.

Not much is known about the work of early black poets in Mississippi during the period 1865–1899, the era of the first and second generations of "free" black Mississippians. The 437,406 blacks in Mississippi, compared to 353,899 whites, in 1860, faced a harsh set of realities during the Emancipation period. These included economic, political, social, cultural, and psychological issues and concerns; all tied in with the task of defining and securing black freedom in the state.

The writers of the period were instrumental in aiding the communication, social and cultural needs of the black masses by helping in the establishment of black newspapers, educational institutions, and other social institutions such as fraternal organizations. It was from such humble efforts made from the 1860s through the 1890s by Mississippi's largely self-educated writers, workers, ministers, teachers and businessmen that encouragement was given to the growth and development of the physical and spiritual needs of black people in Mississippi after the long centuries of bondage and deprivation.[1]

The role of the black poet and writer during the last quarter of the nineteenth century was especially important in the area of the black newspaper in Mississippi. The press served as the major outlet for works by black poets, journalists, politicians, etc. Between 1867 and 1899, over 50 black newspapers were published in Mississippi.[2] Without these journals, black poets and other writers would have had a very difficult—if not impossible—task of securing publication of their poems, short stories, essays and other works.

Since many of the black journals in Mississippi during this period were church-related, religious themes played an important part in the materials which were published. This trend would remain an important element in twentieth century black Mississippi poetry.

W.E.B. DuBois' powerful essay "Of the Sorrow Songs" in *The Souls of Black Folk* reminds us of the unknown qualities of the individual, invisible creators, if you will, of much of the Afro-American's music-song-poetry.[3] This was certainly the case for many of the nineteenth century black poets. Nonetheless, we are given a small indication of their interests and talents by the work of the early black Mississippi poets of the twentieth century.

The major problems associated with the development of black poets in Mississippi during the nineteenth century continued on into the twentieth century. As the plight of blacks increased in the period of 1890–1949, so did the general condition of their creative writing in Mississippi. The Age of Segregation was harsh, and its negative impacts were felt by all Afro-American institutions in the United States. Not the least of these was the black newspaper, which had experienced a tremendous growth, even in Mississippi, during the years 1870–1920. However, after World War I, and between the years of the Great Depression, the black press in the state sharply declined. This was bad news to Afro-American writers in Mississippi who depended on the state's black press as their major outlet for publishing opportunities.[4] Perhaps the greatest consequence of Mississippi's economic, political and social oppression of black people was the mass movement of tens of thousands of blacks from the state during the "Great Migration"; this meant the loss of many talented individuals to the cultural development of black Mississippians.[5]

A number of poets and writers who did not migrate from the state during the 1920s and 1930s appear to have been influenced by the "New Negro" movement of New York City, Chicago, Washington, and other cities. Several factors stand out. The leading Northern black newspapers, such as the *Chicago Defender* (which encouraged blacks to migrate from Mississippi to points North), the *Pittsburgh Courier*, and the Baltimore/Washington, D.C. *Afro-American*, and other papers did reach blacks in Mississippi, even though the papers were sometimes removed from the mail by white Southerners. The works of Alain Locke, W.E.B. DuBois, Langston Hughes, and other figures of the "New Negro" movement were read and discussed in Mississippi, and this too, may have encouraged other Blacks to leave the state.

The Garvey Movement also found an audience in black Mississippi. By 1926, the Garvey Movement had 39 divisions and 5 chapters in Mississippi. They were located in, or near, all of the major cities.[6]

Also during this period, black creative talent in the state received a tremendous boost from the impact of the growth and development of the "Delta blues" as an art form from the 1920s onward. The "blues" artists, who are really special "poets," must be considered apart from the academic, or writing poets. They deserve their own special place in the history, literature and music of black people.[7]

Finally, a word on the impact of the major black institutions during this period, on the development of black culture and black poets in the state. Black women's organizations in Mississippi, especially under the umbrella of the Mississippi branch of the National Council of Negro Women, Inc., were very active between 1900 and 1949 in promoting social programs (i.e., education, human relations, the needs of youth) among black people in Mississippi. These broad efforts by many black women in the state had an important impact on the related concerns of cultural development: the school, the church, the press, black music and writing. The key to the importance of such groups lay in the fact that they were organized throughout Mississippi, and thus could reach all segments of the black population in the state. Equally significant during the period were the various black fraternal orders, which continued to play an important part in press and banking activities among black people, as they had in the nineteenth century.[8]

As in the nineteenth century, many of the early black poets in Mississippi who wrote between 1900 and 1949 are lost to us. Few black newspapers and other journals from this period have survived. These important records of their publishing activities are thus not available for use by modern readers, and many of their original manuscripts have not been collected by universities and archival institutions in the United States.

Between 1900 and 1939, eight black poets lived and worked in Mississippi. They include Samuel A. Beadle (1859–?), a local Jackson poet who, although trained as a lawyer, also had an interest in writing poetry. In 1912 his poem, "If I Had a Million" appeared in a very important collection of works by Mississippi Blacks, *Multum In Parvo*. Beadle writes of youth and love and "...the old familiar ways" plus "better days" to come. By 1912, he was the author of four books: *Fragments*, *Sketches from Life in Dixie*, *Adam Shuffler*, and *Lyric of the Under World*.[9]

Charles P. Jones, of Jackson and a minister by profession, also appeared in the 1912 edition of *Multum in Parvo*. His seven poems in the collection all have a religious theme. Stanza three of this poem, "A Little Girl," sums up his religious expression very well:

> Our lovely Bible teaches us
> If we our parents will obey,
> That we shall live long on the earth,
> And live with God in Heaven always.[10]

Three other poets who also wrote during this period were Effie T. Battle, Eudora V. Marshall Savage, and George W. Lee (1894–1976). Battle was the author of the 1916 collection, *Gleamings from Dixie*. Savage wrote poems which appeared in Mississippi journals such as *The Spirit of Mississippi*, in which she offered praise and celebration of a black religious journal and group in the state by the same name. Savage concludes her deeply religious poem with a special note of appreciation for the founder of the group, Anselm Joseph Finch:

> Thy Editor was blessed,
> By God's Holy will,
> 'Twas through Divine power
> Thy pages were filled.

George Washington Lee, born in Indianola, Mississippi, in 1894, may have written poetry during this time period. He was known during the 1930s for the novels *Beale Street, Where the Blues Began* (1934), and *River George* (1937).[11]

One of the most widely published black poets connected with Mississippi during the 1930s was Jonathan Henderson Brooks (1904–1945). Brooks was born near Lexington, Mississippi. Educated at Jackson College, now Jackson State University (Mississippi), Lincoln University (Missouri), and Tougaloo College (Mississippi), his work was recognized by many of the leading poets of his day, including Arna Bontemps (1902–1973), Langston Hughes (1920–1967), and Countee Cullen (1903–1946).[12] Throughout the late 1920s and the 1930s, his work appeared in *Opportunity* (fifteen poems were published in the journal between 1927 and 1937); and also in the *Crisis*, as well as several anthologies. Brooks wrote about many themes, but religious matters were important to him. In fact, he was also a Baptist minister, in addition to having had an interest in teaching. The religious theme is perhaps best expressed in his poem, "The Resurrection," where "...Calvary was loveliness..."[13] Part of Brooks' lasting fame in Mississippi, however, lies in the fact that he wrote the words to the Tougaloo College alma mater, "Eagle Queen, We Love Thee."

Thomas D. Pawley (1917–) is best known for his works in drama; however, during the 1930s he also published poetry. Born in Jackson, Mississippi, Pawley published "American South" in the October 1935 issue of *Crisis*. Other published poems would follow in the next decade.[14]

Richard Wright (1908–1960) also wrote poetry during the 1930s, after having departed from Mississippi in 1925 for points north, including Arkansas and Memphis, Tennessee, and then finally to Chicago, Illinois. The noted black critic, Blyden Jackson (1910–), suggests that after the Negro Renaissance of the 1920s, the greatest black writer to emerge was Wright. He calls this period the "Age of Wright."[15] Wright, of course, was especially important during the 1930s for his excellent short stories, collected in *Uncle Tom's Children* (1938). Wright's poetry took a Marxist twist during this period, due to his interest in and work with the American Communist Party of the 1930s. The critical literature on Wright is vast and growing, and the critics on his poetry of the 1930s generally conclude, that for the most part, his poetry was not his strongest art form. Nevertheless, several of Wright's poems from the 1930s are outstanding and have appeared in many anthologies since that time. One which has stood the test of time is "I Have Seen Black Hands" (1934).[16]

During the 1940s, a number of local black poets emerged in Mississippi. Their poems appeared in local and national black journals and in some of the leading anthologies of the decade, such as the *Negro Caravan*. Some of the local poets were Anslem Joseph Finch (1902–1969), of Brandon, a teacher and principal; Geneva Smith Wade of Myrtle; Annie Elizabeth Butler, Jackson; Isabella Maria Brown (1917–), of Natchez; Mary Wilkerson Cleaves, Jackson; Amos J. Griffin, a serviceman stationed in Mississippi at Keesler Field; Ruth Roseman Dease (1912–1994), Jackson, a teacher; Alice Brown Smith, a teacher; Joseph Clifton Brown (1908–1994), of Picayune and later Oxford, a teacher and high school principal; and Richard Pitts (1910–), of Holly Springs. Richard V. Durham (1917–) although born in Mississippi, left the state during his early years when his family moved to Chicago. These local poets wrote on such themes as religion, the value of education, death, love, World War II, black soldiers, citizenship, dreams, freedom and justice, teaching and teachers.[17]

In assessing the national black poets of this period, Blyden Jackson notes that the following poets must be studied during the "Age of Wright": Sterling Brown (1901–1989), Frank Marshall Davis (1905–1987), Melvin Tolson (1900–1966), Robert Hayden (1913–1980), Gwendolyn Brooks (1917–), Owen Dodson (1914–1983), Margaret Walker (1915–), and M. Carl Holman (1919–1988). Walker and Holman are connected with Mississippi.

When Margaret Walker (1915–) arrived in Mississippi in 1949 to assume a teaching position in the department of English at Jackson State College (now University), she was already world-famous for her 1942 collection of poetry, *For My People*. M. Carl Holman (1919–1988) was born in Minter City, Mississippi, but grew up in St. Louis, Missouri. He displayed an early talent for poetry and won several writing awards. His poetry was accepted by Arna Bontemps and Langston Hughes in 1949 for the *Poetry of the Negro*, an anthology.[18] Walker certainly was the most noted of the two. Her poetry of the 1930s and 1940s has been noted for its historical vision, and for its sense of black struggle and hope. "For My People," her most famous poem, ranks among the best poems written by a black writer since 1900. Its power and vision have seldom been matched by other poets. Holman also had an interest in these same themes, but wrote about them in a less direct way. His early work indicates a commitment to the poor and the suffering, but poems such as "Song," "Letter Across Doubt and Distance" and "Picnic: the Liberated" speak as well for the individual as they do for the masses.

The poetry of the period was influenced by the many events of the second World War. Of the war, M. Carl Holman wrote: "Let the drums dwindle in the distance." While blacks in the Southland were: "Mounting their private myths of freedom ... prisoners in a haunted land." The war to save democracy for a second time would not, perhaps could not, save them too; but there was the future.

There was a need, felt by some poets such as Eudora V. Savage and Anselm J. Finch (1902–1969), for blacks to settle with the present on a policy of accommodation with the power structure of Mississippi. Of the state's governor in the 1940s, Paul B. Johnson (1880–1943), Savage wrote:

> He was our favorite leader,
>   Because he was so kind,
> And let us enjoy free textbooks
>   To elevate the mind.
> He was our greatest Governor
>   To protect boys that roam,
> After committing petty crimes,
>   They're trained in a delinquent home.

Other poets, such as Isabella Maria Brown (1917–), wrote on religious themes, too. However, unlike many of her contemporaries, Brown's "Prayer" asked when the age for good prayers would come:

> ...because during these times
> there is almost always none.[19]

The 1940s was a decade of mixed voices; however, the 1950s would bring an age of silence in terms of the work produced by the black poet in Mississippi.

The decade of the 1950s was an extreme time for many blacks in Mississippi. On the other hand, the most positive development was the national growth of the Civil Rights movement during this time; however, it would take another dozen years before the full impact of the movement could directly challenge the segregation system of Mississippi.

On the negative side, economically, politically and socially, the basic conditions remained hard for most of the nearly one million blacks who lived in the state. During the 1950s segregation continued in place; the state of

Mississippi was also at the bottom on every national measurement of education, per capita income and housing standards; thus, the great migration of blacks from the state continued. Dr. T.R.M. Howard, a black Mississippi leader, expressed the mood of the 1940s and 1950s when he noted in 1952, "Mississippi lost 455,000 people during the past ten years and over 350,000 of these were Negroes and our people are still going in large numbers."[20] During the mid–1950s Dr. Howard and his family were forced to flee the state; they settled, like so many others, in Chicago, Illinois.

Culturally, besides black music, things were at a standstill for blacks in Mississippi. The great and promising black poets and writers had long ago departed the state. This list included Richard Wright, Richard V. Durham, Joseph Clifton Brown, William Attaway (1912–), M. Carl Holman, George W. Lee, and Thomas D. Pawley.

Margaret Walker remained the only major black writer in the state during the 1950s, and it was very difficult for her to get work out, due to her heavy teaching load at Jackson State. Nonetheless, Walker was able to bring a number of national black writers to Mississippi during the week of October 19–25, 1952, for a literary festival in honor of the 75th anniversary of the founding of Jackson State. The list of names was an impressive one, and included Owen Dodson, Arna Bontemps, Gwendolyn Brooks, Sterling Brown, J. Saunders Redding (1906–1988), Melvin Tolson, Robert Hayden, Era Bell Thompson (1906–1986), and a local talent, Ruth Dease. Perhaps Walker's greatest contribution for the decade came in her willingness to teach three or four courses per academic semester. In this regard, she was truly a cultural worker since she came into contact with so many students over the years.

Poetically, of the age, Margaret Walker would write "A Litany from the Dark People," echoing the earlier theme of her masterpiece "For My People" in its expression of the faith of black people in:

> ...the coming of that day when all mankind
> shall be
> United under God in love and charity...[21]

Thus the themes of human freedom and the majesty of black religion were continued in her work of this period.

Poems by local black poets continued also to appear in the black press of Mississippi during the 1950s. But the black press of the state had also experienced a sharp decline. From a high of 87 papers between 1900 and 1920, the figure for 1941–1959 was 17.[22] Local Mississippi black poets, such as Frank B. Hood and Eugene Beasley, published in Delta papers such as the *Sentinel* of Mound Bayou. Other poets published works in such papers as the *Mississippi Enterprise* of Jackson, and the *Jackson Advocate*, which had a weekly column devoted to a "weekly poem" by Rev. John R. Perkins. All of Rev.

Perkins' work was of a religious nature, such as his poems "Lift Up Jesus" and "Take God Some Work."[23] Rev. Perkins' column was representative of many black papers in the South. Yet, other local black poets were able to express themselves on a variety of themes, such as youth, nature, beauty, education and justice, in the state's black press.

A number of local poets found an outlet for their work in the black college journals of Mississippi. All of these institutions had student newspapers, and these often devoted a page or a section of each issue to the work of students, faculty and staff members. All of the major black colleges of the state were helpful in developing black student talent in this regard. These schools include: Alcorn State University, *The Alcorn Herald*; Jackson State University, *The Blue and White Flash*; Mississippi Valley State University, *The Valley Voice*; Rust College, *The Sentinel*; and Tougaloo College, *The Tougaloo News*. Many of Mississippi's black poets were educated at one of the above institutions. The age of segregation in the area of education in Mississippi, for all practical purposes, really only ended during the early 1970s. Thus, most of the blacks who attended college in Mississippi did so at a black school in the state, or at another black college in a nearby state.

Three other black poets of the 1950s must be noted in the history of black poets in Mississippi. Although John A. Williams (1925–) was born in Jackson, Mississippi, his parents left the state shortly thereafter for Syracuse, New York, where he was "raised from age one." Thus, Mississippi's "claim" to him rests largely on the fact that he was born in this state. Williams is best known as a novelist, especially for *The Man Who Cried I Am* (1967); but he has also written poetry during his career. In 1951, he published a collection of poetry, *Poems*.[24] The role of history in human experience is a key facet in Williams' poetry.

Ruth Roseman Dease of Alcorn State University during the 1950s, published poems in such journals as the *Mississippi Educational Journal* (the organ of the Association of Black Teachers in Mississippi), the *Delta Sigma Theta Sorority Journal*, and the *Christian Recorder* of the A.M.E. Church.[25] Religious images are an important theme in her early work, which extends back to the 1940s.

A north Mississippi poet, Richard W. Pitts (1910–), of Holly Springs, Mississippi, published a small collection of poems, *Above the Clouds*, but the exact date of its publication is unknown. He believed that the chief aim of his poetry was to give "inspiration" to "poetry admirers."[26]

The 1950s were a depressing time for black poets in Mississippi. Many had left the state for more promising opportunities elsewhere; those that remained, mainly Margaret Walker Alexander and Ruth Roseman Dease, had to connect themselves to black colleges in order to survive. They also had to overcome the isolation of being in Mississippi. It was a time of silence.

The 1960s were a time of action, for change in Mississippi—a time to break the silence of the 1950s. A long century of segregation and deprivation had to be broken in Mississippi and the South, and then the North.[27] As the Civil Rights movement grew stronger during the 1960s, a rising tide of black creativity also took place in black Mississippi. Part of this new awakening among black artists in and from Mississippi took place in the area of poetry. Although a large number of the state's best poetic talent had long since abandoned Mississippi, a new crop of poets emerged now to take their place in the struggle to create new words and interpretations on the meaning of the black experience. Two groups stand out in this connection. First, there was a large group of young black civil rights workers, mostly associated with the Student Non-Violent Coordinating Committee (SNCC), who came to the state in the early 1960s to aid the movement there. Many of these young people were also poets. This list included: Doris A. Derby, John O'Neal (1940–), Tom Dent (1932–), and Alice Walker (1944–). Another activist who came to Mississippi in 1969 and has had a wide impact as a cultural worker in the state is Nayo (Barbara Watkins) (1940–), a strong poetic voice from the Black Arts South Movement.

Secondly, a huge number of young blacks from Mississippi were encouraged to write during the 1960s. Much of this work took place in Mississippi's black colleges and in freedom schools, designed to increase the positive aspects of learning for an oppressed people. Out of this movement, thousands began to record their own words on paper; some of this material was published in the freedom journals of the period. The new poets proclaimed for all the world to hear: "I wish that I was free" and, in order to receive their freedom, they had to: "Fight on ... fight on ... keep straight ahead ... to win the fight...."[28] This proclamation was the great challenge of the times which the young put forth and sought to answer in words and deeds to positively overcome the age of segregation.

The older poets in the state continued to write during this period. Margaret Walker and Ruth Roseman Dease are among this group. Arthur P. Davis (1904–), one of the twentieth century's leading black critics, wrote in 1974 that Margaret Walker's work of the 1960s was "...the best poetical comment to come from the civil rights movement..." Thus, like the youth of Mississippi who were fighting to win in the struggle to overcome oppression, Walker's work was also at the front of the ranks. Her poems of the 1960s were about the themes of the times: "Street Demonstration," "Sit-Ins," "Jackson, Mississippi," "At the Lincoln Monument in Washington, August 28, 1963," "For Malcolm X" and of "Prophets for a New Age."[29]

One of the few book-length collections by a black poet living and working in Mississippi, appeared during the 1960s; this was the collection of poetry entitled *Scan-Spans*, by Ruth Roseman Dease, in 1967. Dease's work pulls from the rich tradition of black religious poetry, but also concerns itself with images of the family, and of motherhood and peace. While on life's highway, she suggests in "Bridges," and in the search for fulfillment (peace), we should "...build a strong bridge and then cross over."[30]

Other black poets who lived and worked in Mississippi during the 1960s were the young poets Willie Cook (1929–) at Alcorn State University, later at Jackson State, and Charles Rowell (1940–) at Tougaloo College; Aurelia N. Young (1915–) at Jackson State University; Isabella M. Brown (1917–), at Natchez; and Dilla Irwin (1910–1990), at Vicksburg, and editor of a local black newspaper in that city, the *Citizen's Appeal*, during 1964–67.

A large number of the best known national black poets of the 1960s who were born in Mississippi but no longer lived in the state created a brilliant record of poetic creations before and during the Black Arts movement of the 1960s. This list includes: Richard Wright (1908–1960), who created over 4,000 *haiku* poems before his death in September 1960; Etheridge Knight (1931–1991), perhaps the major poet of the prison experience to emerge during the 1960s; Lerone Bennett (1928–), the popular historian of the black experience in the United States and an excellent poet; Sterling Plumpp (1940–), one of the best users of the folk tradition in literature, and a poet who often writes about Southern themes; Al Young (1939–), a widely published, leading American poet from the West Coast; two voices from the "Black Fire" anthology days, E. H. Jones (1925–) and Clarence Franklin (1932–); M. Carl Holman, long recognized as a significant poet, and a former editor, staff member on the U.S. Commission on Civil Rights (1962–68), and a key former official of the National Urban Coalition; Angela Jackson (1951–), a major poetic voice who lives in Chicago; Loyle Hariston (1926–), a major critic and excellent writer in all the major genres; and Beah Richards (1933–), an actress and poet of New York City during the 1960s.[31]

Audre Lorde (1934–1992), of New York City, was generous with her time and talent to the cause of black poetry in Mississippi. She spent the summer of 1968 as a poet-in-residence at Tougaloo College.[32]

Perhaps the greatest impact of the work of black Mississippi poets during the 1960s was in the area of promoting a new sense of consciousness among black people everywhere. This single theme runs through the best of their poetry. This is especially true of the SNCC poets, Margaret Walker, and the greatest of the black Mississippi poets who were in exile from Mississippi during the 1960s. In addition, the majority of the poets viewed their work as a part of the struggle of black people in the United States for freedom. Consciousness and struggle are key terms in understanding the spirit and the mood of the 1960s and the work of black poets; however, an even larger body of professional work would appear in the 1970s.

By the close of the 1960s and the beginning of the 1970s, blacks in Mississippi had succeeded on many fronts in opening up the "closed society," as the state of Mississippi has been called. But, while blacks in Mississippi and elsewhere were able to end many of the social and political barriers of segregation and powerlessness, they found in the 1970s that the economic barriers were still in place. In addition, the decade proved to be a time of conservative reaction, perhaps even a counter revolution by the old guard to impede, or undo, as much of the positive work of the 1960s as possible.

Nonetheless, the promising growth and development of the Black Arts movement in Mississippi, especially among the poets, would continue during the 1970s. In this respect, the decade proved to be a golden one. With a few more jobs available in Mississippi as a result of the Civil Rights movement, more talented younger blacks remained in Mississippi during the 1970s and some blacks even moved to the state.

The poets, on the whole, were still concerned with the 1960s issues of consciousness and black struggle; however, during the 1970s a number of other major themes made their entrance upon the poetic scene. Black women poets of Mississippi expressed a need during the 1970s to redefine and reinterpret their lives, roles and relationships, not only with black men, but with each other, and with all of the institutions of society. A number of black women writers in Jackson created a special group to focus upon the concerns of black women. They called themselves the Black Women's Art Collective.[33] As on the national scene, some of the black Mississippi poetry of the period also expressed a deep concern for individual problems and needs of the writers.

Nearly 100 black poets connected with Mississippi wrote and published poetry during the 1970s.[34] The major voices remained on the scene, namely, Margaret Walker, Ruth Roseman Dease, Willie Cook, Dilla Irwin, and Aurelia N. Young. Alice Walker continued to turn out excellent work during the early 1970s, but she departed the state for Cambridge, Massachusetts, and later New York in 1973.[35] A number of black poets who were born in Mississippi but continued to live elsewhere also enjoyed success with their poetry during the 1970s. This group included: Etheridge Knight, Sterling Plumpp, Angela Jackson, Al Young, Marion A. Nicholes and Ahmos Zu-Bolton (1935–); and new work by such figures as Beah Richards, the leading black actress; Lerone Bennett, Jr., Nate Johnson of Washington, D.C., Myrtle "Moss" Humphrey (1934–) of Los Angeles, California, Helen H. King (1931–), of Chicago, and Helen Pulliam (1945–), of Detroit, Michigan.

Dozens of the new local Mississippi poets appeared in Jackson, the capital and economic, political and social center of Mississippi. Among poets in this group were: Jerry W. Ward, Jr. (1943–), a noted black critic and the most widely published black poet living and working in Mississippi, and former chairperson of the English Department at Tougaloo College; Virginia Brocks-Shedd (1943–1992), a noted poetic voice of the state and head librarian at Tougaloo College; Nayo (Barbara Watkins), perhaps the leading black woman poet during the 1970s in Mississippi, after Margaret Walker and Alice Walker; the author of this chapter, Julius E. Thompson (1946–), a widely published poet during the 1970s who taught history at Jackson State University,

1973–1980; L.C. Dorsey (1938–), a social worker who committed a large part of her energies during the 1970s toward prison reform in Mississippi and the South; Jonetta Turner, a Jackson poet; and Burns Machobane, a poet and historian at Jackson State University during the mid–1970s.

Toward the end of the 1970s, a second strong component of poets emerged in Jackson. Noted poets in this group were: E. Yvonne Foreman (1940–), an education specialist at Jackson State; Charles Tisdale, publisher of the *Jackson Advocate*; Sinclair O. Lewis (1930–), a professor of psychology at Jackson State; and Doris E. Saunders (1921–), who assumed a teaching position in mass communications at Jackson State in the mid–1970s after a long career at Johnson Publishing Company in Chicago.

The other leading black poetry centers of Mississippi during the 1970s were Vicksburg, with poets Tommy Whitaker (1949–), Barbara Townsley (1946–), and Harrison Havard, Jr. (1939–); Gulfport, where Benjamin John Williams (1947–), continued to live and write; and Oxford, with Joe Delaney (1940s? –).

The black colleges of Mississippi continued to produce hundreds of student poets during the 1970s. The influences of the national black poets of the 1960s, such as Haki R. Madhubuti (Don L. Lee) (1942–), Nikki Giovanni (1947–), and others, was evident in some of the new work by the younger poets, but many of them also had their own ideas about black poetry and the meaning of literature.

Jackson, with two of the major black colleges in Mississippi, Jackson State University and Tougaloo College, was the state scene of much of the poetry activity among black students. Jackson State's large size for a black college in Mississippi and the South (8,000 students yearly during most of the 1970s), and a diversified student body and faculty (also the largest at a black institution in Mississippi), gave it many advantages. In addition, the school also had Margaret Walker, and in 1968–69, Alice Walker. Tougaloo's Jerry W. Ward, Jr., was a strong voice for promoting black poets at that institution, and Alice Walker also gave support to the college. With the support of interested Jackson State faculty, Patricia Grierson, a professor of English at Jackson State, and John Burrows, director of the writing center at Tougaloo, aided students at those institutions in publishing their own literary magazines. *New Visions* appeared in 1975 as the major literary outlet for Jackson State students, and at Tougaloo, *Pound* was the major voice for student poets during the 1970s.[36]

More collections of poetry, in book form, were produced by Mississippi's black poets during the 1970s than in any other previous decade. In 1970, three volumes appeared: *Prophets for a New Day*, by Margaret Walker; *Half Black, Half Blacker*, by Sterling C. Plumpp; and *Hopes Tied Up in Promises*, by Julius E. Thompson. In 1971, Marion Alexander Nicholes published *Life Styles*, and *The Song Turning Back Into Itself* was published by Al Young. Nineteen-seventy-three was a banner year, with three major collections: *Belly Song and Other Poems*, by Etheridge Knight; *Revolutionary Petunias and Other Poems*, by Alice Walker; and *October Journey*, by Margaret Walker. During 1974, Angela Jackson's *Voo Doo/Love Magic* volume appeared, and Sterling Plumpp was the author of *Steps to Break the Circle*. The major book of 1975 by a black Mississippi poet was Ahmos Zu-Bolton's *A Niggered Amen*. Nineteen seventy-six brought Sterling Plumpp's *Clinton* and Al Young's *Geography of the Near Past*. Iyanju (Easley Quinn), was the author in 1977 of *Reality, You Guessed Wrong! It's Poetry*, and Julius E. Thompson's *Blues Said: Walk On* also appeared that year.

The influence of the above poets was also expressed in their poetry readings, teaching, lecturing and work with various black organizations in Mississippi during the 1970s.

The black poets of Mississippi wrote about a variety of themes during the 1970s, but it was mostly a time for reflection, not only on the American Bicentennial, but, as Easley Quinn noted, the black American reality of "Still being oppressed." In "Heavy Feelings," Jerry W. Ward, Jr., argued, after years of hard fighting during the Civil Rights movement "...to raze this country, this prison...." Still, for the long-term struggle, blacks had to "...Live through [the] flack, the Happy Heavy Feelings / on being here now and Black." They also had to be aware, Benjamin John Williams wrote, that "...on a cosmic scale nothing's altered Here." He was talking about the human condition, the lives of many blacks and whites, in all parts of the United States. Still, Sterling Plumpp suggested, that blacks had to create the correct "Steps to Break the Circle."[37]

The decade of the 1970s was a time of increased activity among black poets in Mississippi. By 1979, they could look back on a decade of several advances for black poets in the state. A number of black cultural organizations emerged during the decade in such cities as Natchez, Meridian, Vicksburg, Greenville, and Jackson. Their work was aided by the formation in 1979-80 of the Mississippi Cultural Arts Coalition, a black state-wide organization created to promote the interests of black culture in Mississippi. Other areas of progress were seen in the creation of new black magazines, such as *Sunbelt* and *Rhythm*, although most of the new journals only survived for a short period of time. Nevertheless, they were useful as outlets for black poets in Mississippi. A final sign of encouragement during the 1970s was the movement to Mississippi of poets like Doris Saunders, Julius E. Thompson, Jerry Ward, Jr., Sinclair O. Lewis; and others who remained in the state during all, or a part of, the decade, including Alice Walker, Nayo, and L.C. Dorsey. These poets were helpful in keeping black poetry alive in Mississippi and in encouraging others to write and publish. Their influence would reach from the 1970s into the 1980s.

The major themes and concerns of Mississippi's black poets in the 1970s have continued during the 1980s. These include: a concern for black consciousness (broadly defined); the special issues of black women; the problems of racism in America and the world (e.g., South Africa); black and world survival in the nuclear age; the poverty of blacks in Mississippi; religion (broadly defined, in all areas: Christianity, Islam, African); and the individual concerns of the poets, such as peace, truth, love, and happiness.

While the number of new black poets in Mississippi increased during the early 1980s, their publication outlets, nationally and locally, suffered a decline. This encouraged the growth of more black writers' workshops and cultural organizations in Mississippi, with the development of their own literary organs, or small publishing companies to publish the work of the members of each organization. This is a new development for black Mississippi's poets in terms of the scope of the work which is being produced. Again, Jackson is at the forefront of this movement, but work by other workshops has been produced by black poets in such cities as Vicksburg, and more are likely to appear in the future from such locations as Meridian, Greenville and Oxford, since there are strong colonies of black writers in all of those cities.[38]

On the economic, political and social scale of matters, conditions in the 1980s concerned survival for many blacks in Mississippi. The impact of a new age of conservatism, and the general recessions of the 1970s, the 1980s, and now the 1990s, have had a very negative impact on black culture in Mississippi. Funds for cultural arts are always in short supply; funds for black culture are almost always invisible. Many blacks in Mississippi are also disturbed over the current predicament of the black college in Mississippi. The mood in white America has been to consolidate the educational institutions of the South. Many blacks in Mississippi, and elsewhere, now wonder: how long will most public (and private) black colleges survive; and, if they do survive beyond the 1990s, will they still continue to have their traditional mission of serving black education?[39] The question is a significant one for black culture, because the black college has always served as a major training ground for black writers. Can white institutions serve this function?

Overall, the situation has not been an encouraging one generally for the black arts in Mississippi; and black poets often find themselves today, as a group, with difficult decisions to make, especially in terms of each poet's personal, day-to-day economic survival in Mississippi.

Many of the significant black poets who lived and worked in Mississippi for the period 1960–1979 had by the early 1980s departed the state for a variety of reasons. Some left the state to continue their education; others for economic considerations; some for new positions in government, business and education. Still others left to escape what some consider to be the special burdens of living in Mississippi itself: an open/closed society; a sense of isolationism and the small town atmosphere of most Mississippi cities; and the continuing impact of the state's violent racial history of segregation and racism. Among the poets and writers who have departed Mississippi are the following figures: Alice Walker, Doris Derby, Charlie Cobb (1944–), Charles Rowell, John O'Neal, Anne Moody (1940–), Burns Machobane, Jonetta Turner, and Julius E. Thompson.

Nineteen eighty witnessed the retirement of Margaret Walker from Jackson State University, after 30 years of service to that institution. Margaret Walker was the light at Jackson State. At least now, in retirement, she can devote all of her energies to her poetry and other writing projects.[40]

Nevertheless, in spite of the recent departure of a number of excellent black poets from the state, and the continued long exile of others, still a group of the most noted of the national black poets—Etheridge Knight, Lerone Bennett, Jr., Sterling Plumpp, Beah Richards, Angela Jackson, and others— have remained in Mississippi. This list is impressive and includes: Jerry W. Ward, Jr., Margaret Walker, Ruth Roseman Dease, Willie Cook, Aurelia N. Young, Virginia Brocks-Shedd, Worth Long (1936–), Benjamin John Williams, L.C. Dorsey, Tommy Whitaker, Barbara Townsley, and others.[41]

To the above list must be added the names of 50 new voices of the 1980s. Of this group, Deborah LeSure (1957–), Theodore Bozeman (1955–), and Aurolyn Jacobs (1957–) are representative of the best which this group has produced, and the promise which they hold for tomorrow.[42]

The underlying themes in the work of black Mississippi poets during the 1980s continued to be as varied as those of the 1970s. Black Mississippi women continue to write on their special concerns. For example, Mary Ann Adams questions the meaning of marriage in "Reflection":

> you stood there in holy matrimony
> little girl meshed into womanhood
> wearing
> your ivory and your pearls
> and
> your face for the lenses
> Reflections
> of you
> on display for public consumption...

Others, such as Virginia Brocks-Shedd, demand that love and relationships assume an equal status, therefore the "Casanova Man" must be informed that:

> At least one woman in your life
> will make you cry, too!

But Melvin Turner (1948–) cries that too many of the brothers are "street corner philosophers," who are high "...on dreams / and / words that flowed higher / than the good smoke" of their lives. Others, L. C. Dorsey sings, are behind "Cold Steel," where "the dirt, filth, the pain and misery" are the "stark reality" for too many black men. A time of reflection thus continues in the 1990s. Yet, in spite of all the pain and frustrations, the poets write on, dreaming and struggling for the day when black strength will:

> Let a new earth rise. Let another world be born.
> Let a second generation full of courage issue
>   forth; let a people loving freedom come to growth.
> Let a beauty full of healing and a strength of final
> clenching be the pulsing in our spirits and our blood.
> Let the martial songs be written, let the dirges
> disappear. Let a race of men now rise and take control.[43]

Since the 1860s, Mississippi has been the home of several hundred black poets. The historical significance of their work extends from the vision that each poet created over a lifetime of writing poetry. Often, they have not been appreciated, nor understood. Their publication outlets have been few and in between, and, in some parts of the country, it has been assumed, incorrectly, that other than Margaret Walker, few black poets have lived and worked in Mississippi. Historically, the state's leadership class has had little use for the arts, and according to their outlook, black culture did not deserve a place alongside white culture.

Nevertheless, black culture has survived, and so have black poets. Many, unfortunately, for one reason or another, have had to leave Mississippi; a home, as Tennessee Williams (1911–1983) suggests: "You love it, but can you live it?"[44] For many of the state's best black poets, Mississippi remained a "closed society" too long—one where the growth and development of poets was not seriously observed—for either black or white writers. Yet, as this chapter reveals, many black poets have continued to work in Mississippi and promote the study and interpretation of the black experience in that state. An impressive list of such writers includes Margaret Walker, Jerry W. Ward, Jr., Benjamin John Williams, Deborah LeSure, Willie Cook, Worth Long, Aurolyn Jacobs, L.C. Dorsey, Theodore Bozeman, and Ruth Roseman Dease.

Furthermore, any assessment of the poetic contributions among black people in various states of the United States has to consider the black poets produced by Mississippi. In addition to the poets mentioned above, important black poets living and writing outside of Mississippi today include Al Young, Sterling Plumpp, Angela Jackson, Julius E. Thompson, John A. Williams, Lerone Bennett, Nayo, Marion Alexander Nicholes, and Ahmos Zu-Bolton. The total sum of their work is a powerful statement about the contributing influence and contribution of the Mississippi African American experience to the national culture of the United States.

NOTES

1. United States *Census*, 1860. See Thompson, *The History of Negro Baptists in Mississippi*; Thompson, *Hiram R. Revels, 1827–1901: A Biography*; Lynch, *Reminiscences of an Active Life, The Autobiography of John Roy Lynch*; Wells, *Crusade for Justice*; Harrison, *A History of the Most Worshipful Stringer Grand Lodge: Our Heritage Is Our Challenge*.

2. Thompson, "The Black Press in Mississippi," 178. The social, political and economic obstacles which faced blacks in Mississippi from 1865 to 1899 are well covered in the literature on Reconstruction. The best known work remains Wharton, *The Negro in Mississippi, 1865–1890*. However, Wharton does not consider the role of the black poet during this era; nor does McMillen in *Dark Journey*. Documentation on the period remains a major problem for students of the black experience in Mississippi. For example, of the 50-odd black newspapers which were published in Mississippi during the 35 years after the American Civil War, no copy is known to have survived.

3. William E.B. DuBois, *The Souls of Black Folk* (Greenwich, Connecticut: Fawcett Publications, 1968; reprint from the 1903 edition.) Also see Lawrence W. Levine, *Black Culture and Black Consciousness, Afro-American Folk Thought from Slavery to Freedom* (New York: Oxford University Press, 1977); John R. Sherman, *Invisible Poets, Afro-Americans of the Nineteenth Century* (Urbana: University of Illinois Press, 1974).

4. Thompson, "The Black Press in Mississippi," p. 181. The rates for the decline were as follows: 1900–1920: 87 papers, 1921–1940: 18 papers, and 1941–1953, 11 papers. In educational matters, blacks suffered greatly during the early years of the century. In 1915, they had only six public high schools in the state; seven, if one counts the high school division at public supported Alcorn College. Mather, *Who's Who of the Colored Race, 1915*, p. xxiv. In 1930, Mississippi's per capita income was $202, for the United States as a whole, the figure was $619. Of course, the figure for blacks was much less than $202 in Mississippi. (Mississippi remained at the bottom in terms of per capita income for 1930, 1940 and 1950.) *Clarion Ledger/Jackson Daily News*, September 18, 1983.

5. In fact, the migration began as early as 1879. See Nell Irvin Painter, *Exodusters, Black Migration to Kansas After Reconstruction* (New York: Alfred A. Knopf, 1977), pp. 153–159. For the Great Migration, see Henry, *Black Migration: Movement North, 1900–1920*.

6. Wolsely, *The Black Press, U.S.A.*, 38. Also see Martin, *Race First, the Ideological and Organizational Struggles of Marcus Garvey and the UNIA*, 364–365; and Gheodore G. Vincent, ed., *Voices of a Black Nation, Political Journalism in the Harlem Renaissance* (San Francisco: Ramparts Press, 1973), pp. 20–38, 382.

7. William Ferris, *Blues from the Delta* (Garden City, New York: Anchor Books, 1979); and Paul Oliver, *The Story of the Blues* (Radnor, Pennsylvania: Chilton Book Co., 1975).

8. *What the Mississippi Women Are Doing*, 1–27; Harrison, *A History of the Most Worshipful Stringer Grand Lodge*.

9. Crawford, Thompson, and Ballou, *Multum In Parvo*, 40–42.

10. Ibid., pp. 170–178.

11. Effie T. Battle, *Gleamings from Dixie Land* (Okalona, Mississippi: By the Author, 1916). See Work, *Negro Year Book, 1918-19*, 482; *Mississippi Snaps* 1 (1947): 7; Mosley, *The Negro in Mississippi History*, 92; Sewell and Dwight, *Mississippi Black History Makers*, 163–170; George W. Lee, *Beale Street Where the Blues Began* (New York: Robert O. Ballow, 1934), *River George* (New York: The McCauley Co., 1937); M. Marie Booth Foster, *Southern Black Creative Writers, 1829–1953, Biobibliographies* (Westport, Connecticut: Greenwood Press, 1988), p. 46.

12. Brooks' work appeared in the leading anthologies of the period, including, among others: Langston Hughes and Arna Bontemps, eds., *The Poetry of the Negro, 1746–1970* (New York: Doubleday and Company, Inc., 1949: revised edition 1970, pp. 236–241, 595); Arna Bontemps, ed., *American Negro Poetry*, pp. 95, 188; Sterling A. Brown, Arthur P. Davis, and Ulysses Lee, eds., *The Negro Caravan* (New York: The Dryden Press, 1941; reprint ed., New York: Arno Press and the New York Times, 1970), pp. 364–366; and Countee Cullen, ed., *Caroling Dusk* (New York: Harper and Row, 1927), pp. 192–196; Foster, *Southern Black Creative Writers, p. 9*.

13. Theressa Gunnels Rush, Carol Fairbanks Myers, and Esther Spring Arata, *Black American Writers, Past and Present: A Biographical Dictionary*, 2 vols. (Metuchen, New Jersey: The

Scarecrow Press, 1980), 1:102; Mary Mcace Spradling, ed., *In Black and White, A Guide to Magazine Articles, Newspaper Articles, and Books Concerning More Than 15,000 Black Individuals and Groups*, 2 vols. (Detroit: Gale Research Company, 1980), 1:118; and Ethel M. Ellis, ed., *Opportunity, Journal of Negro Life, Cumulative Index, 1923–1949* (New York: Kraus Reprint Co., 1971), p. 70. For a critical review of Brooks' work, see Erma Young Perkins, "Analysis of the Poetry of Jonathan Henderson Brooks" (M.A. thesis, Jackson State University, 1980), pp. 1–77.

14. Thomas D. Pawley, letter to Julius E. Thompson, Summer 1979, and December 5, 1983. Mr. Pawley's parents moved the family to Virginia when he was 13 months old. He has been a resident of Missouri for more than 50 years.

15. Blyden Jackson, *The Waiting Years, Essays on American Negro Literature* (Baton Rouge: Louisiana State University Press, 1976), pp. 203–204; and John Griffin Jones, ed., *Mississippi Writers Talking*, 2 vols. (Jackson: University Press of Mississippi, 1983), II:135.

16. Wright remained a member of the Communist Party for nine years, before he renounced his membership in 1942. On Wright, see the following significant works: Ellen Wright and Michel Fabre, eds., *Richard Wright Reader* (New York: Harper and Row, 1978), pp. xi–xii; Addison Gayle, Richard Wright, *Ordeal of a Native Son* (Garden City, New York: Anchor Press/Doubleday, 1980); Yoshinobu Hakutani, ed., *Critical Essays on Richard Wright* (Boston: G.K. Hall and Co., 1982); and Margaret Walker, *Richard Wright, Demonic Genius, A Portrait of the Man, A Critical Look at His Work* (New York: Warner Books, 1988). The major themes in Wright's poetry of the 1930s were: black and white solidarity, the struggles of the masses, protest against racism and injustice, and revolution. Also see Dorothy Abbott, ed., *Mississippi Writers, Reflections of Childhood and Youth*, vol. III (Jackson: University Press of Mississippi, 1988), pp. 16, 421.

17. *Mississippi Snaps*, p. 22; *Jackson Advocate*, September 13, 1947; Arna Bontemps, ed., *Golden Slippers* (New York: Harper and Row, 1941), p. 207; Beatrice M. Murphy, ed., *Ebony Rhythm, An Anthology of Contemporary Negro Verse* (Freeport, New York: Books for Libraries Press, 1948; reprint, 1968), pp. 15–16, 45–47, 74–75; Hughes and Bontemps, *The Poetry of the Negro*, pp. 341–342, 596; *Soldiers of Faith* 1 (1945): pp. 3, 5, 7, and 15; Thompson, *The History of the Mississippi Teachers Association*, pp. 161–163; Richard Pitts, *Excelsior, Book of Poems* (Holly Springs, Miss.: privately printed, 1944); Foster, *Southern Black Creative Writers*, p. 56.

18. Jackson, *The Waiting Years*, p. 203–204. On Margaret Walker see "The Margaret Walker Collection," Jackson State University, Jackson, Mississippi; Jones, *Mississippi Writers, A Talking*, pp. 120–240; Lina Mainiero, ed., *American Women Writers, A Critical Reference Guide from Colonial Times to the Present* (New York: Frederick Ungar Publishing Co., 1982), pp. 315–316; *Clarion-Ledger*, February 18, 1980; Leaonead Pack Bailey, ed., *Broadside Authors and Artists, An Illustrated Biographical Directory* (Detroit: Broadside Press, 1974), p. 120; Robert Holt, "Variations on a Theme: The Literary Art of Margaret Walker" (Ph.D. dissertation, George Peabody College for Teachers, 1976) and *Contemporary Authors*, vols. 73–76 (Detroit: Gale Research Company, 1976). On M. Carl Holman see Rush, Myers, and Arata, *Black American Writers*, I:387–88; *Who's Who in America, 1982-83* (Chicago: Marquis Who's Who, 1982), p. 1156; *Who's Who Among Black Americans, 1980-81* (Northbrook, Illinois: Who's Who Among Black Americans Publishing Co., 1981), p. 381; *Jackson Advocate*, November 19, 1981; New York Times, August 11, 1988; Abbott, *Mississippi Writers*, vol. III, pp. 21, 416.

19. Hughes and Bontemps, *The Poetry of the Negro*, pp. 341, 362, 396; Eudora V. Savage, "Paul Burney Johnson," *Soldiers of Faith*, p. 3; Anselm J. Finch, *Mississippi Negro Ramblings* (Chicago: Adams Press, 1969), p. 59. The black press of Mississippi survived the Great Depression, however; during the 1940s, there were only four major black papers in the state. They were the *Jackson Advocate*, the *Mississippi Enterprise* (Jackson), the Mound Bayou *Southern Advocate*, and the Greenville *Delta Leader*. These papers continued to serve as organs for the expression of black writers. For example, during 1942, the *Jackson Advocate* ran the entire book of *Native Son*, by Richard Wright, in ten excerpts, in the paper. See the *Jackson Advocate*, March 2, 1942; Thompson, "The Black Press in Mississippi," p. 182.

20. *The Commercial Appeal*, January 29, 1962; Mississippi Regional Council of Negro Leadership, *Prospectus of the First Annual Meeting of the Mississippi Regional Council of Negro Leadership, Delta Area* (Mount Bayou, Mississippi, May 2, 1952), p. 8. The age of lynching continued for blacks in Mississippi during the 1950s. The cases of Willie Magee (1950), Emmett Till (1955), the Rev. George Lee (1955), Lamar Smith (1957), Clyde Kennard (1957), and Mack Charles Parker (1959), all served as reminders to people of the times of just how hard the future

struggles for freedom, justice and equality would be, in Mississippi and the United States. See Wilhoit, *The Politics of Massive Resistance*; Loewen and Sallis, *Mississippi: Conflict and Change*; McMillen, *The Citizens' Council: Organized Resistance to the Second Reconstruction*; William M. Simpson, "Reflections on a Murder: The Emmett Till Case," in *Southern Miscellany: Essays in History in Honor of Glover Moore*, ed. Frank Allen Dennis (Jackson, Mississippi: University Press of Mississippi, 1981), pp. 177–200; and Silver, *Mississippi: The Closed Society*.

21. *Jackson Advocate*, October 18, 1952; Margaret Walker, *October Journey* (Detroit: Broadside Press, 1973), 38. The poem, "Litany from the Dark People" was first published in 1952, by *Phylon*. Walker also published another poem during the decade, "Dear Are the Names that Charmed Me in My Youth," in the *Virginia Quarterly*, 1955.

22. Thompson, "The Black Press in Mississippi," p. 181.

23. The Mound Bayou *Sentinel*, January 17, 1953, February 21, 1953, and March 14, 1953; *Jackson Advocate*, June 14, 1952, and January 12, 1952. Rev. J. R. Perkins' poems also appeared as early as 1930, in the *Mississippi Weekly Recorder*, Jackson. He was also a teacher at Lanier High School during the 1930s. See Jackson Chamber of Commerce (Jackson, Mississippi: Department of Archives & History, Subject File, quoting the U.S. Census of 1930).

24. John A. Williams, letter to Julius E. Thompson, Summer 1979; W.P. French, M.J. Fabre, A Singh, eds., *Afro-American Poetry, 1760–1975, Afro-American Drama, 1850–1975* (Detroit: Gale Research Company, 1979), p. 244. For an interesting statement by John A. Williams on the state of his birth, see Earl A. Cash, *John A. Williams: The Evolution of a Black Writer* (New York: The Third Press, 1975), p. 6. John A. Williams returned to Mississippi in 1946, and again in 1963. See John A. Williams, *Flashbacks, A Twenty-Year Diary of Article Writing* (Garden City, New York: Anchor Press, 1973), pp. 36, 76.

25. Ruth Roseman Dease, letter to Julius E. Thompson, July 17, 1979. *The Mississippi Educational Journal for Teachers in Colored Schools*, was established at Jackson in 1927. It served as a major outlet for the poetry written by black teachers in Mississippi. See Thompson, *The History of the Mississippi Teachers Association*, pp. 106–108.

26. Richard W. Pitts, *Above the Clouds, Poems that Live* (Holly Springs, Mississippi: By the author, date unknown), p. 2.

27. In fact, Mississippi served as a major testing ground during the black struggle of the 1960s. Blacks in the state paid a heavy price in the struggle to obtain justice. Lives were lost— Medgar Evers, Herbert Lee, Vernon Dahmer—many thousands went to jail, and people risked everything in the effort to obtain equality and freedom. See J.H. O'Dell, "Life in Mississippi, An Interview with Fannie Lou Hamer," pp. 231–242; Joyce Ladner, "What 'Black Power' Means to Negroes in Mississippi," pp. 7–15; Mrs. Medgar Evers, *For Us, The Living*; and Ann Moody, *Coming of Age in Mississippi*.

28. *Freedomways* 5 (Spring, 1965):341; *Freedom's Journal* (August 3, 1964) p. 2. The most significant state-wide cultural movement to occur in Mississippi during the early 1960s was the establishment in 1963 of the Free Southern Theater, at Tougaloo College, located near Jackson, Mississippi. The FST was created in order to offer a legitimate touring theater experience to blacks in Mississippi and other Deep South states. The range of FST's activities helped to promote the work of playwrights, actors, directors, poets, and other artists in the South. In order to increase its options, the FST relocated at New Orleans, Louisiana in 1964, where it continued its operations throughout the 1960s and the 1970s. See Thomas C. Dent, Richard Schechner, and Gilbert Moses, eds., *The Free Southern Theater* (Indianapolis: The Bobbs-Merrill Co., 1969), pp. 3, 23, 33.

29. Arthur P. Davis, *From the Dark Tower* (Washington, D.C.: Howard University Press, 1974), p. 184; Margaret Walker, *Prophets for a New Day* (Detroit: Broadside Press, 1970), 7–32. Also see Walker, *October Journey*. The black colleges of Mississippi continued to serve as training grounds for black poetic talent during this period. Several significant poets emerged in the state in the 1970s who received their college training in the 1960s at black colleges in the state (i.e., Jerry W. Ward, Jr., Julius E. Thompson, and Benjamin John Williams, among others). Margaret Walker, Ruth Roseman Dease, and other black teachers in Mississippi, such as Eula J. Danzy at Alcorn State University (now at Stillman College, Tuscaloose, Alabama), had a positive influence on the development of many of the student poets of the 1960s and 1970s. On the Black Arts Movement in the South, see Eugene B. Redmond, *Drumvoices, The Mission of Afro-American Poetry, A Critical History* (Garden City: Anchor Press/Doubleday, 1976), pp. 376–380;

Abraham Chapman, ed., *New Black Voices* (New York: New American Library, 1972), pp. 370_390. The national black debate of the 1960s among black poets and writers on a definition and inter- pretation of the "black aesthetic," also had an audience in black Mississippi, especially among the young SNCC poets and many of the black Mississippi college poets, and of course, Margaret Walker. See Addison Gayle, Jr., ed., *The Black Aesthetic* (Garden City: Anchor Books, 1972).

30. Ruth Roseman Dease, *Scan-Spans* (New York: Vantage Press, 1967), p. 13.

31. On Richard Wright's haiku poetry, see Robert Tener, "The Where, the When, the What: A Study of Richard Wright's Haiku," in *Critical Essays on Richard Wright*, ed. Yoshinobu Hakutani (Boston: G. K. Hall and Co., 1982), pp. 273–298; Ellen Wright and Fabre, *Richard Wright Reader*, pp. 251–254. Also see Rush, Myers, and Arata, *Black American Writers*, 1:387; *Freedomways* 4 (Winter, 1964):58.

32. Bailey, *Broadside Authors and Artists*, p. 80; Ted Wilentz and Tom Weatherly, eds., *Natural Process, An Anthology of New Black Poetry* (New York: Hill and Wang, 1970), 75.

33. *Jackson Advocate*, February 1–7, 1979. This group includes Gigi Hines, Elaine Peacock, Nayo (Barbara Watkins), Herticene Clay, Linda Buford, L.C. Dorsey, Yvonne Swaine, among others.

34. The list of publications for this work includes the following Mississippi publications: the *Jackson Advocate, Pound, New Visions*, the *Jackson State University Review*, the *Alcorn Herald*, the *Blue and White Flash, Furrows, Harambee, Reaction Magazine, Sunbelt Magazine*, the *Merid- ian Memo Digest*, the *Moss Point Pas-Point Journal*, and the *Natchez Bluff City Post*. National pub- lications include: *Freedomways, Phylon, Essence, Yardbird Reader, Painted Bride Quarterly, Black World, First Works*, the *Journal of Black Poetry, Callaloo, Obsidian, Hoo Doo, Y'Bird, Black Cre- ation*, etc. Their work also appeared in many of the anthologies of the period, such as *A Broad- side Treasury* (1971); the *Forerunners, Black Poets in America* (1975); *Soulscript* (1979); *Cavalcade* (1971); *Black Out Loud* (1970); *Understanding the New Black Poetry* (1973); *Black Literature in America* (1971); the *New Negro Renaissance* (1975); *Black Writers of America* (1972); *Right On!* (1970); *On Being Black* (1970); *Nommo* (1972); *I, Too, Sing America* (1971); *The Black Poets* (1971); *The Poetry of Black America* (1973); *Black American Literature* (1970); *The World Split Open* (1974); the *American Poetry Anthology* (1975); *The Ardis Anthology of New American Poetry* (1977); *An Anthology of Mississippi Writers* (1979); *New Voices in American Poetry* (1973); *I Hear My Sisters Saying* (1976); *Black Love's Black Wealth* (1974); *Today's Negro Voices* (1970); *New Expressions in Black Poetry* (1974) and others.

35. Margaret Walker's influence as the leading cultural worker in Mississippi continued during the 1970s. She directed two important national conferences at Jackson State University during the decade: the Phillis Wheatley Poetry Festival, on November 4–7, 1973; and the Con- ference on the Teaching of Creative Writing and a Literary Festival, during the week of Sep- tember 19, 1977. See the special issue on the Phillis Wheatley Poetry Festival, *Jackson State Review* 6 (Summer 1974):1–107; Charles H. Rowell and Jerry W. Ward, "Ancestral Memories, the Phillis Wheatley Poetry Festival," *Freedomways* 14 (Second Quarterly, 1974):127–145; and Deria Margarite, "A Look at JSU's Literary Festival," *Jackson Advocate*, October 1, 1977, p. 3. Alice Walker notes in a recent interview with novelist David Bradley, that before her escape, she found life in Mississippi had "just about driven her around the bend." See David Bradley, "Novelist Alice Walker, Telling the Black Woman's Story," *New York Times Magazine*, January 8, 1984, sec. 6, p. 36. But, 1973 was also the year of the publication of Walker's major poetry collection, *Revolutionary Petunias* (New York: Harcourt Brace Jovanovich, Inc., 1973). Her Mis- sissippi years also produced significant poems on Fannie Lou Hamer (1917–79) and Aaron Henry (1922–), two giant figures in post–World War II Mississippi and Southern history.

36. *New Visions* (Fall/Winter 1975), 1–32, (Spring/Summer 1976), 1–51, and (Winter, 1976– 77), 1–63; *Pound* (Fall 1978), 1–24. Students at Alcorn State University, Mississippi Valley State University, and Rust College also produced a large volume of poetry during the 1970s, as did black students at junior colleges in Mississippi, and there were black poets among the several thousand black students who attended the historically white universities and colleges of Mis- sissippi. It is interesting to note, however, that the largest volume of activity appears to have occurred on black college campuses. The majority of Afro-American presence at the Mississippi black colleges probably helps to explain the poetic freedom which developed among some of the black students at those institutions.

37. Iyanju (Easley Quian), *Reality You Guessed Wrong! It's Poetry* (Jackson: By the Author, 1977), 27; Jerry W. Ward, "Heavy Feelings," *Hoo Doo* 1 (1972), p. 28; Benjamin John Williams,

"The Odd Menagerie," *Hoo Doo* 2 (1975), p. 19; Sterling Plumpp, *Steps to Break the Circle* (Chicago: Third World Press, 1974).

38. Examples of small black publishing companies in Mississippi are: Visions, Inc., Jackson; Earthworks Publications, Jackson; and Nu-South Typesetting, Jackson; and Vicksburg, Javekcher Press. Much of this new work is in the tradition of pamphlet/manifesto poetry. See Carolyn Fowler, "A Contemporary American Genre: Pamphlet/Manifesto Poetry," *Black World* 23 (June 1974):4–19.

39. See the *Clarion-Ledger*, August 21, 1983, November 19, 1983; and the *Jackson Advocate*, April 1, 1982, November 3–9, 1983, and November 17–23, 1983.

40. "Jackson State University Honors Faculty Retirees" (Jackson: Jackson State University, May 9, 1979), 2; *Clarion-Ledger*, July 11, 1980; "Margaret Walker Alexander Jubilee," (Jackson: Jackson State University, July 12, 1980).

41. Theodore Bozeman, Jackson, Mississippi, letter to the author, December 17, 1983; Willie Cook, Jackson, Mississippi, letter to the author, December 15, 1983; Rhoyia Hope Crozier, Jackson, Mississippi, letter to the author, December 10, 1983; Ruth Roseman Dease, Jackson, Mississippi, letter to the author, July 17, 1979; Doris Derby, Urbana, Illinois, letter to the author, July 10, 1979; L.C. Dorsey, Jackson, Mississippi, letter to the author, August 25, 1982; Minnie L. Harp, Greenville, Mississippi, letter to the author, September 17, 1982; Harrison Havard, Jr., Vicksburg, Mississippi, letter to the author, December 19, 1983; Roland Havis, DeQuincy, Louisiana, letter to the author, November 30, 1983; John Author Horhn, Jackson, Mississippi, letter to the author, August 20, 1983; Larry Hudson, Jackson, Mississippi, letter to the author, July 9, 1979; interview with Dilla E. Irwin, Vicksburg, Mississippi, June 7, 1981; Aurolyn Charise Jacobs, Bolton, Mississippi, letter to the author, December 13, 1983; Deborah D. LeSure, Coldwater, Mississippi, letter to the author, July, 1980; Charles Victor McTeer, Greenville, Mississippi, letter to the author, December 8, 1983; Pamela D. Mack, Greenville, Mississippi, letter to the author, October 28, 1982; Barbara Watkins, Jackson, Mississippi, letter to the author, October 18, 1982; Sterling Plumpp, Chicago, Illinois, letter to the author, August 27, 1982; Melvin Turner, Jr., New Orleans, Louisiana, letter to the author, December 5, 1983; Virginia Brock-Shedd, Jackson, Mississippi, letter to the author, August, 1980; Jerry W. Ward, Jr., Tougaloo, Mississippi, letter to the author, November 2, 1981; Aurelia Norris Young, Jackson, Mississippi, letter to the author, December 14, 1983; Ahmos Zu-Bolton, Galveston, Texas, letter to the author, January 15, 1983. The data sources are incomplete on the military and foreign travel experiences of the poets. Space limitations will not allow a complete listing here of the over 200 black poets produced by Mississippi since the nineteenth century. On contemporary black poets in Mississippi, also see Abbott, *Mississippi Writers*, vol. III, 25, 30–36, 42–47, 77–78, 90–92, 129–130, 138–153, 163–168, 177–180, 195–211, 281, 295–337, 350–358, 363–366, 368–373, 376–423.

42. Book-length collections of poetry by Mississippi's black poets in the early 1980s include works by: L.C. Dorsey, *Cold Steel* (Jackson: Dorseys, Inc., 1982); Etheridge Knight, *Born of a Woman, New and Selected Poems* (Boston: Houghton Mifflin Company, 1980); Sterling Plumpp, *The Mojo Hands Call, I Must Go* (New York: Thunders Mouth Press, 1982); and Al Young, *The Blues Don't Change* (Baton Rouge: Louisiana State University Press, 1982).

43. Mary Ann Adams, "Reflections," in *Mississippi Earthworks* (Jackson: Earthworks Publications, 1982), pp. 3–6; Virginia Brock-Shedd, "Casanova Man," in *Mississippi Woods* (Jackson: Visions, Inc., 1980), p. 6; Melvin Turner, Untitled in *Mississippi Woods*, p. 18; L.C. Dorsey, "Cold Steel," in *Cold Steel*, p. 1; and Margaret Walker, "For My People," in *For My People* (New Haven: Yale University Press, 1942), p. 14.

44. Rolling Stones (April 14, 1983):124. The Jackson Advocate served as the major black newspaper outlet for black poets in Mississippi during the 1980s, but other active papers during this period were: the *Mississppi Enterprise*, the *Memo Digest*, the *PasPoint Journal*, the *Claiborne*, *Bluff City Post*; and magazines, such as *Sunbelt, Black Life in the South*. See Thompson, *The Black Press in Mississippi, 1865–1985: A Directory*, pp. 3, 19, 50, 64, 76, 83. Julius E. Thompson, *The Black Press in Mississippi, 1865–1985* (Gainesville, Fla.: University Press of Florida, 1993), pp. 113–47.

List of Contributors

DELORES P. ALDRIDGE is the Grace Towns Professor of Sociology and African American Studies at Emory University. Prior to that position, she was the founding director of the African American Studies program from 1971. Her most recent books include a co-edited volume titled, *River of Tears: Politics of Black Women's Health Issues*; her books include *Black Male-Female Relationships: A Resource Book*; and *Black Focusing: Black Male-Female Relationships*. In addition, she has published widely in the areas of sociology, African American Studies, and Africana Womanism.

MOLEFI KETE ASANTE is professor and chair of the department of African American Studies at Temple University. His books include *Afrocentricity: The Theory of Social Change; The Afrocentric Idea*; *Kemet, Afrocentricity and Knowledge*; and *A Historical and Cultural Atlas of African Americans*. He is also the co-editor of *African Culture: The Rhythms of Unity*; and *Thunder and Silence: The Mass Media in Africa*. In addition, Asante is the architect of the first doctoral program in African American Studies in the United States.

HOUSTON A. BAKER is the Albert E. Greenfield Professor of Human Relations at the University of Pennsylvania and director of the Center for the Study of Black Literature and Culture. His books include *Modernism and the Harlem Renaissance* and *Black Studies Rap and the Academy*. He is the co-editor of *Afro-American Literary Studies in the 90s*.

JAMES L. CONYERS, JR., is an associate professor of Black Studies and chair of the department of Black Studies, at the University of Nebraska at Omaha, and founding director of the Malcolm X Research Institute on Black Biography. He is the author of *The Evolution of African American Studies* and numerous articles on the African American experience.

SHAWN R. DONALDSON is an associate professor of sociology at the Richard Stockton State College in Pomona, New Jersey. She is the author of numerous articles that focus on Africana Studies and Gender. She is currently working on a book on African women in South Africa.

VIVIAN B. GORDON, now deceased, was formerly professor of Africana Studies at the State University of New York at Albany. She is the author of *Black Women, Feminism and Black Liberation: Which Way?*.

NORM HARRIS is professor of African American Studies at the University of Cincinnati. He is the author of *The Sixties: A Black Chronology*.

DARLENE CLARK HINE is the John A. Hannah Professor of American History at Michigan State University. Her books include *Black Women in White: Racial Conflicts and Cooperation in the Nursing Profession, 1890–1950*; *Black Victory: The Rise and Fall of the White Primary in Texas*; and *When the Truth Is Told: A History of Black Women's Culture and Community in Indiana, 1875–1950*. She is also the editor of *The State of Afro-American History: Past, Present, and Future*, Carlson Publishing's two volume series *Black Women in America*; and Carlson Publishing's sixteen volume series *Black Women in United States History: From Colonial Times to the Present*.

WILLIAM E. NELSON is professor of Black Studies and political science at Ohio State University and formerly the department chair for over a decade. He is the co-author of the book *Electing Black Mayors*.

CLYDE ROBERTSON is director of African American Studies for the New Orleans public school system. He also teaches African American Studies at Tulane University. He is currently a doctoral candidate in the Department of African American Studies at Temple University.

JAMES B. STEWART is vice provost and associate professor of labor studies and industrial relations at Pennsylvania State University and was the former director of the Black Studies Program. He is also the co-editor of the books, *Black Families: Interdisciplinary Perspectives*; *Research on the Black Family: A Holistic Perspective*; and *The Housing Status of African Americans*.

WARREN SWINDELL is professor and director of Afro-American Studies at Indiana State University. He is the author of numerous articles in the field of Afro-American Studies and Ethno-musicology.

JULIUS E. THOMPSON is director of Black Studies and History at University of Missouri at Columbia. His books include *Percy Green and the Jackson Advocate*; *The Black Press in Mississippi*; and *Hiriam Revels: A Biography*. He has recently completed a literary biography of Dudley Randall and the Broadside Press (to be published by McFarland in 1997).

AHATI N.N. TOURE is a community activist in Albany, New York and columnist for the *New York Sojourner-Herald* newspaper and author of the monograph titled, *The Impact of Criminal Justice on New York State's African and Latino Populations: A Focus on Corrections*.

JAMES TURNER is an associate professor of Africana Studies in the Center for Africana Studies and Research at Cornell University. He is the editor of *The Next Decade: Theoretical and Research Issues in Africana Studies*. He has published widely in the fields of sociology, political science and Africana Studies.

Index

Adams, Mary Ann 222
Adams, Russell 61, 137–138
administration 16–28, 45–48
administration of programs 16–66
aesthetics 75–76, 82–83, 112
affirmative action 105
Africana, defined 94
Africana Studies: academic niche for 130–139; administration 16–28, 45–48; cultural aesthetics 195–228; culture studies 195–205; development 49–59; discipline, as 60–66; epistemology 91–106; language issues 195–205; methodology 69–89; overview 7–15; rationales 29–44; understanding of 108–126; *see also* Africana womanist studies; Africology
Africana Womanism: activism and 145–146; Biblical sources of sexism 181–187; black/white women's issues 156–162, 168–170; color conflict 167–170; defined 144–145, 176–177; economic oppression 164–166; female deity, history of 187–189; feminism compared 14, 36, 110, 144–145, 155–156, 169, 176–179; goddess in early religion 187–189; male supremacy myth, analysis of 180–190; oppression 163–170; power relationships, analysis of 156–162, 167–170; racism 164, 168–170; rape as issue 171–173; self-definition 175–179; sexism 164, 169, 180–190; sexual politics 170–173; slavery, legacies of 168–170; socio-historic record 166–167; status conflict 167–170; stereotyped images of black women 165, 169; white feminism compared 14, 36, 110, 144–145, 155–156, 169, 176–179; *see also* Africana Womanist Studies; feminism

Africana Womanist Studies 13–14, 110; Black Studies compared 145–146; black women poets of Mississippi 208–223; black women scholars, obstacles to 146–147; curriculum issues 148–150; exclusion of 146–150; inclusion in Africana studies 151–152; literature of 147–148; professional organizations and 150–151; sexism and 146–147; womanist defined 144–145; women's studies and 145–146, 162–163; *see also* Africana Womanism
African diaspora 196–197
Africology: discipline of 60–61, 132; *see also* Africana Studies; Africana Womanism; Africana Womanist Studies; Afrocentricity
Afrocentricity: aesthetics 76, 82–83; art as factor 75; axiology 75–76; class as factor 74; cosmology 73–74; cultural issues 74, 82–83, 195–206; curriculum, as basis for 46–48, 136–137; dance as factor 75; defined 119–122, 135; disciplinary matrix, in 122–125; discipline, as 60–61, 108–109, 121–122; epistemology 75, 91–106, 121–122; Eurocentricity compared 70–71; gender as factor 74; language and 195–200; language as factor 75; methodologies for 69–90; music as factor 75; myth as factor 75; place as concept in 71; process of becoming Afrocentric 121; race as factor 74, 80–81; terminology reflecting 198–200; theory of 46–48, 119–122; value systems 75–76; *see also* Africana Womanism
Akbar, Na'im 77, 195
Aldridge, Delores P. 143–154

Women's Liberation movement 143–144
Women's Studies 13–14, 23, 30, 36, 110, 143–144; civil rights movement and 162–163; *see also* Africana womanist studies
Woodson, Carter G. 93, 98, 130
Wright, Bobby 22
Wright, Richard 212, 214, 217

Yamato, Gloria 176
Yerkes, Robert M. 84
Young, Al 217–219
Young, Aurelia N. 217–218, 222
Young, Carlene 17, 152

Zu-Bolton, Ahmos 218, 220